CW00341098

Dr Abby J Waterman is an 85-year-old retired consultant pathologist who has also been a Harley Street dentist, an entrepreneur and director of a Cancer Research laboratory, as well as the mother of four. She lives in London with her husband, while her children and grandchildren are scattered around the globe.

To read more about Abby visit her blog http://abbyjw.com

WOMAN

in a

WHITE

COAT

—

A Memoir

—

Dr Abby J Waterman

Copyright © 2017 Dr Abby J Waterman

All rights reserved,
including the right to reproduce this book, or portions thereof
in any form. No part of this text may be reproduced, transmitted, downloaded,
decompiled, reverse engineered, or stored, in any form or introduced into
any information storage and retrieval system, in any form or by any
means, whether electronic or mechanical without the
express written permission of the author.

Dr Abby J Waterman is a pseudonym.
The names of friends, family, colleagues and patients have been changed
as have the names of places and hospitals, although all the
events in this memoir are true to reality.

Cover design by Nathan Burton
Typeset in Garamond by M Rules

Printed and bound in Great Britain by
Clays Ltd, St Ives plc

ISBN: 978-1-5272-1628-0

A Doberman Elliott Associates Book

For the real Joshua,
the children and their partners
and the grandchildren.
I love you all.

CONTENTS

1	The Watermans	1
2	My First School	13
3	Petticoat Lane	31
4	A Country at War	45
5	To Dawlish	60
6	Grammar School	76
7	Music Studies	94
8	Hither Green Isolation Hospital	106
9	A Working Girl	118
10	A Girl at the Boys' School	135
11	St Margaret's Hospital Dental School	151
12	Real Patients at Last	161
13	Dentistry Finals	178
14	At Medical School	187
15	Villefranche-sur-Mer	201
16	The Obstetrics Firm	213
17	Ear, Nose and Throat House Surgeon	225
18	Medical House Physician	239
19	Starting a Family	247
20	John Dobbie Toyshop	261
21	Fireworks	272
22	Facing Bankruptcy	287
23	St Justin's Cancer Hospital	305
24	Back at St Margaret's	318
25	Illness Strikes	335
26	Further Education	355
27	Recurrence	372
28	Death Knocks at My Door	381

CHAPTER 1

The Watermans

My mother said she cried for days when I was born. I wasn't the son she wanted, the son who would carry on the family name and say the prayer for the dead (the *Kadesh*) at her funeral. She didn't need a third daughter.

My elder sister, Rebecca age 12, burst into tears when my mother brought me home from the Jewish Maternity Hospital in White-chapel. I wasn't the brother she had been looking forward to and I had a nasty rash on my face.

'We're going to call her Abigail,' my father said.

'It's a stupid name,' Rebecca said.

I screwed up my eyes to cry and the blotches on my face glowed bright red.

'She's ugly,' Hannah, my six-year-old middle sister said. 'Take her back.'

Thursday October 8th, 1931 was not an auspicious day to be born. The mild sunny weather of September and early October had turned

1

cold and wet, and the Great Depression was at its height. My father was laid off from his work as a journeyman printer, so he tried to get temporary work in the docks but he was turned away. He had to take work where he could, some of the time as a road sweeper.

My family lived at 116 Wentworth Dwellings, a development of cold-water tenements on the corner of Wentworth Street and Goulston Street in what was known as *Petticoat Lane*. However, Petticoat Lane as such hadn't existed as a thoroughfare for over 160 years. Originally near pig farms and called Hog's Lane, it was where the Huguenots living in Spitalfields sold their petticoats and lace. In 1846, during a boundary rearrangement, its name was changed by the prudish Victorians to Middlesex Street. *Petticoat Lane* now refers only to the street market.

During the week, the shops and stalls were mainly in Wentworth Street and Goulston Street, but, on Sundays, they spread into the surrounding streets.

Our flat was on the third floor, with an entrance in Goulston Street. Many years later I discovered that in the doorway of 119 Wentworth Dwellings, two floors above us, at 2.55 am on Sunday September 30th, 1888, PC Long found a blood-soaked piece of Catherine Eddowes' apron. Her murderer, thought to be *Jack the Ripper,* had left her mutilated body in Mitre Street, some distance away. His reign of terror in the East End of London, killing and disembowelling local prostitutes, finally ended three years later, with the murder of Mary Jane Kelly.

There were six of us living in our small three-roomed flat – my parents, my grandmother, my two older sisters and me. We washed, cooked and ate in the kitchen. In the evening, we sat around the oilcloth-covered table to read, gossip or listen to the wireless.

We had a black, coal-fired range for cooking and heating. I would spend hours looking into the flames, watching the writhing shapes and making up stories about the images I saw in them. A set of fire-irons stood on the hearth – a poker, a pair of tongs and a shovel. Come winter, we used a long-armed fork to toast slices of stale bread in front of the fire.

The porcelain butler sink only had a cold-water tap, so we had to heat water in a kettle on the range for doing the dishes, washing or shaving. My father would make up a thick lather in his shaving cup rubbing the soap with a badger-haired brush. I watched fascinated as he used a cut-throat razor to scrape off the thick white foam in long swirling stripes. If he nicked or grazed himself, he touched up the area with a caustic stick to stop it bleeding onto his detachable stiff white collar.

In one corner of the kitchen there was a mahogany gramophone chest surmounted by a turntable gramophone with a big curly horn. It took metal needles which my father sharpened from time to time. We had few records. The record we played most was Caruso singing opera – scratchy and enchanting.

The kitchen door gave on to a small balcony, with a coal bunker on the left and an outside toilet on the right. As the youngest, it was my job to cut our newspapers into squares, thread them onto a length of string for toilet paper and hang them on a nail hammered into the lavatory wall.

The parlour, which led off the other end of the kitchen, was used as a bedroom for my grandmother, my two sisters and me. A proper bedroom, with my parents' twin beds, was beyond that. Until I was six, when my grandmother died, she and I slept in the mahogany double bed that had belonged to my parents, before they changed to more fashionable twin beds. My sisters shared a pull-out sofa.

No hot water, no central heating. In winter, we put china hot water bottles in our beds to take off the chill. We sisters all had painful chilblains on our toes that didn't go away until the warmer weather came. On the coldest days, the lacy fern-like patterns of *Jack Frost* decorated the window panes.

There was a rubbish chute on each floor. You pulled down an iron gate about twelve inches square and tipped in your unwrapped rubbish. It ended up in the basement which was accessed by a door just inside the entrance to each block. The dustmen emptied it twice a week but feral cats as well as rats were always rooting through it. When I came home from school, it was to be greeted by the smell of cat pee and rotting food.

My grandmother was an intelligent, fiercely independent woman. She insisted on doing more than her fair share of the cooking and housework. The tenants of the two flats on each floor took turns to clean the stone steps that led down to the next level.

'Her next door! She never cleans the stairs properly,' my grandmother complained. 'She should clean out the corners. And it wouldn't hurt for her to change the water now and then.'

In 1937, when I was six, my grandmother had a stroke while she was scrubbing the stairs. She was dead on arrival at The London Hospital.

The neighbours blamed my mother.

'How could you let your mother clean the stairs, and her half-blind? No wonder she had a stroke, May She Rest in Peace.'

But there had been no talking my determined grandmother out of doing anything she wanted to do.

She could speak little English and she never spoke her native Russian. She spoke to me and my sisters in Yiddish and we answered in English. Though both our parents could speak Yiddish, we understood but couldn't speak it.

My grandmother was a tall, commanding woman with dark hair piled on top of her head. As a deeply orthodox Jewish woman it would have been a *sheitel*, a wig. I always went to bed before she did, so I never saw her without it. I loved her and looked forward to curling up against her warm back in the big double bed we shared.

She was kind to us but very tough. She'd had to be. In 1903, together with my ten-year-old mother, she fled the small town of Mogilev and the widespread pogroms in Belarus, one of the areas forming part of the Pale of Settlement. Established by Czar Catherine the Great in 1791, the Pale was the only area in Russia where Jews could live, unless they had some special employment, such as jeweller to the Crown. The Pale included present-day Poland, Latvia, Moldova and Ukraine, as well as Belarus, but it formed only a small part of Imperial Russia.

My grandmother had few happy memories of Mogilev. After her mother died giving birth to her, she'd had a miserable childhood as the unwanted stepdaughter of her father's second wife. She fell in love and married my grandfather when she was seventeen, but her happiness was short-lived. My grandfather died of pneumonia when her baby daughter, my mother, was just two.

After she was widowed, my grandmother made a poor living taking in lodgers. They slept on shelves around the central pot-bellied stove and ate at the long wooden table her husband had made for her as a wedding present. A careless shard of glass from the windows of the synagogue, shattered when the Cossacks rode through the town pillaging and burning, pierced my grandmother's right eye not long after she got married. It left her with an unsightly white scar. She was virtually blind in that eye.

She scraped together enough money to book a passage for herself and my mother on a ship bound for America. Their miserable voyage in the filthy, crowded steerage section was interrupted by a stop in the Port of London but, instead of continuing the journey to America they had paid for, they were forced off the ship by jeering Russian seamen. It was a frequent practice – to sell tickets to the USA, but only take the emigrants as far as England.

They wandered the streets of East London, sleeping in doorways, until an elderly Jew took pity on them and offered them shelter in his basement in Old Castle Street. They shared it with his family of six.

The Jewish Board of Guardians gave my grandmother the money to buy a willow basket and she got a pitch to sell bagels in Petticoat Lane Market on the corner of Wentworth Street and Goulston Street. She was at her pitch every weekday, summer and winter, leaving home at four in the morning to get her bagels from the baker. On a good day, she sold out by late afternoon but, when the weather was bad, she'd have to trudge home with some unsold. She would pick up barely damaged fruit and vegetables from the market refuse and with the leftover bagels, that would be their food until she'd sold enough to pay the baker what she owed.

There was no question of my mother going to school when they came to England. Soon after they arrived, my grandmother apprenticed her, then aged eleven, to a dressmaker who paid her threepence a week. My mother didn't tell my grandmother that the dressmaker treated her as a servant, cleaning her house and running errands for her.

In her second year, the dressmaker started to teach my mother how to cut out fabric and make up the garments. My mother learned quickly. When she started to earn a proper wage, she bought my grandmother a large black umbrella, and the man from the hardware shop made a stand for it. Before that, when it rained, my grandmother draped herself and the basket in a big grey tarpaulin. She even went out in the snow, when there were hardly any passers-by.

'What do you think we did in Russia then? Sit indoors all day? Your father, May He Rest in Peace, had to deliver ice on his back to the rich people in all weathers. That's why he got pneumonia and died.'

My mother soon had her own clientele and she was paid a more reasonable wage. Finally, she could set up her own workshop in the flat she and my grandmother could now afford. They turned the parlour into a cosy workroom where, unless the weather was very warm, a coal fire burned in the grate.

My grandmother refused to give up her pitch until 1918, when my mother got married. My parents moved to Old Kent Road with her and my father's younger brother, Nathan. By the time I was born, my uncle had married and moved away, and my parents had moved back to Petticoat Lane.

My mother spoke English with a slight Cockney accent, though there was just a trace of her Russian background in her pronunciation.

When she was 20, she fell in love with Harry, an ambitious young tailor she met at the synagogue. He was determined to better himself and emigrate to America. He said he would send for her when he'd found a job and had somewhere for them to live.

My mother spent months saving for the trip and making her trousseau – chiffon blouses, wool skirts, silk camisole tops, lacy nightdresses and elegant negligees. Harry met her when she arrived in New York. He was accompanied by the daughter of the factory owner where he worked.

He found my mother a room and a job with a dressmaker nearby. He said he loved her and would marry her when her mother joined them.

Ship owners were required to have a doctor available to examine would-be emigrants to confirm that they were healthy. My grandmother bought a ticket to follow my mother to New York, but she was turned back by the steamship doctor. He said she had trachoma, a highly infectious eye disease, and that they didn't need any more sick Jews in America. In fact, she had cataracts as well as her corneal scar and didn't have trachoma at all. There was nothing she could do but get off the boat.

My mother soon discovered that Harry and the daughter of the factory owner were seeing each other. Harry said he was sorry, but he was in love, so my mother was glad my grandmother hadn't been allowed to come. She could return to England with her head held high. She was the loving daughter, coming back to look after her half-blind mother, not crawling back rejected by Harry, humiliated.

My mother married my father on the rebound. She was introduced to him by a matchmaker, a *Shadchen*.

For as long as I remember, my mother's dark hair had grey streaks in it, though in the photos she had taken before she went to America she had raven-black hair pulled back into a bun at the nape of her neck. She was a small woman, not plump but not thin either. My father was six-foot-tall and if you look carefully at their wedding photograph, you can see the bump made by the box the photographer put under the carpet so that the disparity in their heights didn't look so obvious.

My father came from a more assimilated family, but my grand-mother took him in hand, and made an orthodox Jew of him. My father's relationship with my grandmother was one of mutual respect rather than affection, but when she died he was as desolated as the rest of us.

He was the sixth, and last but one, son of a wealthy Hebrew book printer. Samuel Waterman, my paternal grandfather, was a Freemason and an important member of his synagogue. He frequently travelled abroad, ostensibly on business, though in fact, it was to visit his mistress in Paris.

The housemaids, if they were young and pretty, never lasted long. Soon the sons would be lined up and asked who was responsible for the girl's pregnancy. None of them ever owned up, and the maid would be dismissed without a reference.

My paternal grandparents died long before I was born; their daughter and one son having died of tuberculosis some time before. The two eldest sons kept the printing business as their inheritance. The rest of the money was divided between the other sons.

The *Shadchen* had told my mother that my father was from a wealthy family, but not that he was a gambler. When they married, there was very little left of his inheritance. Fortunately, his gambling was just a passing fancy and, by the time my sisters and I came along, if he gambled at all it was just to do the Football Pools with an occasional bet on the Grand National.

My mother saw no reason to go on working as a dressmaker after they got married, even though they could have done with the money. In any case, at that time married women didn't work. It reflected badly on their husbands.

My parents bought a newsagent and tobacconist shop in the Old Kent Road, but neither was cut out to be a successful shopkeeper.

They bickered over whose turn it was to dress the window or sort out the stock.

My father and his brothers had been trained in the various branches of the printing trade, so when my parents finally sold the shop my father went to work as a compositor – one who sets the letters for books and newspapers by hand. The letters are cast in lead, and put into a carrier one by one, or phrase by phrase. Working in a newspaper was better paid but my father needed a job in which he didn't have to work on Saturdays and could go home early on Fridays before the Sabbath began. He earned just about enough to pay for the rent and our food.

My grandmother made things worse by constantly criticising him for not being sufficiently Orthodox. She also complained about my father's younger brother, Nathan, who lived with them until he married my Aunt Jenny in 1924.

When Nathan was a baby my father and his brothers took him for outings in his pram. My father said that they would climb Tower Hill and then let the pram go. He never said the baby fell out, although he did say that letting the pram runaway down the hill was why Nathan was a little strange and could never hold down a job for any length of time.

I remember my father as a quiet kindly man, rather overwhelmed by the five women in his life – my mother, my grandmother and we three sisters. If he minded not having a son, he never said so to me. In his wedding photo, he had a mass of straight black hair, but I only remember him being bald, with a fringe of greying hair around the edges.

On Saturday afternoons, when my mother had a nap and my sisters went off with their friends, he used to take me for a walk. Sometimes we'd go to Liverpool Street station and stand on the bridge over the railway tracks and watch the steam trains shunting in and out. I'd hold my breath in case they didn't stop in time to avoid crashing into the large round buffers at the end of the tracks. Other times we'd walk through the City of London, the great financial houses now quiet and shuttered. We'd sit in Finsbury Square, a piece of stale bread in our pockets for the sparrows and watch them picking at the crumbs. If there were any road works around, we'd go and stand near them. The smell of tar was supposed to be good for your lungs.

I tried to tell my father how unfair I thought my mother was, and how she preferred my sisters to me.

'You know your mother,' he said, patting me awkwardly on the shoulder. 'But remember, Abby, your name in Hebrew means *Father's joy.*'

My parents' marriage was not a loving one though my mother doted on my elder sister, Rebecca, who was born in 1920. My mother became resigned to her lot and as my grandmother was living with them, she had help with the cooking and housework.

Harry returned to England in 1922, when Rebecca was two. He came to my parents' shop after waiting until my father left to collect supplies from the wholesaler.

'I made a terrible mistake, Sarah,' he said. 'I never should have married her, but her father promised me a partnership when we got engaged. I was greedy and stupid. Come back to New York with me and bring your little girl. I can see how sweet she is. Leave him. You don't love him.'

'I can't, Harry,' she said. 'I want to say yes, Harry, I do, but my mother wouldn't be able to come with us, and I would never leave her again, not even for you. I'll just have to stick it out. And I have got my little Rebecca.'

I knew she didn't feel the way about me as she did about Rebecca. I was a bottle-fed baby. In 1931 bottle-feeding was all the rage and breast-feeding looked down upon. Instead of sucking my thumb. I always had a dummy. My earliest memory, as a two-year old, was of being wheeled up Bell Lane in a grey metal pushchair, a dummy pinned to my coat with a large safety pin at the end of a long pink ribbon.

My mother stopped the pushchair on the corner of Brune Street and suddenly my dummy was gone. I scrambled out of the push-chair to look for it, peering under the cushion on the hard seat. I didn't find it and cried and cried. Although it happened so long ago. I can still recall that awful feeing of loss.

CHAPTER 2

My First School

I started at Jews Free Infant School in Toynbee Street just before my third birthday. Holding tight to my grandmother's hand as we went through the market, I skipped along chattering to her, to the stall holders, to anyone who would pay me attention.

Being born in October, I was always one of the youngest in the class. My sister Rebecca had taught me to read and at the end of my first school year I won a prize for reading, a book of pressed flowers. The covers were of inlaid polished wood, hinged together with a brown tasselled cord. The words *Flowers from the Holy Land* were embossed on the front over the design of a tree. Its stiff cream pages were interleaved with translucent embossed tissue and a different delicate flower was attached to each page. Though a few petals and leaves dropped off from time to time, I treasured it for years.

I loved school, but I hated having to take a nap in the afternoon. We had to pull down the smelly rubber-covered mattresses stacked around the assembly hall and line them up neatly, leaving a space for our shoes between.

When the teacher drew the curtains, I tried hard to stay awake, hating every moment of doing nothing in the half-dark, but I soon fell asleep.

'Sh-h,' my mother whispered. 'Get up, Abigail, and be careful how you climb over Hannah. I don't want you waking her up. And wash your hands and face properly.'

After my grandmother died, Rebecca was given the sofa-bed to herself and Hannah and I shared the mahogany double bed. I slept next to the wall, so I had to climb over her to get up. She grunted and turned over, but didn't wake up.

I came into the kitchen as my father was leaving for work. I was surprised when he dropped a quick kiss on my head and wished me luck. We didn't kiss in our family.

When I got out some cornflakes and milk, my mother snatched them away.

'No eating. You're going to the hospital today and you mustn't eat before an operation. Have a drink of water, then hurry up and get your clothes on.'

I wanted to know what an operation was but I didn't ask my mother in case she got crosser still. I got dressed but I couldn't find my shoes. They weren't by the front door or next to the shoe cleaning box.

'Six years old, you should be dressed by now, a big girl like you,' my mother said. 'Where have you put your shoes this time?'

She found my shoes under the bed.

'I don't know how they got there. I left them by the front door when I took them off,' I said.

'Always dreaming,' she said. 'You don't know what day it is, half the time.'

I put on my cardigan and pushed my feet into my brown lace-up shoes. I was so nervous it took me ages to tie the laces. My mother dragged a comb through the tangles in my hair and pushed my arms into my coat.

'We'll be late,' she said.

But we were always late. We'd arrive at the synagogue for the High Holydays just after the service had begun, and have to push past the other women in the Ladies' Gallery. It was the same at the cinema. We often missed the beginning of the main film and had to wait for it to come around again.

We caught the tram in Commercial Street. There was a big notice inside saying *DO NOT SPIT*. Hannah said that if you spat you'd get tuberculosis and die.

The tram went swaying and clanging up to the beginning of Gray's Inn Road. We got off, and walked towards the Royal Free Hospital for Women.

'Come on, Abigail,' my mother scolded as she pulled me along, nearly wrenching my arm out of its socket. 'You never listen. You should have been dressed ages ago. Always with your head in the clouds.'

We waited at the reception desk as the clerk slowly wrote 'Abigail Josephine Waterman of 116 Wentworth Dwellings, Goulston Street, E.1., date of birth October 8th, 1931, religion Jewish.'

'Go up to the first floor,' she said. 'You'll find a door marked *Admissions*.'

The nurse in a blue dress and starched white apron was cross too.

'You were due here thirty minutes ago, Mrs Waterman. Your daughter isn't the only child having a tonsillectomy today. We can't

15

run a ward properly unless we keep to time. I hope you haven't given her anything to eat.'

My mother mumbled that she was sorry, that it was hard making a dreamy girl get a move on and that I'd had nothing to eat since the night before. She left without looking back.

The nurse took my hand and led me to a bed in the corner of a huge ward. Long windows stretched from the ceiling practically to the floor. It was scary in such a big room. I tried hard not to cry but I couldn't help it. I was afraid the nurse would tell me off for crying. I hated being told off – it made me feel sick. At home if I cried for nothing, my mother slapped me.

'Come on, love. No need to cry. Look around. Lots of other boys and girls here,' the nurse said.

She helped me off with my clothes and swapped them for a long white cotton gown that tied up down the back.

'You pop into bed and I'll put your clothes in the cupboard.'

When she came back she tucked a small teddy bear in beside me. I wished my mother was nice like her.

She stroked the hair off my forehead and told me to roll over onto my side. She put something in my bottom that made me sleepy.

Soon I was sitting up in bed, my throat hurting so much I couldn't help crying again.

'Awake now, are we, love?'

A nurse was bending over me. She gave me some warm milk and I fell asleep again.

Next morning, I woke to see her holding a dish with two scoops of ice cream, one vanilla and one strawberry.

'Have some of this. It'll make your throat feel better. When you feel up to it you can go and play with the others. Put this dressing gown on.'

I'd never had a dressing gown. I put on the soft white towelling robe and the nurse tied up the belt for me.

Some of the boys and girls were still in bed, while three of them, two girls and a boy, were sitting on a grey blanket in the middle of the floor playing *Ludo*. I went over to them, a bit afraid they'd shoo me away.

'Come on, you can be *Red*,' one of the girls said.

I didn't win at *Ludo* but I won at *Snakes and Ladders*.

'Come on children. Tidy up now. Dinner time,' a nurse called.

The gritty minced meat and watery mashed potatoes didn't taste very nice but I managed to get some down, even though my throat was sore. I was worried that the nurse would be angry when she took my plate away. At home, I always had to finish what was on my plate or I couldn't leave the table.

'Never mind, love,' the nurse said. 'Maybe you'll eat more tomorrow. Time for a nap.'

I was sure I'd never get to sleep but then the nurse was waking me for supper.

Each morning a nurse brought a mug of warm salty water to gargle with and an enamel bowl to spit in. The second day, as I was holding the bowl on my knees, it tipped over and spilt. The nurse came over to collect the bowls and mugs.

'What's this then, Abby?' she asked, pointing to the big wet patch.

'I'm sorry,' I said. 'It's white sick.'

She laughed.

'That's a new one. Come on out then. We'll get you some dry bedding.'

I enjoyed the days I spent at the Royal Free. All the other children's parents came during visiting hours, but no-one came to see me that day nor for the rest of the time I was there. But I had the teddy bear to cuddle and a shelf of children's books to choose from – Rupert Bear Annuals, all the Peter Rabbit books, Mother Goose, the Golden Treasury and a pile of comics – and I played with the other children outside visiting hours. We were shouted at when we got too noisy or when we chased each other around the ward and under the beds.

Then it was time for the children who'd had their operations the same day as me to go home. The nurses helped us get dressed in our own clothes, and took us into the waiting room. I was the only one left after all the other children's mothers and fathers arrived to take them home. A nurse came to get me.

'No point waiting here, dear. Come on back to the ward. We'll send you out when your mother comes.'

Ashamed and frightened that my mother was never going to come for me, I had to go back and sit in the ward, afraid that she was going to leave me there for ever.

After a long, long time the nurse said, 'Your mother's here' and took me back to the waiting room.

'Come along, Abigail,' my mother scolded. 'I haven't got all day and I've still got get your father's dinner on.'

We always had a cat. Most people in *The Buildings* kept a cat, because we all had mice, even on the third floor. I never caught sight of a mouse in our flat, but often there would be a few mouse droppings. Now and again my father baited two or three mouse traps with cheese, but he rarely caught a mouse. They were too wary. They had learned how to steal the cheese without getting trapped.

Tabby was over ten years old when she started refusing her food. She even turned her head away from her favourite foods and only wanted to lie in her basket. Hannah came with me to the RSPCA.

The vet, an old man with snow-white hair, was very gentle with Tabby.

'I'm really sorry, girls. She's a lovely cat and I can see she's been well looked after, but for a cat, she's very old and I'm afraid her kidneys have practically stopped functioning.' Tabby purred as he stroked her and went on. 'I know it's a hard decision for you to make, but it would be a kindness to put her down. Do you want to come back with your mother or father, or will you leave her with me?'

Hannah told him that our parents were too busy to come and yes keep her, but please don't hurt her.

We kissed Tabby goodbye.

We held hands as we walked home, too miserable to get on a bus and have strangers see us cry.

At first, I felt I never wanted a cat again, but then I realised how much I missed a friendly face, a cat always pleased to see me and never cross or angry. My mother said she'd had enough of cats and to stop nagging.

'Please, Mummy,' I begged. 'I'm sure I saw mouse droppings under the kitchen table.'

'It's too much trouble having a cat and getting it trained properly. When the shops open, I'll go down and buy a couple of mouse traps.'

I hated the wooden slabs with their cruel iron springs, but I was pleased when two days later the trap under the table finally contained a dead mouse.

'Now can we have a cat, please? Please?'

'We'll have to see,' my mother said, 'but you'll have to look after it and clean out its tray.'

During school, I kept thinking about having a cat again. I was sure there'd be a cat waiting for me when I got home and I looked everywhere in case it had fallen asleep in a corner.

'No good looking,' my mother said. 'There's no cat here and stop crying, you silly girl.'

I got out my homework and sat down at the kitchen table.

'Mind you put all that away when your father comes. He'll be wanting his supper as soon as he sits down.'

As soon as I heard my father's whistle on the stairs, I tidied my books away.

The doors to our flats had heavy iron U-shaped knockers, but we never used them. Hannah taught me how to whistle and we each had our own tune. As we got to the entrance to our block, we whistled our special tune and my mother would have the door open by the time we got up to the third floor.

'Have you been a good girl, Abby?' my father asked. 'Not been cheeky to your mother? Do you deserve a present?'

As he spoke, he pulled out a little black bundle from inside his jacket.

'Oh Daddy,' I cried, reaching up to it, and then 'Ouch' as the kitten dug its sharp little teeth into my thumb.

'Is it a boy or a girl?'

'It's a boy. Jimmy at work gave it to me. It's already house trained.'

'I'll call it Rupert, after Rupert the bear,' I said.

Black, except for a white spot on his forehead, he was gorgeous and he was mine. I rubbed my face in his soft warm fur.

'Don't let it near your face,' my mother snapped. 'You'll catch something.'

Nothing could spoil the day for me, not my mother's bad temper, nothing.

I put some milk into a saucer and watched Rupert lap it greedily, leaving a bead of milk on his chin. I picked him up.

'Silly old thing,' I said. 'Can't even keep your chin clean.'

I made up a bed of old rags in the corner of the kitchen and tucked Rupert in.

It was wonderful coming home from school to be greeted by Rupert who would wind himself round and round my ankles, delighted to see me again.

When I went to the toilet on our little balcony, Rupert would follow me and walk along the brick support at the bottom of the protective railings. As he grew bolder, he started climbing over the coal bunker and up to the bar at the top, weaving in and out of the upright spikes. I could hardly bear to watch him. Sometimes he walked along the railings to our neighbour's balcony. She usually had a few scraps for a cat who was always hungry, even when he had just been fed.

'Be careful,' I told Rupert. 'I know you've got nine lives, but we're on the third floor, and it's a long way down.'

Rupert said nothing and stalked into the kitchen, but when I did my homework he came to sit on my lap, purring loudly.

One day, when I was standing on the balcony watching as Rupert put one careful foot in front of the other on the top bar of the guard rail, my mother called me.

'Abby, come in at once. What's all this?' she said, pointing to the scrunched-up drawings I'd left on the kitchen table.

As I turned towards her, Rupert lost his footing and fell. I was paralysed; couldn't move.

'Mummy, come quickly,' I screamed. 'Rupert's fallen off.'

'He'll be dead, for sure, but you'd better go down and see.'

I raced down the six flights of stairs, out into Goulston Street, round into Wentworth Street and into the entrance of our court-yard. Rupert was sitting there, nonchalantly licking a paw, as if falling from the third floor was nothing.

'You're a naughty, naughty, kitten,' I said, as I picked him up and hugged him.

The nosy old woman who was always sitting on her first-floor balcony, looking out and gossiping about everyone, said:

'They've got nine lives and no mistake. You should look after it better, Abby. You tell your mother I said so.'

Rupert licked my hand with his rough little tongue.

'You're to stop walking along the railings,' I told him.

But an hour later he was winding in and out of the spikes again, as if to show he wasn't a scaredy cat, even if I was.

We went up to the Junior School when we were seven. The entrance was in Frying Pan Alley, opposite the salmon smoke houses. The smell seemed heavy and unpleasant on the way to school, when I'd just had breakfast, but delicious on the way home to dinner (we referred to our mid-day meal as 'dinner') when I was ravenous. On a lucky day, I would catch the eye of one of the men working there.

'A little piece of smoked salmon to taste, miss? Something to keep you going till you get home?'

At morning break, crates of small bottles of milk with shiny blue tops were stacked outside the playground door. I liked milk, unless it had been boiled and had a skin on top, but my best friend, Phyllis, hated it, so I drank hers as well as mine, trying not to get caught. We were told off if we gave our milk away.

I was never bullied at school, nor teased for being clever. We were smacked for being naughty, but girls were never caned. A smack on the hand or bottom was something we expected.

It was much worse at home. At school, you got punished immediately. You didn't have to wait for hours dreading your father's footsteps on the stairs. If I did something naughty, or if I was cheeky either to my mother or to Rebecca, my mother would threaten me.

'Just you wait until your father gets home. He'll give you a good hiding.'

He never smacked me hard, but it was the waiting that was so awful, and the disgrace.

We had smoked salmon at home only on special occasions, like when Uncle Joe and Auntie Dora came to tea. I would be sent to the delicatessen to buy two ounces or even a quarter of a pound (4 ounces) of smoked salmon. I would stand fascinated, watching the shop assistants pick out the bones with eyebrow tweezers. If you asked nicely, they gave you the trimmings – the skin that couldn't be sold, but had enough salmon left on it to scrape off with your teeth.

I hated Uncle Joe. He wasn't a real uncle – we always called older people Auntie or Uncle. I dreaded his visits. Small and thin, with a tobacco-stained grey moustache, he was dwarfed by fat Auntie Dora. She would smother me with wet kisses and then Uncle Joe would lift me up, rub his bristly moustache across my cheeks and slip his rough hand under my knicker elastic and stroke my bottom.

'What a lovely *tuchus* the child has,' he'd say, giving my bottom a pinch.

When I was sent to the delicatessen to buy pickled herrings, the assistants always added some of the sliced onions that were pickled with them. I didn't like herrings, but pickled onions are delicious between slices of rye and caraway bread.

Rye bread cost twopence three farthings and black bread cost threepence ha'penny. If I had to buy one of each, and hadn't brought a farthing with me, the assistant would say:

'Never mind, *bubbele*, bring it in next time.'

But my mother said we must never owe money and that I must go back down to pay the farthing we owed.

We didn't own any reading books. The only books we owned were the Pentateuch (the five books of Moses), six daily Prayer Books and six copies of a beautifully illustrated *Haggadah*, the book of the service for Passover- one for each of us. The *Haggadah* told the story of the Israelites in Egypt, the Ten Plagues, the parting of the Red Sea and the Exodus. They were printed with Hebrew on one side and an English translation on the other.

I joined Whitechapel library as soon as I was five. Once a week I bundled up the library books I had read and walked down Wentworth Street to the Commercial Street crossing.

'Find a big man to take you across the road and make sure you hold his hand tight,' my mother said. 'No skipping or messing about as you go.'

Whoever was holding my hand always said how little my hand was and how the books were nearly as big as me. All I wanted, was to hurry up, get to the library as quickly as possible and borrow some more books.

The children's library was huge, with bookshelves stretching from floor to ceiling. You needed one of those rolling step-ladders to reach the top. We could take out six books. I always chose at least one book of fairy tales and one book of myths and legends. The Andrew Lang fairy books were my favourites and I was fascinated by the Aubrey Beardsley illustrations. At first, I'd choose a book or two from the Angela Brazil's girls' boarding school stories but over the years I moved on to boys' books. I learned the rules and positions of cricket and rugby, and thrilled to the *Biggles* books.

I had to be brave if I wanted to look up something in the Children's Encyclopaedia, which was kept upstairs in the Reference Library. I'd climb the steps up to the Reference section, hurrying past the glass cases filled with stuffed animals. The foxes, with their big teeth and staring eyes, were especially frightening and I hated seeing tiny stuffed birds stuck on twigs.

I was wary of the grubby old men who sat around the centre table reading newspapers. I avoided catching anyone's eye and hurried past to get to the encyclopaedia.

Everyone who lived in Wentworth Dwellings – *The Buildings* – was poor, but at least we had our own toilet.

The Buildings consisted of three blocks. The flats in the outer two blocks were arranged in pairs on each floor. None of us had a bathroom, but each had a toilet on our balcony.

Flats in the centre block were arranged in long corridors. They didn't have individual toilets. Instead, in the centre of each floor, there were two pairs of shared backto-back lavatories, fastened only by black lift-up latches. The door was just too far for you to be able to hold it shut while sitting on the toilet.

We children would run from lavatory to lavatory trying to catch someone with their knickers down. Polly's father was furious when we caught him with his trousers around his ankles, smoking a Wills' Woodbine, and reading the *News of the World*.

'You wait till I get you home, Polly my girl. You're in real trouble now.'

We edged away. Polly's father was a frightening man. We'd seen the red marks and tear stains on her face when she came down to play.

'I'm sorry, Dad,' Polly whispered. 'I promise I won't do it again.'

'Make sure I don't catch you at it then.'

Lily was my best friend in The Buildings. She, her mother and older sister lived in the tenement above ours. We used the wash room on the topmost floor as a dressing-up room and theatre. My mother, being a dress maker, there were no old clothes lying around – she remade or re-used everything. But Lily's older sister was always buying new outfits and we used her old clothes. Sometimes we made up plays; sometimes we just sang and danced.

The neighbours said that Lily's sister was really her mother and that her sister had got into trouble when she was only 14. They'd sent her off into the country and, when she brought the baby back, her mother said it was hers.

My mother said: 'What do you expect? They're *Dotchkas* (Dutch).

There was a hierarchy amongst the Jews of the East End. The wealthiest, those that came to England from Spain and Portugal long ago, were at the top. Then came the Eastern European Jews with the Dutch at the bottom.

'They don't believe in anything,' my mother said.

Not true, but they tended to be less Orthodox than Jews like my mother and grandmother who were from Russia.

We had all the streets as a playground though, until Petticoat Lane market closed, our playground was confined to the courtyard between the blocks of flats.

Only rich people had cars before the war, so we didn't have to worry about traffic. After the stall holders packed up, we'd rescue a discarded orange box from which to make a wicket and bat. Once the dustmen had cleared away the rotten fruit and debris, someone would bring down a much-used tennis ball and we'd play cricket in the street.

Sometimes we'd play leap frog over each other, over the tall bollards on pavement corners and over the waist-high electrical junction boxes. The metal left a sour smell on your hands that was hard to wash off.

We chalked squares for *Hopscotch* on the pavements or in our courtyard. You threw a dried-up piece of orange peel into the next numbered square and jumped first with two legs and then one until you reached the peel. Then you turned around and came back again.

Girls played *Higher and Higher* and other skipping games. We sang:

> *I know a boy.*
> *He's double jointed*
> *He kissed me and made me disappointed*
> *When he died I found another one*
> *His name begins with . . .*

chanting ABCDE . . . until the girl skipping caught her foot in the rope. We then had to guess the name of the boy she loved, beginning with the letter we'd stopped at.

Cat's Cradle was played with long pieces of clean string picked up from the debris the stallholders left. We tied it into a loop and lifted it over each other's outstretched hands in ever more complicated patterns.

The aim of *Knock down Ginger* was to bang on a door with its heavy iron knocker and run away just as the occupant came to the door. If you were lucky, you caught a woman still in her curlers and underwear.

If it was sunny we played on the flat roof until we got told off by the people in the topmost apartments for making too much noise. When I got older, I took up a chair and a book so I could read in peace without my mother giving me some chore or other as I was 'wasting time, doing nothing'.

Everyone in *The Buildings* did their washing on Mondays. We had a big copper tub that boiled and hissed on the hob as my mother stirred the washing with a big wooden paddle. The dirtiest things were rubbed on a washboard which had a wooden frame and metal rubbing surface. We loved the sound it made as we rubbed our nails across the surface. A mangle was tucked away above the coal bunker on our balcony. It was a special treat to turn the big handle and feed through the clothes, careful not to get my fingers trapped.

Come Monday, assorted underwear, shirts, and nightdresses flew in the breeze on every balcony. Anything a bit grey or torn was kept to the back so none of the neighbours had an excuse to call out rude comments. Washing soda was added to the wash to soften the water and help remove stains. It came as rough, cloudy lumps of sodium carbonate. You could rub off the white powder on the surface with a wet finger to reveal a clear transparent crystal. It tasted nasty if you made the mistake of licking your finger afterwards. We used *Reckitt's Blue* to whiten the washing. The blue dye compound came as a little block in a muslin sack called a *Dolly Bag*.

Ironing was done with a flat iron. We had two irons – used alternately. They sat on the cooking range until the sole plate hissed when my mother touched it with a moistened fingertip. She said that spitting on the iron to test it was a dirty habit. My task was to fold the freshly ironed handkerchiefs, taking care to match the corners exactly. The biggest pile was my father's and I'd proudly show him the folded handkerchiefs before putting them away in the mahogany chest of drawers.

We sent sheets and tablecloths to the laundry. It must have been cheap or we couldn't have afforded it. The laundry man collected and delivered the laundry to our flat on the third floor. Dirty washing was sent in one of our large square pillowcases and it came back tightly folded and wrapped in stiff white paper. The paper was too stiff for toilet paper but it was just right for drawing on or covering school books.

Long before duvets became popular in this country, Russian immigrants had the feather duvets, *paranas,* they had brought with them from the old country. Each spring we tipped out the old feathers and replaced them with new ones collected from the poultry yards. The feathers flew everywhere, getting up our noses and making us sneeze.

We all caught measles, chicken pox and whooping cough. The only immunisation we had was against smallpox – it left an ugly scar on your upper arm.

There was an outbreak of Infantile Paralysis (Polio) every summer and in all the schools there were children with leg braces to support limbs damaged by the disease. It wasn't until 1955 that Dr Salk's anti-polio vaccine became available.

One day that June, I knocked at Violet's door to ask if she could come out to play – my best friend, Lily, had gone shopping with her elder sister. Violet's mother said she wasn't well and soon an ambulance came blaring its way into the street outside. Minutes later I saw Violet being carried out on a stretcher.

The caretaker was sweeping the courtyard when I went down to play after supper.

'Poor little thing,' he said. 'She's got infantile paralysis. They've put her in an iron lung. They only put you in an iron lung when it gets to your chest and you can't breathe. They've closed all the swimming pools because of the epidemic.'

The whole tenement was hushed. No-one knew what to say to Violet's parents. They had lost their little boy in a dreadful swimming accident the year before and they'd only had the two children.

Three days passed and then I saw men in black suits carrying in a small white coffin. Violet's was the only Catholic family in the flats and no-one was sure what we were supposed to do. Our parents called and paid their respects, but children were kept away from their flat.

We stood by the gate as Violet's little coffin was carried out into the waiting hearse. The man who worked in the fabric shop just outside our gate was in tears, twisting his cap in his large hands. Violet had been a special favourite of his. He used to carry her around on his shoulders, playing horses.

For days afterwards, our mothers gathered in worried groups wondering who would be next, but it was only little Violet who caught polio and died. She was younger than me and we didn't always play together, but the playground seemed empty after she died.

CHAPTER 3

Petticoat Lane

The stalls on our side of Goulston Street sold chickens. Trapped in crates under the stalls, they squawked and cackled until it was their turn to have their heads chopped off and their entrails pulled out. The intestines were thrown away but sometimes, when the stall-holder pulled out the liver and heart to give to you, there would be some soft yellow eggs, not yet hardened.

'Look at these, *bubbele*,' the stallholder would say, giving my cheek a quick pinch. 'They'll be delicious in your mother's chicken soup.'

My mother said Rebecca needed to keep her strength up, so she would be given a couple of the eggs. Hannah and I would squabble over whose turn it was to have any left over.

A religious inspector, a *Shomer*, wandered up and down the Goulston Street stalls all day, making sure none of the chickens was diseased or abnormal. If the stallholder had any doubts about a mottled liver or an unusual swelling, the *Shomer* would be called

over to pronounce on whether Jews could eat that chicken or not.
If not, it had to be sold off for cat or dog food.

There were fish stalls on the other side of the street. I hated the
fishy smell and avoided walking on that side of the street, though
the feral cats loved it over there. They would snatch unwanted fish
heads from the rubbish under the fish stall and sit there gnawing
away at them with that special concentrated look cats wear when
they are chewing something tough.

In Wentworth Street, most of the stalls displayed highly polished fruit and neatly arranged vegetables, the costermongers
shouting their wares, 'Ripe tomatoes, threepence a pound',
'Lovely strawberries, melt in your mouth'. There were two baker
shops, Kossoff's and Grodzinski's, wafting out an enticing smell
of freshly baked bread. Mark's, the delicatessen, with its array of
different spicy odours, stood on the corner of Wentworth and
Toynbee Street. The hardware shop always smelled of disinfectant. It was stocked with mouse traps, *Flit* spray and fly papers
for the summer flies, and turpentine to deal with the bed bugs
that infested all the tenements. Other shops sold religious books,
clothes, fabric or trimmings.

Meat was sold only in shops displaying certificates from the *Beth
Din*, the Jewish body that authorises Kosher butchers and restaurants. The biggest butcher shop, Barnett's, was in Middlesex Street.
Upstairs there was a large restaurant where you could have a full
three course meal or a salt beef sandwich and lemon tea. We never
had the money for such luxuries.

It's against Jewish dietary laws to eat meat and milk dishes at the
same meal. You couldn't have rice pudding or custard after meat,
nor follow your meal with a drink with milk in it. We drank lemon
tea after meat meals instead. Russian immigrants, like my mother,

sucked their tea through lumps of sugar or stirred in a spoonful of homemade jam.

Food such as fruit and vegetables and fish were *Pareve* and could be eaten with either milk or meat meals.

You couldn't use the same cutlery, plates or pots and pans for meat that you used for milk dishes. Every orthodox family, however poor, had two sets of each.

Actually, it was four sets. Passover commemorates the flight of the Israelites from Egypt and the gift of the Holy Land. After the visitation by God of the Ten Plagues, the Israelites were finally allowed to leave Egypt, but had no time to wait for their bread to rise. To commemorate this, on the eight days of Passover, Jews don't eat normal risen bread, only *Matzos*, unleavened bread made without yeast. No trace of bread must be left in our homes for those eight days.

On the day before the Holyday, we had a great hunt for any remaining crumbs, shining our torches in every corner. Then all everyday pots and pans, crockery and cutlery were 'sold' in a token sale to a non-Jew. Everyday items were wrapped in newspaper and stored out of reach, and the special set of Passover meat and milk dishes brought out. At the end of the Holydays the small coin given in payment at the beginning of Passover was returned and the crockery, cutlery and pots and pans were redeemed.

On Sundays, the character of Petticoat Lane changed. The market expanded to Middlesex Street, Bell Lane and the cross streets. There were stalls selling leather, clothes, crockery and linen and there were always mock auctions.

We kept clear of the market on Sundays. We looked down on the gullible people who bought all that junk.

'Those people are not from round here,' my father said, 'and on Sundays the market is full of con-men.'

A crowd would quickly gather around a huckster standing at the open mouth of his van, balancing a tea set on one hand – six cups, six saucers and six tea plates.

'Who'll give me ten, no, five? Who'll give me a sovereign (£1) for this genuine Royal Doulton tea service?' he would yell.

'There are always stooges in the crowd paid to buy a set and start him off,' my father declared. 'If you look around the back, you'll see them return the goods while everyone is listening to him. Thieves the lot of them. Royal Doulton, my eye. Hong Kong Chinese more like.'

There was a gold and silver market in Cutler Street, just off Middlesex Street. My father would get up at dawn to prowl around the London flea markets before going to work. He'd spend hours in the evenings polishing his finds – silver jugs, bowls and brooches. The following Sunday he'd set up his wares in Cutler Street on a large baize-lined wooden tray with trestle legs. He didn't like me coming there every week – children were discouraged – but some Sundays he took me with him as long as mother didn't tell him I'd been naughty or cheeky that week. My mother said he wasn't a good businessman and it was all a waste of time.

Prince Monolulu often wandered the market – a tall imposing black man originating from the Danish West Indies. Dressed in a medley of colourful clothes and wearing a tall feathered headband, he had a small drum hung around his neck and carried a chieftain's fly whisk.

He was a tipster. You could hear his cry 'I gotta horse' from the other end of the street. Everyone thought he brought them luck.

My dad said Prince Monolulu won the enormous sum of £8,000 in 1920, betting with odds of 100-6 in the Derby.

There was also an escape artist, a big brawny bare-chested man. He would climb into a large sack and invite someone from his audience – no doubt a stooge – to tie up the opening of the sack with several knots. His assistant would then come forward with a heavy chain, wind it several times around the sack, padlock it and call for someone in the crowd to check the fastenings.

The sack would wriggle and twist and in minutes, the escapologist's flushed face would appear and he would step free to loud applause. On a good day, he would be showered with coins.

I loved it when the coal man came. We could hear him calling 'Coal for sale' from streets away and I would be sent down to ask for a bag of coal. The coalman, his face black from the ingrained coal dust, would follow me up the stairs and through our kitchen to the balcony. He'd then heave the hundred-weight sack of coal off his shoulder and pour it into our coal bunker. My mother always grumbled about the trail of coal dust he left on the kitchen floor.

About every other week a tired horse pulling a cart piled high with unwanted possessions came through the lane. The driver cried what sounded like 'Ragabo' – in fact Rags and Bones. We rushed home to sort through our few belongings to see what we could swap for a comb, a handkerchief or a small celluloid doll. He never gave you cash for your small offerings.

The knife grinder came regularly too. His grinding wheel was mounted. on a bicycle chassis. We stood enthralled by the sparks that flew off the big wheel as he pedalled away. Anyone who had brought a knife or pair of scissor to sharpen could ask to have a go on his bicycle. I could only just about reach the pedals when it was my turn and had to pedal standing up.

Our enamel saucepans and kettles all finally developed holes at the junction of their sides and bottom. Mostly we mended them with small round discs of flexible metal and washers which were screwed in, but when the tinkers came we took them down to be mended properly.

At the beginning of the winter the chimney sweep called. He would first cover the grate and the hearth in front of it with an old blanket. Then he would take out his bundle of telescopic sticks, screwing each in turn to his large circular brush. We watched enthralled as he pushed his brushes further and further up the chimney and then pulled them out accompanied by clouds of soot. Once a dead pigeon came tumbling out with the soot.

'No wonder your fire wouldn't draw,' he said, laughing. 'We see plenty of those.'

The milkman carried his trays of milk up and down the stone stairways to all the flats. Milk was delivered in tall glass bottles closed with foil discs. We only had the Gold Top milk, the full cream milk, for the special occasions when we had tinned peaches or tinned pineapple for pudding. My mother would pour the cream off the top of the milk onto the fruit. Mostly we drank the cheaper Silver Top milk.

'Abby, make sure you listen out for the milkman and take in the milk as soon as he comes, or the birds will get at it and peck through the tops.'

They liked the cream as much as we did.

None of the tenements had a fridge. We tried to keep butter and milk cool in a square wooden box with a mesh door we kept on the balcony.

We stood the butter in a dish containing cold water and covered

36

it with a muslin cloth. The evaporation from the soaked cloth helped to keep the butter cool, but by the end of the day it was always a squashy mess.

When the milk turned sour – as it often did – my mother would allow it to separate into the white curds and the thin clear whey. She'd tip off as much of the whey as possible and then empty the curds into a muslin bag that she hung over the kitchen tap to drain. After a couple of days, we had a bag of curd cheese – delicious on a slice of black bread.

Each year my mother made my sisters and me new clothes – skirts and blouses or dresses – for *Rosh Hashanah*, the Jewish New Year. My mother combed the shops and stalls in the Lane for remnants, and then there would be long sessions of standing on a chair for the fittings. She made us hold a length of thread in our mouths if she needed to tack the garment while we had it on. She said if we didn't hold the thread in our mouths as she sewed, our brains would be sewn together.

It was the highlight of the year having new clothes of my own. Being the youngest, it was hand-me-downs otherwise.

Although we kept away from the Sunday market, we often went on Sundays to Club Row, on the corner of Brick Lane. There you could buy puppies, kittens, rats, mice, guinea pigs, snakes and birds of all kinds and there was always a crowd around the budgies, especially towards Christmas. A budgie in a cage was just the right present for Grannie.

One man had a trained budgerigar that told your fortune for twopence. The budgie would choose one of the tiny envelopes stacked on the tray in front of it, and the man would open it and read its message.

I handed over my twopence and the budgie picked out a small pink envelope,

'Your future looks good, girlie. You are going to get married, have four children and win the football pools.'

I managed two of the three.

We went to the Mayfair cinema in Brick Lane every week. Sometimes I would go with my sisters and, as I grew older, with a friend. We saw whatever was on – a main film, a supporting B film – usually a Western – plus the news and trailers for the next week. The programmes ran continuously with no break. If we came in late we could stay on and catch up on what we had missed. I often needed to go to the toilet while the film was showing, pushing past a row of angry knees to get to the gangway, and then having to squeeze past to get back again.

On the way to the pictures we always went into Woolworth's, at the corner of Commercial Street and Whitechapel Road, to buy chocolate money. It was a very special treat, having a whole bag of chocolate money to myself, instead of a small bar of chocolate being divided between me and my sisters. I would undo the ribbon that tied up the bag of chocolate money very carefully so I could use it to store small treasures.

The gold foil covering the chocolate discs was in two circles – the smaller one just fitted one side of the chocolate coin and the larger one went on the other side and wrapped over the edge. If you smoothed out the foil very carefully, you could use it to wrap little presents or swap it with your friends for wrappers from toffees or sweets. Sometimes we bought little bags of chocolate rectangles wrapped in silver or gold foil instead. They had a central hollow you could run your nail across and split the foil before you unwrapped them.

We children couldn't buy our own tickets if the certificate was A for Adults rather than U for Universal. We had to be accompanied by an adult, so we would wait outside the cinema until we saw someone on their own.

'Take us in, sir/ miss?' we would plead. Mostly the answer was 'Yes '. We'd whisper 'Thanks', press our cinema money into their hand and find a seat near the front. We never tried to see horror films. No-one would take us in to see those.

Sometimes we went to the Rivoli in Whitechapel instead, though it was more expensive. My dad kidded me that he hid out in the Rivoli to avoid being called up for World War 1.

At the Rivoli, before the programme began, an electric organ rose out of the floor. Lit by an array of coloured spotlights, the organist, his hair slicked back with brilliantine, played current hits for the audience to sing along.

Johnny Isaacs' Fish and Chip shop was just up the road. After the film, we bought two pennyworths of chips wrapped in newspaper. We had to stand on tiptoe to reach the vinegar bottle and salt shaker on the zinc covered counter.

'That's enough, you kids,' one of the men behind the counter would shout, as we smothered our chips in salt and vinegar.

They were crisp and delicious, almost too hot to put in our eager mouths. I never had enough money to buy a piece of fried fish to go with the chips. I told myself I didn't really care for their fried fish – the fish my mother cooked for Friday nights tasted better.

On Friday afternoons, my mother, my sister Hannah and I went to the Public Baths in Goulston Street to be clean for the Sabbath. Rebecca went separately after work.

We always bought Second Class tickets. The water was controlled by the attendants, and turned on and off with the brass detachable handles they carried with them. Hot water gushed out of a wide gleaming tap into the deep porcelain baths which always had deep chips in their surfaces.

Hannah and I shared a bath to save money. Once we'd had our bath we waited on a bench in the corridor and my mother would call out for more hot water and have her bath. That way she only paid for one ticket.

The attendants, large perspiring women in immaculate white wrap-around overalls, were tyrants. If you crossed them, they'd turn on the cold water instead of hot. All the brass taps and fittings gleamed and any water on the floor was wiped up immediately.

Everyone in the tenements where we lived used the Public Baths. You just had to say to one of our neighbours 'More hot water Number 22' for them to burst out laughing.

The First Class baths had hot and cold taps you could control yourself and they even had hair driers. I promised myself I would buy a First Class ticket as soon as I earned my own money.

We didn't wash our hair at the baths. My mother said we'd catch cold walking home. We washed our hair on Friday nights after we'd been to the baths. We called them *Amami Nights* after the advertisement for Amami shampoo. We washed our hair in the kitchen, heating the kettle on the range and pouring jugs of hot water over our heads. The water that streamed off us was black with dirt and soot from the smog-filled East End – this was long before the Clean Air Act of 1956 that forbad burning coal in the centre of London.

The coal fires and the factories belching smoke, combined with the November mists coming off the River Thames, created thick choking fogs – 'pea-soupers'. If you had to go out, you took a torch.

Sometimes you would hardly be able to see a hand in front of your face.

We all had black rings around the necks of our shirts and blouses after we'd worn them for only a day.

When we got home my mother would peel the potatoes, add a little water and chicken fat and put the saucepan on a low gas. They would cook all night – if you didn't actually light the gas but left it on from the day before the Sabbath it wasn't considered work – that would be forbidden on the Sabbath. The result was a delicious fruity potato stew – *cholent*.

I always loved Friday nights – had looked forward to them all week since I was little. The Sabbath runs from sunset on Friday to sunset on Saturday. It is so early in the winter that orthodox Jews need to take Friday afternoons off work. From then on, no work of any kind is permitted until the Sabbath ends.

A few minutes before sunset my mother pulled a scarf over her head and recited the Sabbath blessing as she lit the candles.

'*Baruch ata Adonai Elohenu, Melech ha'olam, asher kid'shanu b'mitzvotav v'tzivanu l'hadlik ner shel Shabbat.*' 'Blessed art Thou, Oh Lord our God, King of the Universe, who sanctified us with His commandments and commanded us to light the Sabbath candles.'

On an enamelled tin tray stood two embossed silver candlesticks, inherited from my father's parents, and two simple brass ones my mother had bought with her first earnings. They were the precious ones and she lit those first.

The dripping candle wax, soft and translucent, was irresistible. I always tried to break off a small piece. My elder sister, Rebecca, slapped my hand away.

'You know you mustn't. It's *Shabbat*.'

She was too late. I would hide my hands under the stiff white tablecloth, rolling the ball of wax between my fingers.

A large shiny plaited loaf, a *challah*, was covered by a satin cloth with gold fringes. '*Lichvod Shabbat Kodesh*'- 'To Honour the Holy Sabbath' – embroidered across it. The Hebrew letters were surrounded by satin-work flowers in pink and red.

We had to wait for my father to come home from the synagogue to bless and pour the *Kiddush* wine. My sisters and I watched hungrily as he cut the loaf, the black poppy seeds on the top bouncing off onto the tablecloth. Breaking off a piece for each of us, he passed around the antique cut glass goblet for us to take a sip of the sweet kosher wine.

Supper was always cold fried fish with *chrane*, a fiery mixture of horseradish and beetroot. We tried to make each batch of *chrane* last as long as possible. Peeling and grating the long horseradish root makes tears pour from your eyes.

When the supper things were cleared away, we sat around the kitchen table, talking and arguing by the flickering candlelight. My mother told us off for all talking at once, so we sisters had to take turns. Rebecca told stories from work, Hannah, my middle sister, and I gossiped about school.

'You should have seen our teacher making eyes at the school inspector. She's really old, at least 40.'

We all had something to say about the films we'd seen that week.

Hannah and I went to bed first. It was forbidden to switch on a light on the Sabbath, so the bedroom we sisters shared was dark.

I was in awe of Rebecca. I would be scolded if I was cheeky to her. I had to be respectful to my elders, but I loved Hannah.

Sometimes Hannah would say she wasn't Hannah, she was Cynthia Levy, an evil girl who held my sister prisoner in the light bulb hanging from the ceiling. She would whip Hannah until she bled if I didn't do exactly what she told me. Even though it was the Sabbath, she would say I must flick the brass light switch on and off three times, or creep under the bed amongst all the dust balls and stay there until she said I could come out. It was years before I stopped believing in Cynthia Levy. I would do anything this other girl asked, rather than let her do anything bad to Hannah.

When Hannah said, 'I'll tell you a nice story' often she'd tell me a ghost story; about things that pinched you in the night, headless knights in armour and ghosts that hid in the toilet. Her favourite was the one about the ghost who strangled the man who stole the golden arm from his coffin.

I was afraid of making my way in the pitch dark through the kitchen to our toilet on the balcony. I'd put it off until I was bursting, sure a ghost was waiting to pounce. The long iron lavatory chain clanked as I pulled it – just like the sound of shackles being dragged along the ground. I kept my eyes shut until I was safely back in bed. If I couldn't see the ghost, it wasn't there.

I knew there were ghosts inside the arm of the chair that stood by our black coal-fired range. If I put my ear on the wooden arms I could hear them talking. Hannah spoiled it for me.

'You're hearing the people downstairs, Abby Lalla,' she said.

I hated the nickname. Luckily only my sisters used it.

Every summer my mother, Hannah and I caught the steam train from Fenchurch Street Station to Southend-on-Sea, though my mother told our friends and neighbours that we were going to the posher suburb of Westcliff. We stayed for a week in a Kosher bed and breakfast, always a long walk from the seafront. My father couldn't afford to take a week off work and there were no paid holidays pre-World War 2. He came down on the Sunday at the end of our holiday, spent the day and took us home.

On rainy days, we'd huddle in cafes or by the bandstand. You weren't allowed back into the B & B until supper at 6.30pm.

One afternoon, my mother took Hannah and me to the Kursaal, the huge funfair on the seafront. I suddenly found myself alone in front of the big wheel. At first, I was too fascinated watching the cages going up and over and up and over to be upset, but then I realised my mother and sister were gone and I was all alone. My dad said I should ask a policeman if I got lost but I couldn't see one anywhere. Everyone was so tall, I couldn't see past them.

Had they gone back to the Lane and left me? I was in tears by the time they found me.

'You naughty girl,' my mother scolded. 'Always dozy. Next time don't let go of my hand. There must be hundreds of people here. You could get lost for good.'

CHAPTER 4

A Country at War

We were tired and hungry, my sister Hannah and I, as we stood waiting in Littleport Village Hall, waiting to be chosen by someone, anyone.

'Don't snivel,' Hannah said. 'No-one will take us in if they see you crying.' She pushed my hand away. 'You're too old to hold hands Abby, and anyhow your hands are always wet and sticky.'

'*Operation Pied Piper*', the plan for the evacuation of children from areas likely to be bombed, was in place long before World War 2 was declared. People in safe areas with spare bedrooms were urged to take in evacuees. They would be paid 10/6d a week for the first child and 8/6d for each subsequent child. Nearly a million children were evacuated on Friday September 1st, 1939. London railway stations were packed with children and whole trains were commandeered.

Parents had been given a list of clothing to pack. Girls needed 1 spare vest, 1 pair of knickers, 1 petticoat, 1 slip, 1 blouse, 1 cardigan, a coat or Mackintosh, nightwear, a comb, towel, soap, face-cloth, boots or shoes and plimsolls.

Hannah hadn't yet started at the local grammar school, Central Foundation School for Girls, so she came with me to my school, Jews Free Junior School. She carried the brown cardboard suitcase we shared. Our teachers marched us to Liverpool Street station and onto the train to Littleport. Many mothers and a few fathers came to the station with their children. Hannah and I were alone.

'You're old enough to go on your own,' my mother said. 'I've put a stamped and addressed postcard in your case for you to send me your address as soon as you're settled.'

I was seven, nearly eight and Hannah was thirteen. She wore her new school uniform and I was in my dark green skirt and jumper and my navy serge coat, the one with the collar that rubbed. Our gas masks in their square brown boxes hung on tapes around our necks and we had identity labels printed with our names and evacuee numbers tied through our buttonholes.

We waited and waited. Maybe no-one wanted to take in two sisters from the East End of London. Then, when we were beginning to dread that no-one would ever choose us, a young couple beckoned us over. The husband, a big man with a bushy red beard, lowered the tail-gate of an open-bed lorry and put in our suitcase.

'Jump in girls. The farm's only a couple of miles from here. You can sit on those potato sacks. Don't mind the straw. It's this year's and quite clean.'

We clung to the side of the lorry as he hurtled through the narrow country lanes. Empty fields stretched for miles, right up to the horizon. The harvest had been gathered in, and most of the fields were brown, though the verges were still green. Ripe purple blackberries hung from brambles at the side of the road.

They ushered us in to a large brick-built farmhouse. It was completely surrounded by fields and there were no other houses in sight. Back home in Petticoat Lane, there were tightly packed buildings wherever you looked.

We had a fried egg on toast for tea and at 7.30 they shooed us off to bed in a little attic bedroom. Horses snuffled in a nearby field and there was a herd of cows in the distance. I was scared when I heard an owl hooting. I crept closer to Hannah and pulled the blankets over my head. When dawn came, the birds woke us. It was so noisy and different.

After porridge for breakfast, they took us in their lorry back to the Village Hall. We were to spend the day there with the other evacuees from our school. The farmer and his wife were going off to a wedding.

'What's that horrible smell?' Hannah asked the farmer, as we climbed into the lorry.

'Don't you worry your little head, miss. It's only Fred's piggeries.'

I hoped no-one would expect us to eat pork. Jews weren't allowed. We'd been taught that pigs were filthy animals, non-Kosher, *traife*.

It was Saturday, *Shabbat,* so we had a short service, lunch and some games. After tea, we were sent back to our billets.

One of the teachers pointed out the way.

'The farm is straight along that road. They said you can't miss it.'

We trudged back to the farmhouse and knocked on the door but no-one answered. We went around the back but the back door was locked. We peeped into the kitchen but no-one was there. As the blood-red sunset gave way to night, we cowered in a corner of the porch away from the huge Alsatian that strained at his chain, trying to get at us, snapping and barking. We were terrified, alone in that vast expanse. Finally, the farmer and his wife came home.

'Sorry we're late. We forgot all about you.'

They gave us milk and biscuits, and sent us up to bed.

The next day the farmer's wife said it wouldn't work.

'We can't be baby-sitting you every night. You're going to have to stay with my mother. She lives in the village and she'll take you in.'

Once again, we climbed into the back of the lorry. They didn't talk to us or smile. We never knew their names.

Mrs Hopwood, a tiny white-haired woman, not quite as tall as Hannah, was waiting at the door of her stone cottage. She had bright blue eyes, lots of wrinkles and a big smile.

'Come in. Come in,' she said, giving Hannah and me a hug. 'I'll show you around. My little cottage is tiny compared with the farmhouse.'

On the ground floor at the front there was a parlour. At the back, there was a kitchen and a pocket-sized garden with an outside toilet at the far end. Butterflies hovered over borders ablaze with colour. The lawn was smooth and bright green. We could smell newly cut grass.

On the first floor, there were two bedrooms. Mrs Hopwood took us into the front bedroom.

'This will be your room, my dears. I've no need for it now that Mr Hopwood has passed away.'

A big brass double bed, a tall mahogany wardrobe and a dressing table crowded the room. A porcelain bowl with a border of roses and a large ewer stood on the dressing table, while a matching chamber pot peeped out from under the bed. The wallpaper was pale pink and decorated with tiny roses. It was all lovely and cosy.

'We don't have a bathroom, my dears. I still use my tin bath. We'll have a big coal fire going in the kitchen, and you'll be warm

48

as toast. You can leave your things for now. Come on down and we'll have a bite to eat.'

We had scones still warm from the oven, as much butter as we liked, strawberry jam and strong sweet tea. When we'd eaten all the scones, Mrs Hopwood wiped the crumbs and jam off my face with a damp flannel.

'There now,' she said. 'That's better, isn't it?'

She took us over to a large sepia photograph on the wall. There were two rows of children with a man and a woman in the centre.

She pointed to the man with a long white beard.

'That's the late Mr Hopwood, God Rest His Soul, with his hand on my shoulder, and there are all the children – had 22 and raised 19. We had to eat in shifts, we did. There was never enough room for us all to sit down at once, save at Christmas, when we all squeezed up.'

I'd never heard of anyone having that many children. *The Old Woman who lived in a Shoe,* popped into my head.

> *There was an old woman who lived in a shoe,*
> *She had so many children she didn't know what to do;*
> *She gave them some broth without any bread;*
> *She whipped them all soundly and put them to bed.*

I smiled at my thoughts. Hannah dug me in the ribs.

'Don't be rude. What are you laughing at?'

'Nothing,' I said. 'That hurt.'

I couldn't imagine Mrs Hopwood whipping her children or not giving them any bread.

When it was bedtime, Hannah and I snuggled up underneath the patchwork eiderdown and were soon fast asleep.

The wail of an air raid siren woke us up. We jumped out of bed, found our gas-masks and pulled them on. We were sure we were about to be bombed or gassed. Maybe the Germans had already landed.

Mrs Hopwood came to check that we were OK. She stood in the doorway trying to catch her breath. She was laughing so much that tears ran down her face.

'You should see yourselves, my lovelies, looking for all the world like a couple of monsters. It's only a practice. Do take those nasty things off. I'll tuck you in and you must go straight back to sleep. You'll want to be up bright and early in the morning.'

Next day was Sunday September 3rd. Mrs Hopwood had the radio on in the kitchen and we listened to Mr Chamberlain's speech.

'I am speaking to you from the Cabinet Room at 10 Downing Street. This morning the British Ambassador in Berlin handed the German Government a final note stating that, unless we hear from them by 11 o'clock that they were prepared at once to withdraw their troops from Poland, a state of war would exist between us. I have to tell you now that no such undertaking has been received, and that consequently this country is at war with Germany.'

Mrs Hopwood put her arms around us.

'I never thought there'd be another war in my lifetime. Our war was the war to end all wars. Those Jerries. They'll never learn, but we'll beat them again like we did last time.'

The few weeks we spent with Mrs Hopwood were all sunshine. On Fridays, she gave us the money to go to the fish and chip shop on the corner for cod and chips and a bottle of Tizer. I'd never tasted Tizer before. At home, my father sometimes bought me a glass of the red, slightly sour drink, sarsaparilla, in Petticoat Lane market.

It tasted like hot, sweet medicine and was supposed to be good for you. Tizer was quite different – fizzy and very sweet. It dyed your tongue bright orange.

Then it was decided that it wasn't sensible for the CFS girls billeted in Littleport and other villages to catch the bus into Ely every day. Hannah and I were to move to Ely. We would be billeted with Mr and Mrs Stonemartin and I would go to the local junior school.

Next day a slight man with a small mousey moustache drew up.

'Have you got them ready?' he asked Mrs Hopwood with a shy smile.

Hannah and I were both crying as we kissed her goodbye and got into Mr Stonemartin's small black car. A wire-haired terrier sat on the front passenger seat and we squeezed into the back.

'Must be nice people, if they have a lovely little dog like that,' Hannah whispered.

Mr Stonemartin turned around.

'She's called Jill. Mrs Stonemartin dotes on her.'

He stopped the car in front of a semi-detached 1930s house, one of a long stretch of similar houses on the outskirts of Ely.

Mrs Stonemartin, a tall thin-faced woman, opened the door. She had a bright red turban tied around her head and wore a patterned wrap-around apron.

'Welcome girls,' she said. 'Take off your shoes in the house, please, and be careful how you walk on our new stair carpet. It was only laid two weeks ago. When you're going up and down, make sure you walk on the sides to save wear.'

The stair carpet had an all over vivid floral design that clashed with the large chrysanthemums on the wallpaper. The glaring colours made me feel ill.

'I'll show you to your bedroom and you can put your things away. Mind you always clear up after yourselves and keep everything tidy. Even our lovely dog, Jill, knows not to make a mess.'

The bedroom had twin beds. I'd never slept on my own. At home, I'd been sleeping in the large double mahogany bed with Hannah after my grandmother died. What if I was scared in the night?

'Hurry up girls and fold your things nicely. Supper will be ready at six. The bathroom is along the hall. Wash your hands properly before you come down.'

By now I was starving. We'd had some paste sandwiches before we left Mrs Hopwood, but that was hours before.

We sat down at the dining table and Mrs Stonemartin brought in four plates and a dish for the dog. She ladled out some cold lumpy mashed potatoes and served each of us two tinned sardines swimming in oil. The look of them made me feel queasy. Sardines on toast sprinkled with lots of lemon juice was my favourite supper, but my mother always poured off the oil when she opened the tin.

For afters, we had cold tinned rice pudding with a tiny spoonful of jam. I was afraid I might be sick, but I managed to eat it.

We had grown to love Mrs Hopwood. She was the exact opposite of our new billet lady, Mrs Stonemartin, and her cooking had been delicious.

'It's seven o'clock. Time for you girls to go to bed. Make sure you brush your teeth and say your prayers before you get into bed. Luckily you have a nice clean carpet to kneel on. I don't suppose you have that where you come from.'

It wasn't something Jews did – kneel down to pray – but I prayed that night that we wouldn't have to stay with the Stonemartins. She was horrible, though Mr Stonemartin tried to be friendly and smiled at us when she wasn't looking.

Next evening, we had cold lumpy mashed potatoes again, this time with a small slice of pale meat that had a thick rim of fat. I hate fat. Although the Chief Rabbi said Jews were allowed to eat non-Kosher meat in wartime, I left the meat on the side of my plate.

'Your sister's eating hers. Why aren't you?'

'I'm not allowed to eat meat,' I said.

'All the more for the rest of us,' Mrs Stonemartin said, putting my meat onto her plate.

The next two months were miserable, but when the Stonemartins went away for a weekend they asked their neighbours to have us from Friday night to Sunday night. Mr and Mrs Johnson were completely different from the Stonemartins. As soon as you walked into their half of the semi-detached house you could feel how warm and friendly they were.

We had shepherd's pie for supper and golden syrup pudding with hot creamy custard for afters. It seemed too rude to ask for seconds, though I would have liked to.

'Come on girls,' Mrs Johnson said. 'Let's get you a nice warm bath and into pyjamas.'

It snowed heavily that weekend. The four of us threw snowballs and we made a huge snowman. We never had enough snow at home to make one. We wished we could stay with the Johnsons forever but on Sunday night we had to go back.

Then I did something awful. I wrote to my parents about how wonderful it had been staying with the Johnsons, and how horrible Mrs Stonemartin was, and left the letter lying on top of the chest of drawers in our bedroom.

Dear Mummy and Daddy

We had a lovely time with Mr and Mrs Johnson. It snowed and we made an enormous snowman. We gave him two pieces of coal for eyes, a carrot for his nose and two little curved sticks for his lips. He looked cold, so Mr Johnson tied a scarf around his neck and put a pipe in his mouth. We wish we could be billeted with them, but they're both teachers and they said they wouldn't be able to take us in permanently. We had to go back to the old sourpuss, Mrs Stonehearted, and her horrid food.

Love to everyone.

Yours sincerely

Abigail Waterman

When we got home after school Mrs Stonemartin was livid.

'That's all the thanks I get, after taking you in, you ungrateful child. *Mrs Stonehearted* indeed. You can go straight to bed. Don't even think about supper.'

I didn't mind. I hated her food and I was glad not to have to eat it.

My father came to see us two weeks before Christmas.

'Abby, you look like a skeleton. What have you been up to? Aren't you eating?'

'Please take me home, Daddy, please. I hate it here. Mrs Stonemartin is horrible. Mr Stonemartin says she likes Jill, her dog, better than him. If he's sitting in front of the gas fire she makes him move away so that Jill can get warm. He's got some shrapnel in his leg from the trenches, and it leaks nasty yellow stuff. He needs to change the bandages every few days. Mrs Stonemartin said she can't bear to see it and he must do it himself. He knows Hannah is going to be a doctor, so he lets her help him. She doesn't

54

like children. She hates them. Hannah says she only took us in for the money.'

'You'd better come home, Abby, but you should stay here, Hannah. You need to get on with your schooling, now that you've got into grammar school.'

'I'm not staying if Abby's going,' Hannah said. 'But why can't she stay? She's just being stupid about not eating.'

'You can see the state she's in. I won't stop you coming home, if that's what you want, Hannah, but you know it's the wrong thing to do.'

On the train back to London I snuggled up to my father. Hannah ignored me and sat staring out of the window.

'I'm never, ever going to be evacuated again,' I said.

In the New Year, I went to the temporary junior school at Toynbee Hall. It was the time of the so-called Phony War. The bombing hadn't started, and children had begun to trickle back to London. Makeshift classes were set up where there were large enough rooms, but there were no grammar school places. Grammar schools were all still evacuated. As Hannah was now fourteen, she left school. My parents sent her to Pitman's College to learn shorthand and typing. She could become a secretary, like our elder sister, Rebecca. No way could she become a doctor now.

I shivered as I crossed Commercial Road. My hands were like ice. Since I came back from Ely, I couldn't seem to get warm.

'It's because you let yourself get so thin, you silly girl,' my father said. 'We'll have to fatten you up.'

My father left for work at seven in the morning so he couldn't take me to school on my first day.

'Now you've turned eight you're old enough to go on your own,' my mother said when I asked her to take me instead.

I walked up the paved path to Toynbee Hall and pushed as hard as I could, but the door wouldn't give. I knocked and a large smiling woman opened it.

'Come on in, girlie,' she said. 'Are you for the juniors?'

When I nodded, she rubbed my cold hands in her large warm ones, and took me upstairs to a room full of children. They sat at small wooden tables with separate chairs, not at all like the school desks I was used to.

The teacher standing at the front came over.

'You must be Abby Waterman. We've been expecting you. Say "Hello" to Abby, children.'

Some muttered 'Hello', while a boy near the front put his hand over the side of his mouth so the teacher couldn't see, and poked out his tongue.

'You can sit in that empty place there,' the teacher said. She pointed to a table in the middle of the room.

They were doing long multiplication and division which I had learned in Ely. I found the sums quite easy and put my hand up a couple of times with the answers.

When the bell went, I hoped it was break time so I could go to the toilet, but it was Composition.

'I want you all to write about your last birthday.'

I was in Ely for my birthday and Mrs Stonemartin was especially horrid. My father had sent me a big bar of chocolate – his ration for a month – and Mrs Stonemartin took it away. She said it was bad for children's teeth. Mr Stonemartin secretly gave me a shilling. He told me to hide it and not to tell. I bought a tiny teddy in the little shop near school and took it with me everywhere. I hid it in the pocket in my knicker leg.

I sat my teddy on the table in front of me and started to write.

'My last birthday . . .' I began.

In Ely, you had to wait until the mid-morning break to go to the toilet, but I had no idea whether that would be soon or not. I carried on writing for a bit, but I got really upset thinking about Ely and Mrs Stonemartin and everything. I squeezed my legs together, ever so hard, but it was no use. A warm trickle ran down my leg onto the floor.

'Please Miss,' said the boy who'd stuck out his tongue at me. 'The new girl's done a wee-wee.'

Everyone turned round to look and some of them giggled. I wanted to disappear.

The teacher put her arm around my shoulders.

'Don't worry, my dear. Sally can take you to the nurse. She'll find you some nice dry underwear. It's hard – your first day at school.'

The worst thing was going home afterwards. I knew if I told, I'd get a slap for disgracing myself, so I slipped into the girls' toilet and put my wet knickers back on and stuffed the school knickers into my coat pocket. I'd give them back next day.

When I got home I sat down very carefully so the wet part didn't soak my skirt. There was a space under our bed, so I spread my knickers over my shoes, and pushed them to the back, well hidden away. They were dry by morning so my mother never found out.

We were playing tag during morning break when some of the big girls came over and started lifting our skirts. I ran away fast as I could, straight into the corner of a brick wall. For a moment, I couldn't understand what had happened. The other girls in my class gathered round me.

'Your forehead's all bloody,' said Sally, who had taken me to get dry knickers. 'Better go and see nurse.'

I got out my handkerchief and dabbed at my head.

'It's nothing,' I said.

I didn't want to make a fuss and get sent home, but all afternoon my head hurt. I was wearing the new brown leather gloves my father had bought me. As I walked home I took off my right glove and held it over my forehead. That way no-one could see the blood and ask me about it.

By the time I climbed up to our tenement on the third floor, I felt sick and dizzy. I just about got in before I was sick. Luckily, I made it as far as the kitchen sink.

'What have you been up to?' my mother asked.

I was used to being told off, or even slapped, for falling over. I pulled my hair over the sore place on my forehead.

'It's nothing,' I said, but she lifted my fringe.

'Been playing rough games again, have you? How many times have I told you to be careful?'

Soon I was sick again and very dizzy indeed. My father had come home by then.

'You poor wounded soldier,' he said. 'We'd better get the doctor.'

Dr Wilson asked me what had happened. I told him we'd been playing tag and I'd tried to get away from the big girls trying to lift my skirt.

'I've told her so many times to be careful. She shouldn't play with the big girls,' my mother said.

She didn't understand. They broke into our games and chased us. She wouldn't listen.

'Abby's got a bit of a concussion,' Dr Wilson said. 'Keep her off for a couple of days. If she gets worse call me again.'

I didn't get worse, and I went back to school two days later. I made up my mind that if I hurt myself I would never tell my mother. It was no use expecting her to *kiss it make it better,* maybe my father, and maybe Hannah, but never her.

Maybe she wasn't my real mother. Maybe I was adopted or I was a changeling like in the stories.

CHAPTER 5

To Dawlish

The *Blitz* began on September 7th, 1940. The Luftwaffe bombed London on 57 consecutive nights. We tried taking shelter on the platform of Aldgate East Underground station, where we slept in rows tightly packed like sardines, but we hated it there. I often walked in my sleep, and although I knew that the electric current was turned off at night, I was terrified that I might walk to the edge of the platform and fall onto the lines. I hated being hemmed by so many people and the crush on the stairs as we made our way down to the platform where we slept was frightening.

I was right to be scared. A couple of years later, on March 3rd, 1943, the air-raid warning siren sounded and the people who used Bethnal Green Underground made their way down the short flight of steps as usual. However, a panic was caused by the explosion at Victoria Park nearby of a new type of anti-aircraft rocket directed at the Luftwaffe planes overhead. A woman fell and many of the 300 people waiting to descend also tripped. 172 were crushed to death, of whom 62 were children. For wartime security reasons, the incident was hushed up at the time, but later Herbert Morrison, the Home Secretary, published a full report stating that although there were several factors, the main cause was the 'irrational' behaviour of the crowd surging down the stairwell. The report hardly endeared itself to the grieving relatives.

Finally, we were allocated spaces in the basement of a factory in Middlesex Street and started to sleep there every night.

Soon, posters appeared saying that children still in London should be sent to the country. I told my parents I wouldn't go. After the miserable time I'd had in Ely, I absolutely didn't want to be evacuated again.

My seventeen-year-old cousin, Alan, came to our flat.

'You'll love it, Abby,' he said. 'There are lots of boys and girls of your age at the hostels. They're Jewish, so you won't have a problem with the food again.'

I blushed, embarrassed. Had my mother told everyone about me not eating meat when I was evacuated with the Stonemartins?

'Surely you can't like sleeping in the shelter every night?'

He was right. I hated using the smelly chemical toilets and coming up in the morning light to find yet another building demolished and people already clambering over the ruins trying to rescue a few precious possessions. One day we got home to find a bomb had dropped so close that all our windows had shattered. I had to wait in the street until my parents cleared up the glass. My father had to queue to be given some sheets of cardboard to fill the gaps until a glazier could come.

'The hostels are all by the sea,' Alan continued. 'You can learn to swim and have all sorts of adventures.'

'How do you know? It might be awful there,' I said.

'Look, silly. I work in one of the hostels, don't I? I've only come up to London for the weekend. If you say 'yes', I'll take you back with me. I checked. They've got room for you.'

Over the weekend, I got used to the idea of going to the country. Alan was right. I hated sleeping in the shelter with all those people. And it was exciting – the idea of going away all by myself, this time without Hannah.

Alan collected me on Monday morning just before eight. I was up and dressed by six and had my gas mask slung round my neck ready. He had a huge bag of sandwiches and drinks that Aunt Bertha had packed for him. She believed in feeding up her children, though Alan was as thin as a rake. You couldn't say he was handsome, but I loved it when he smiled down at me.

I'd been on short journeys – to Westcliff-on-Sea, where we went for a few days each summer, and to Littleport where I was evacuated before – but never on a long train journey like this one, all the way to Dawlish in South Devon. I sniffed the air as our train chugged its way out of the station. My father used to take me to Liverpool Street station to watch the trains and I loved the smell of steam engines.

Alan let me have the window seat and I sat with my nose pressed against the window. I didn't want to miss a second. When people in the gardens next to the railway line waved. I waved back.

'The people in those houses are so lucky,' I said. 'They can watch the trains all day long. Look! You can see right into their bedrooms.'

I giggled as a large pink lady stretched luxuriously at the window of a bungalow.

'Look. She's got nothing on. You can see her titties.'

My hand went up to cover my mouth. My mother would threaten to wash out my mouth with soap, if I used a word like that.

Alan opened the packet of food – jam sandwiches, cream cheese bagels, two packets of Smith's crisps with their little blue twists of salt, almond biscuits, apples and a huge bottle of Tizer.

'Tizer's my very favourite,' I said. 'Mrs Hopwood used to send us buy it on Fridays to have with our fish and chips. She was our second billet lady and we loved her. We hated it when we had to move to Ely, to the Stonemartins.'

When we finished the sandwiches and all the food, I fell asleep. I woke up as the sea came into view. I dug Alan in the ribs.

'Look, Alan, look. Look how blue the sea is, not all mud like in Westcliff. And why are the cliffs so red? Can we go paddling? Now? Before we go to the hostel? Are you sure they'll teach me to swim? Will there really be lots of children my age?'

He looked down at me.

'I don't know, no, no, yes and no.'

'Please don't tease me. Will there?'

'Well, you'll be the youngest, at least at first. They only agreed to take you because I work in the Teignmouth hostel. But I'll come over and see you on my days off. Anyway, you'll have so many friends you won't miss me at all.'

When we got out at Dawlish station, the air smelled salty and full of seaweed. It was sunny but quite chilly. I shivered in my new dark green coat. My mother had only finished it the night before. The material was stiff and itchy, especially where the collar rubbed. I always had trouble with the collars of my coats. Maybe my neck was too short.

Alan held my hand as we trudged up the hill to my new home.

A long gravel drive led up to an enormous white house with bay windows on either side of double wooden doors. Alan rang the bell and a plump red-faced woman came to the door.

'Alan. It's good to see you. Is this Abby Waterman?' She gave him a loud smacking kiss. 'Come in. Come in. The goulash is nearly ready. You'll stay and have some?'

'Sorry. I must go. My train leaves in twenty minutes. I'll have to hurry or I won't make it.'

I tried to be brave but the tears still fell.

'Can't I come with you, to your hostel? I'll be good, really I will, and I promise I'll eat everything.'

He knelt down and gave me a hug.

'Now you be a good brave girl and stop crying. Our hostel is completely full, too full. I promised I'll come and see you, and I will. You go along now. Gilda will look after you.'

I watched until he disappeared around the bend in the drive. Gilda took my cold hand in her warm one.

'Come on *liebchen*. I'll show you where you'll sleep. Then you can have a bite to tide you over until supper.'

I followed Gilda up the carved dark wooden staircase. I shivered at the sight of a man pierced by arrows in the stained-glass window on the first landing.

'Don't worry about that. You'll soon get used to it. This house used to belong to a very religious Christian family. It's one of their saints.'

I edged away from the window and squeezed myself close to her.

The next landing led onto a long corridor. She pushed open the door of a bedroom containing four black metal bunk beds. Gilda put my case on the lower bunk in the corner and pointed to the basin.

'That's where you'll wash in the morning. Matron will give you a bath once a week. Do you know the Hebrew Alphabet?' I nodded and she went on 'This is room *Aleph*. It shouldn't be difficult to remember – the first letter of the *Aleph Bet*. We have a competition each week for the tidiest room. You'll have to do your bit to make sure *Aleph* comes top.'

I didn't like the sound of any of this. I felt my eyes begin to fill again but I managed to sniff my tears away.

'I promised I'd be good and eat everything.'

'Of course you will, little one. You're talking to the cook.'

Taking my hand, she led me down to the kitchen. A huge cooking range took up the whole of one side of the room. The sound and smell of a huge pot of goulash bubbling away made me feel hungry.

'Does that smell delicious, or does it? You won't only eat it all up, Abby. You'll be asking for more.'

I soon felt at home in the hostel. I was not quite nine and the youngest. For the first time ever, I was made a big fuss of – by everyone, by the older children as well as by the grown-ups in charge of us. Though I had to pass a test to join the gang of the younger children.

'Are you rude?' Sophie asked.

I wasn't sure what she meant but I said 'Yes.'

'Hold out your right hand.'

She took my hand and the other five placed their hands over ours.

'You can join,' she said.

Like all the other children, I had to do my share of the chores. Some did the breakfast washing up and some washed up the supper things. Others swept or mopped the floors. The older boys took turns mowing the grass in the huge back garden.

Each bedroom had a large old-fashioned porcelain pedestal basin with hot and cold brass taps. My job was to clean all the taps before I left for school. There was no central heating, no heating at all in the bedrooms, though we had big wood fires in the dining and sitting rooms. It wasn't so bad in the summer, even if the water hadn't yet heated up. In winter, when you could see the lacy patterns of *Jack Frost* on the window panes, the water was icy. By November I had chilblains on my fingers – red itchy things that throbbed in bed at night and kept me awake. In London, I always had chilblains on my toes in the winter, but they were worse on my fingers. Some mornings I could hardly hold my pencil in class.

It was hard to get all the basins finished and be early for school. Those in the boys' rooms were especially dirty, while, since the girls washed their hair in the basins, the plug holes in their rooms were often blocked with long strands of hair. I had to fish them out with a hairpin. The *Brasso* I used to shine the taps turned the cloth and my hands black. It was agony getting it off my swollen fingers. If I got to school, Dawlish Junior School, with dirty hands, I'd be told off by our headmistress. She always inspected our hands at the end of assembly.

Evacuees had doubled the number of pupils. The space problem was solved by having two classes in one room, separated by a wooden folding screen. You couldn't see the other class, but you could hear them.

I mostly arrived early enough to avoid a black mark. To get to school in time, I ran down the steep hill on the way, often tripping – over a stone, over my laces or over nothing at all. I always had scabs on my knees from falling over and grazing them. The scabs itched like mad. I'd sit picking at them during class until the last bit came off leaving a small bright pink scar.

Victor, the local Dawlish boy who shared my school desk, would wait until I lifted my skirt to scratch and try to lift my skirt higher. We'd scuffle and then we'd both be scolded. If we'd been noisy enough, we would have to write out a hundred times '*I must not be disruptive in class.*'

The bench we sat on, and the support for our desks, were shared, but we had separate lift-up lids and porcelain inkwells. When I wasn't looking, Victor would roll up a strip of paper and stuff it in my inkwell. We were only issued with one pen and one brass nib. If I didn't notice what he had done and pushed my pen into the inkwell too hard, my nib would bend back on the rolled-up paper and be ruined. As he was always getting into trouble for fighting in the playground, I knew sooner or later he'd be called to the front of the class to be told off. Then I'd swap my pen and inkwell for his.

Most of the time we got on well enough, but we competed for being class monitor. It wasn't fair. Unlike me, Victor was never late. He had no chores before school and he lived nearby. To be form monitor and give out the stationery, you had to have the highest number of gold stars and only a few black marks. All stationery in state schools was free and if you were the monitor you could sneak out extra nibs or other goodies for your friends. We called it 'nicking' not stealing.

Sometimes my chores took me so long that I didn't get to school on time and got a black mark, while Victor was always being caught fighting in the playground. He sometimes got more black marks than I did but we were mostly neck and neck with the number of gold stars.

We took turns with Arthur Mee's *Children's Encyclopaedia* and tried to find new things the other hadn't yet discovered.

'What's the most poisonous snake in the world?' 'Where did Napoleon die?'

Then Victor would spoil it by asking if my knickers were navy blue like last week, or were they green, and did they have a pocket in the leg for a handkerchief, like his sister's did.

I had been at Dawlish for about six months when Philip came to the hostel. Gilda came out holding his hand

'This is Philip,' she said. 'Abby will look after you for the morning. Come here Abby and say hello.'

I saw a boy of about my own age with mussed-up hair that badly needed cutting. His blue long-sleeved shirt was pulled tight over his skinny chest and his shorts were so big he had to keep hitching them up. He looked awkward and uncomfortable. We held out our hands and shyly shook them. Philip's hand was hot and clammy.

'I'll show you my favourite places,' I said.

I showed him the bare patch of earth I'd cleared right in the back corner of the garden and told him I'd saved up for a packet of snapdragon seeds.

'They haven't come up yet but the packet said it would take two or three weeks.'

I then took him to my favourite tree. It had a thick low branch that had started to break off the main trunk but it would hold my weight even if I bounced up and down.

'Are you allowed to climb trees here? We weren't allowed to in the orphanage. If you did you got the cane and no supper for three days.'

'You can climb any tree here,' I said. 'This is my secret place. You can share it if you like.'

He took two dusty barley sugars out of the pocket in his shorts and offered me one.

'I want to tell you something,' he said. 'I love you.'

I laughed and gave him a push. He never said it again.

Matron put up a notice saying she had written to our parents asking if they wanted us to learn to play the piano. I didn't think my parents would agree to pay for lessons though they were quite cheap, especially as I had just been in trouble for refusing to wash on the Sabbath.

Three of us girls decided that, as Jews aren't allowed to do any work on the Sabbath or do things as minor as switching on a light, it would also be against the Jewish religion to wash or comb our hair on the Sabbath. On Saturday mornings we got up, dressed and went down to breakfast unkempt and unwashed. Matron wrote to our parents and my father wrote back to say it was all nonsense. I felt let down. He should have supported me.

Matron called me into her office.

'Today is your first piano lesson, Abby. Mind you behave yourself. Your mummy must love you very much to forgive you for that business about not washing on Saturdays. Run along now. Mr Lawson's waiting.'

I knocked on the door of the room where a piano had been delivered the week before.

The smell of cigarettes and mothballs greeted me as I pushed open the door. A short bald-headed man, wearing a rumpled dark grey pin-striped suit, stood by the piano. His waistcoat was tightly stretched across his paunch, a silver watch chain hanging between the pockets. His steelrimmed glasses were held together with sticky tape and perched on the end of his nose. On the top of his forehead, he had a round swelling, about the size of a plum. I tried hard not to stare at it.

'Come in. Come in. You must be Abby Waterman.'

He flicked open his pocket watch.

'Right on time, my dear. I'm Geoffrey Lawson, the organist at St Stephen's.'

He rested his cigarette carefully on the edge of the piano lid and held out a stubby hand for me to shake.

'Nine years old, are we? Ever played before? No? Come and sit yourself down beside me. Tell me what this makes you think of.'

He stuck his half-burnt cigarette back between his lips. As his hands glided over the keys, I was fascinated by the dark curly hair on the backs of his short square fingers. I saw waterfalls, faery grottos, beautiful princesses and knights in shining armour.

'Very good. Chopin of course,' he said, changing to something dark and sinister.

This time the music spoke to me of dwarves toiling in the dark, beating out gold bars in smoke-filled caverns.

'That's it exactly,' he said. 'Wagner.'

He ignored the column of ash dropping off the end of his cigarette. When the cigarette had burnt down, he removed the stub, coughed, and used it to light another, putting the stub into the empty tobacco tin he took out of his waistcoat pocket.

He began by pointing to the black and white keys, explaining that they were named A to G, and that you found middle C by looking for the keyhole below the keyboard. He taught me how to play *London's Burning* as a round, and wrote it out for me letter by letter.

'That's all we've got time for now, my dear. You'll need to practice every day, if you want to be a real pianist. Next week I'll bring a manuscript book and start to teach you how to read music.'

He was a kind and patient teacher. I soon built up a small repertoire of easy pieces. Time slowed at school on Tuesday afternoons until it was home time, and I could rush off to my lesson with Mr Lawson.

One afternoon he played Bach's *Toccata and Fugue in D minor* for me. It was the most beautiful piece of music I'd ever heard.

'Get someone to bring you over to St Stephen's on Sunday

70

morning. I'll be playing it before the service. It's even more magnificent on the organ.'

I nodded, but I knew no-one at the hostel would take me into a church. My orthodox Jewish parents would have been horrified.

Hilda arrived after I had been at the hostel for about a year. She was pretty, with long dark curls and deep brown eyes. I used to write lots of stories and plays. When it was my group's turn to put on the Friday night's entertainment, I'd write a play with her as the beautiful heroine who had to be rescued from danger. The others said I was too small to be the hero, so I'd put in a part for me as a devoted servant or a trusty slave.

Her family had got out of Germany just before war started. She still had a German accent, as well as a German surname, Gotlieb. Three big girls in her class always picked on her. They called her a 'Jerry' and 'Hitler's pet'. 'Why don't you go back to Germany?' they'd shout after her, pinching her arms when the teacher wasn't looking. I told her to tell someone, but she said it would only make things worse. She used to make herself be sick to get out of school. At first Matron allowed her to stay off, but, after the first few times, she made her go just the same.

One day I had a bad sore throat. I couldn't eat or drink and could hardly talk. The nurse took my temperature and put me to bed in the sick room.

Hilda's sickness was bad that day and she said she was too ill to go school. The nurse put her in the bed next to mine, though she still half-thought Hilda was putting it on. Hilda said the light was too bright and her head hurt. When the doctor came, he said she was play-acting again, and told the nurse to give her some aspirin.

71

When I woke next morning, Hilda was curled up in a tight ball, her eyelids swollen shut and she had red blotches on her face and hands. Soon I heard an ambulance arrive to take her to hospital.

After supper Matron called us all into the games room and told us to sit down and be quiet. She said that Hilda had meningitis but that the hospital had a stock of sulphonamides and she'd be OK.

One of the older boys took down the dictionary to look up meningitis. It wasn't much help. It said, 'inflammation of the meninges' so then we had to look up 'inflammation' and 'meninges' and it went on and on.

When we came down to breakfast next day, the grown-ups had red-rimmed eyes and wouldn't look at us. Matron asked for hush. She said that Hilda had died in the night and that everything possible had been done for her.

Hilda's mother and father took her straight from the hospital to London to be buried so I never even had the chance to say goodbye.

In 1942 when I was ten, the school entered me for a Junior County Scholarship. The exam was in three parts: English, Arithmetic and General Intelligence. Until the Education Act of 1944, children had to pay to go to a grammar school unless they won a scholarship. Then their fees were paid and, if they did well enough, their uniform was paid for too. It was the equivalent of the 11+ and taken in the last year of primary school.

The day of the exam fell on *Succoth* (the Feast of Tabernacles), a minor Jewish Holyday. Our matron decided she wouldn't let the four of us sit the Junior County Scholarship on that day and our headmistress agreed to let us take the exam two weeks later.

I was going to be late again. Running too fast down the steep hill, I tripped. My right knee was badly grazed with little pieces of road gravel stuck in the cuts. Blood ran down my shin onto my sock, so I pulled my handkerchief out of the pocket in my knickers and dabbed at my knee. It went on bleeding, so I tied my handkerchief around it and hurried on.

'You're only just in time,' said our headmistress. 'A few minutes later and we would have started without you. You'd have had to wait another year before you could take the scholarship again. Maybe it would do you good to wait.'

'Sorry, Miss Richardson,' I said, and slipped into the side room, where the other three were already at their desks.

I liked tests and exams and I was well into my composition when Miss Richardson came over.

'You've got two of your sums wrong,' she whispered. 'I'll give you that page back.'

I looked at the sums.

'I think they're OK,' I whispered back.

'Well I don't,' she muttered and walked off.

I left the sums as they were and finished the rest of the exam. As the four of us handed in our papers, Miss Richardson glared at me as I passed.

At assembly the next morning, Mr Johnston, our class teacher, called me to the front.

'This is the girl who thinks she knows better than Miss Richardson and who dared to argue with her.'

I looked down, trying not to cry in front of the whole school. Why did he have to tell me off in front of everybody? And I was sure my answers had been correct.

When I went back to my place Victor stuck out his tongue.

'Na, na-na-na, na,' he sang.

I was heartbroken, betrayed. Mr Johnston had always been so

nice to me. He should have known I didn't mean to be impertinent when I'd argued with Miss Richardson. I just hadn't seen anything wrong with my sums.

I'd been wary of Mr Johnston at first. He was the first male teacher I'd ever had, but he had won me round, especially when he started a lunchtime class doing mental arithmetic and spelling. Now I hated him. I would never forgive him, never.

It was a lovely summer's day and I was early. For once I hadn't tripped and I came in without a handkerchief tied around my knee.

'Not a wounded soldier today, I see,' said Mr Johnston, 'and very smart.'

I was wearing the navy skirt and jacket and frilly white blouse my mother had made for me for the previous Jewish New Year.

'You've got your collar half tucked in,' he said, pulling it out and straightening it.

I was standing at the front of the class, waiting to go to my place, wishing he wouldn't touch me.

'Listen up everybody,' he said. 'You too,' he shouted at the noisy class in the other half of the room. 'This clever girl has just won a scholarship to Christ's Hospital School.'

I was confused. I had taken an exam to go to a grammar school, not to Christ's Hospital.

He put his arm around my shoulders.

'Only the cleverest children in the country are offered places to Christ's Hospital School and our little Abby is one of them.'

Victor whistled with two fingers in his mouth. For once he didn't get a clout round the head for whistling in class. Josie smiled as I slipped into my place and said 'Clever Clogs', but in a nice way, as if she meant it.

If Mr Johnston could be so nice today, why was he so horrid before? Why hadn't he been on my side and understood that I wasn't being rude to Miss Richardson?

Christ's Hospital was a boarding school and I was looking forward to going there. I'd read lots of books about girls' boarding schools, and I hadn't been homesick during my two years at the hostel, even though my mother only came to see me three times all the time I was there. I was sure I would be fine at my new school.

My father wrote saying they were trying to find out whether I'd be allowed to take the Jewish Holydays off and eat Kosher food at Christ's Hospital. I was worried about what my mother would say. It made a very orthodox Jew uncomfortable even to say the name 'Christ.'

Then my father came to visit.

'I'm sorry Abby. You won't be able to go to that school. They say they can't make special arrangements for Jews. Stay on here at Dawlish. I'm sure next year you'll get a scholarship to the grammar school.'

'Please Daddy. Don't make me stay. I hate it here.'

Until I'd thought I was going to a boarding school, I'd felt fine about the hostel, been happy there. Now I was so disappointed about not going to Christ's Hospital, I couldn't stand it a minute longer. Tears rolled down my cheeks and I began to sob.

'I don't know what your mother will say, Abby, but you'd better come back with me,' my dad said. 'Can't have you all upset.'

CHAPTER 6

Grammar School

There was no bed for me when I got home. My parents had sold the big double bed that I'd shared with Hannah, and my sisters now slept on the pull-out sofa in the living room. My dad made up a bed by pushing three chairs together, one at each end facing the other, and one in the middle at right angles, laying a child's mattress over the seats. My bed could be dismantled and the sofa closed if one of Rebecca's boyfriends came to tea and we needed to use the room as a parlour again.

What was much more upsetting was that my mother had got rid of the china doll and doll's pram Auntie Jenny had given me for my seventh birthday. It was the first and only birthday present I'd ever been given and I'd loved it and looked after it as if it were a real baby and pram. I was broken-hearted.

'It was mine. How could you give it away?' I cried.

'You're too old for toys, a big girl like you, almost eleven years old. It was taking up too much room,' my mother declared.

And that wasn't all. I was worried about where I would go to school, now my parents wouldn't let me go to Christ's Hospital. I'd won a Christ's Hospital Scholarship, but it didn't come with a free place to a Grammar School.

Luckily, a neighbour was a friend of Miss Abrahams, the gym teacher at Central Foundation School for Girls, the local grammar school that Hannah had attended for one term when we were evacuated to Ely. Miss Abrahams spoke to the headmistress on my behalf.

'Abigail can join the school in September,' the headmistress said, 'but she'll have to take the Junior County Scholarship in the spring. If she passes, she'll be able to stay on. If she doesn't pass the scholarship her parents will have to pay our fees or she'll have to leave. You'll need to drop in her birth certificate in the next few days.'

At first my mother couldn't find my birth certificate but then she found it at the back of the handkerchief drawer. It was just a small piece of paper – a threepenny birth certificate that only registered the birth of a female child on October 8th, 1931 in the Parish of Stepney – no name, no other details. Were my parents so disappointed with me that they wouldn't even spend two shillings and sixpence. for a proper birth certificate? It made me feel like a nobody, as if I didn't really exist.

My mother grumbled about having to make a special trip to Somerset House in the Strand to get a proper copy with my name and the correct details. I took it to the school the next day.

With a bit of taking in, Hannah's CFS school uniform fitted me well enough. I started with the other girls in September and took the scholarship in March.

The names of the girls who'd won a Junior County Scholarship were called out at Assembly. In the corridor afterwards, my best friend, Phyllis, twirled round and round, pulling me towards her.

'Dad promised me a new bike if I passed, and Mum said I could have a party. Will you come? Promise you will.'

When I arrived home for dinner, my father was just leaving for work.

'I've won a Junior County Scholarship,' I said.

'That's good,' he replied, patting me on the head before hurrying off.

'At least if you stay on at grammar school, your uniform won't go to waste,' my mother said. 'Lucky you won that scholarship. We could never have paid for you to stay on if you hadn't got one. Me and your father can't afford that sort of nonsense.'

Maybe it was hard for my mother, seeing me succeed where her favourite daughter, Rebecca, had failed. Though Rebecca was bright, she fell to pieces when she took the scholarship exam. My parents couldn't afford the fees to send her to a grammar school without a scholarship, so she had to stay at Jews Free Senior School until she was 14, when she left to take a Pitman's course in shorthand and typing.

I loved everything about CFS. The classes were small as most of the staff and pupils who had been evacuated to Ely hadn't yet returned to London. Many did not do so until 1945, when WW2 ended.

On my first day, I walked up Bell Lane, through Artillery Row and past Spitalfields Wholesale Fruit and Vegetable Market. I was proud of my school uniform and wide-brimmed black velour hat with its green and red striped ribbon and CFS crest. I didn't mind the whistling and ribbing by the market porters. '*Where did you get that hat?*' they called out in the words of a current popular song.

Where did you get that hat?
Where did you get that tile?
Isn't it a nobby one?
And just the proper style
I should like to have one
Just the same as that
Wherever I go they'd shout "Hello"
Where did you get that hat?

Some farmers still brought in their produce by horse and cart, so there were piles of horse dung to skirt around. There was an overwhelming mixture of smells as I made my way through the market – rotting fruit and vegetables and horse manure. In places the road was slippery, where vegetables that had spilled out of the wooden crates to be crushed underfoot. The porters carried the produce to their customers in large round grey willow baskets, piled up on top of each other in huge swaying towers.

Being in the East End, a high proportion of the girls were Jewish and I never met any anti-Semitism at school. We had joint assembly on Mondays and separate prayers for Christian and Jewish girls for the rest of the week. In the winter, we hurried home on Friday nights to be in time for the Sabbath.

We had exams every year. The results for each subject were announced by the respective teachers one by one and the followers of the brightest girls added up the marks to see who would come top over all – or rather second. I always came top overall but it seemed to cause no hard feelings and I would be congratulated by my closest friends every year as though it was something new. It was a bit unfair really. As a child, I had an almost photographic memory so it was easy to remember what I had been taught. It wasn't until much later when I was in the sixth form that poor teaching resulted in my downfall. I was too used to relying on my memory instead of reading up the subjects in our textbooks.

Miss Jones was our red-haired fiery-tempered Latin teacher who always had us in fits of laughter with her stories about life in a village in Southern Ireland. Most girls in my class hated Latin but I loved it, loved its logic and predictability. We had Virgil's *The Aeneid* and Caesar's *Gallic Wars Book I* as our O-level set books. My friend Phyllis and I took a bus to Marble Arch, meaning to go on to Hyde Park to work on our Latin. We were having tea and chocolate éclairs in J Lyons Marble Arch Corner House when I bet her I could translate the whole of our part of the Gallic Wars. I won and she had to pay for our tea.

'*Gallia est omnis divisa in tres partes*' and '*Horum omnium fortissimi sunt Belgae,*' I chanted.

Miss Brown took us for what was euphemistically called 'Hygiene'. An elderly woman, with her grey hair pulled back in a tight bun, she wore flowered long-sleeved blouses winter and summer, skirts down to the ground and lace-up shiny brown boots. She explained the physiology of menstruation, showed us how to bath a baby doll, told us how important it was to bring children up with love and to know right from wrong and that was it. It was all the sex education that was given to us in the 1940s. We were unbelievably innocent, except for the rare girl who had to leave because she was pregnant.

Miss Woods taught French. She had been brought up in France and we all ended up with a fairly convincing French accent. She often talked about French fashions and was the only one of our teachers with chic. We had young French *assistantes* from time to time. They weren't much older than us and we were horrid to those we didn't like – talking while they were trying to teach us, being rude and generally messing about.

Miss Evans took us for music theory. She was the complete opposite of Miss Simmonds, my piano teacher, who was small, round and motherly. She was skinny and fierce and berated me for solving music questions mathematically.

'Music is an art, not a science. You don't work out your compositions and harmonies by using arithmetic.'

Later I came to understand the beautiful relationship between mathematics and music and how many mathematicians were also talented musicians.

Miss Green was our games mistress. Her legs were like tree trunks sticking out of her navy-blue shorts. I was never much good at Sports and had struggled a bit in P.E. (Physical Education) classes, so it was fantastic when the headmistress announced at Assembly that I had been accepted for the Star Gym class. It met on Wednesdays after school. Perhaps Miss Green had noticed that I had been making a special effort and trying hard to keep up. It couldn't last, of course. I went to a couple of classes but all those acrobatics were really beyond me. I watched with admiration as the others performed vaults and double somersaults with ease. But nothing could take away that marvellous feeling when Miss Johnson read out:

'And Abby Waterman will join the Star Gym Class next term'.

None of my friends was very good at games but we would choose each other to be in our team for netball. That way, none of us got chosen last or felt left out.

In the spring and summer terms we were taken to the swimming pool at Goulston Street baths once a week. I was fine until, having learnt to swim a length doing breast stroke, our swimming instructor said I needed to learn to dive.

'Come on now. You'll be perfectly fine. Try jumping in to begin with and then you can try diving.'

The third week I tried a flat dive, seemed to go down for ever and started to panic. I never tried again, contenting myself with swimming widths across the pool with the beginners.

Miss Gold took us for maths. I always took ages to take in new ideas. I'm sure I was the last to be able to understand decimals or use log tables. I felt I had to understand things thoroughly and make them my own before using them. But in the end, I usually got a star for my homework.

Miss Stone was our history teacher. She taught us history by having us act the characters. We all wanted to take part and as soon as she'd finished talking there would be a forest of hands in the air, hoping to be chosen to perform. I never saw her write down our names but she made sure we all had a turn. However, we didn't mind that the best actress in our class, Josie, was picked most weeks. One week she'd play a tyrannical Queen Elizabeth I and the next week a simpering naughty Anne Boleyn. She was every bit as good at Oliver Cromwell.

Miss Rawlings took us for English. She was tall and thin with grey unruly hair. She looked very old to me but she was probably in her early 50s. At first, I enjoyed writing stories and essays for homework and having them praised and read out to the class, but she frightened me. Maybe I would have stopped being as creative in my writing naturally, but I felt inhibited by her and from having my essays read out at least once a week I was lucky so write one that pleased her enough to be read out once a term. I dried up.

'It's Nitty Nora,' Phyllis hissed.

We all turned to look out of the window. A large, big-bosomed woman in a tightly belted navy raincoat and a wide-brimmed felt hat strode across the playground. Some of the Health Visitors must have been slim and pretty, but mostly they looked like sergeant-majors. We called them all 'Nitty Nora' because they checked us for lice. They also examined the webs of our hands for scabies.

'Girls. Behave yourselves. We need to finish with Henry VIII today,' Miss Stone said.

The bell went and Miss Jones, who was also our form mistress, came in.

'Line up outside the First Aid Room, girls. Alphabetical order please and no running in the corridor. We'll start on *The Aeneid* when you get back.'

We went in one at a time. I was one from last. Only Sophie Yarnstein came after Abigail Waterman. The Health Visitor examined the webs of my fingers for the tell-tale burrows of scabies mites.

'Your hands and nails are very nice and clean, Abigail. You could tell the others a thing or two,' she said.

She asked me to undo my plaits and looked through my hair for nits, the louse eggs that stick to your hair especially behind the ears. Then she called in Sophie, and I went back to our classroom and Latin.

As I stuffed my homework into my satchel, Miss Jones called me back and handed me a brown envelope to give to my parents. I hated those flimsy brown envelopes, especially now that the teachers didn't just lick them down. They used glue so you couldn't steam them open.

My mother would grumble if it was to announce the date of the next prize day.

'Not again,' she'd complain. 'I have to *schlepp* all the way to Hackney Town Hall and listen to those long speeches and the girls scratching away on their violins. You always get a prize for coming top. I'm sure you don't need me there. Do the other mothers go?'

I knew that if Phyllis got a prize her mother would be over the moon and so would the mothers of all my other friends. When Joanne came top of Geography her mother bought her a globe that lit up and Barbara got a new dress for coming first in History.

I walked home as slowly as I could, putting off as long as possible the argument that was sure to come.

When my mother tore open the envelope, she screamed at me:

'You wicked girl. I told you to let me wash your hair. You never listen, and now you've shown me up. They'll think I'm a bad mother, letting you go to school with lice in your hair. And don't think I'm going to go with you to the Cleansing Station. I don't want anyone seeing me there.'

She pushed the letter at me.

My hands shook as I read.

Dear Mrs Waterman,

This is to inform you that your daughter, Abigail Waterman, has been found to be infested with lice. Please take her to the Cleansing Station tomorrow morning. Do not allow her to attend school until she has a written certificate to say she is free of vermin.'

The Health Visitor had said nothing to me. I had no idea there was anything wrong until I read that letter.

My tears brimmed over. I had washed my hair; I had been careful. I threw myself onto my bed. I wished myself out of here, out of this horrible world. My mother hates me and I hate her back and I love her and I want her to love me back.

It had started off as a fabulous day. The sun was shining as I walked to my school in Spital Square. The porters in Spitalfields Market whistled after me and said how pretty I was; I got a gold star for my maths homework and when our English mistress read out my story about our cat getting old and having to be put to sleep, Phyllis said it made her cry. Anna, the girl nobody liked, blew a raspberry of course.

That night my mother insisted on washing my hair, pulling a painful comb through the tangles. She didn't bother heating another kettle when it came to rinsing out the soap: just poured jugs of cold water over my head.

I was so miserable it was hard to get to sleep. The Cleansing Station opened at eight, so I didn't bother with breakfast and caught an early bus, sitting well away from the other passengers, in case they would see lice crawling through my hair.

I was scared that they would shave my head at the Cleansing Station. I'd never known anyone who had lice. Only dirty, uncared for, girls got lice, not a nice clean girl from an orthodox Jewish family.

The brass rail going down the steps to the Cleansing Station shone in the weak winter sunshine, as did the ring around the porthole in the mahogany door. I rang the bell, expecting an ogre of a woman to answer.

A tubby smiling woman opened the door.

'Come in love, come in. You must be Abigail Waterman. I'm Betty. You're my only customer this morning. You must be frozen out there. I'll make us both a nice cup of tea.'

I tried not to cry, but tears still came.

'There, there, dearie. Don't upset yourself. Having lice doesn't mean you're dirty. Plenty of spotlessly clean girls come through here. Anyone can catch lice. Take off your coat and sit yourself down. The kettle's just on the boil now.'

I drank the strong sweet tea and nibbled the Garibaldi biscuits. We always called them 'fly biscuits' because of the currants embedded in them. It wasn't at all what I'd been expecting. I was expecting someone like the matron of one of Charles Dickens' workhouses.

'Finished, love? Then we'll give your hair a good wash and get rid of all those nasty creatures. Lovely strong black hair you've got, and such a pretty girl. I'll bet your Mum's proud of you.'

That made me start crying again.

'Maybe better go to the lav first, dear, and then we'll see to that hair of yours.'

The brass taps in the washroom were as shiny as everything else, and the toilet was spotless. When I got back, Betty gave me a small white towel to hold over my eyes so I wouldn't get soap in them. I didn't like the smell of the shampoo – it smelled like carbolic – but I knew it would kill the lice. The stainless-steel toothcomb pulled at my hair, but at least it was pulling out all the lice and nits.

'I'll towel you off, and then you can sit in the corner and read some of those comics while you dry. Don't want you catching cold now, do we?'

There were copies of the Beano and Dandy and a Girls' Own

Annual. While my hair dried I sat reading them, warm and comfortable.

Betty finally said my hair was dry enough for me to go.

'You have to come back tomorrow, love. Once may not be enough for the lice we have these days. Shouldn't be surprised to hear that old Adolf Hitler sends them over on his bombs. You pop back in the morning, dearie, first thing. I'll check your hair and give you a certificate saying you're free from lice. You'll be able to go straight back to school.'

Betty was so nice to me I started to cry again. I didn't know what to say so I gave her a kiss.

'There, there, my love,' Betty said, flushing bright red. 'It was nothing at all. I can see you're a clean polite girl. It could have happened to anyone.'

When I got home my mother wouldn't speak to me, wouldn't look up from ironing my dad's shirts. Finally, she said:

'Don't you go thinking I'm going to let you wash your hair yourself ever again. That a child of mine should have lice!'

When I went to school next day Miss Jones smiled at me when she called the register and she didn't let on where I'd been the day before.

'We're going to put on *The Wizard of Oz* as our end of term play,' Miss Rawlings said, 'and we'll start reading the book today. Who knows who wrote it?'

I waited to see if anyone else would put up their hand before I put mine up. Noone else did.

'L. Frank Baum,' I said.

'Well done, Abby. Pass around these books and you can read first.'

I got as far as the first sentence

'The Cyclone. Dorothy lived in the midst of the great Kansas prairies, with Uncle Henry, who was a farmer, and Aunt Em, who was the farmer's wife.'

Then I found I had to move my book from side to side to see the whole page.

'What's the trouble?' Miss Rawlings asked as I stumbled over the words.

'I don't feel very well and I can't quite see the words.'

'Oh dear. Phyllis, could you take Abby to the nurse, please.'

As we left, I started to see flashing lights and felt very sick.

'Get me to the toilets,' I gasped.

I staggered into one of the cubicles before bringing up my breakfast.

'You poor thing. Was it something you ate?'

'I don't think so. I think I have to lie down for a bit.'

When we got to the Sick Room the nurse helped me onto a couch and covered me with a blanket.

'See if you can get some sleep, dear. I'm sure you'll soon feel better.'

I slept until mid-afternoon.

'Get your mum to take you to the doctor if you're poorly tomorrow,' the nurse said. 'You run along now if you think you're alright to go home on your own.'

My sight was better but I still felt a bit strange, sort of not quite there.

'Phyllis lives near me. I'll wait for her and we can go home together.'

My mother was never very keen on taking me anywhere, so next morning I went to the doctor's surgery on my own.

I told him what had happened and he shone a light in my eyes and listened to my chest.

'Sounds to me like migraine. You're a bit young but I have seen it in children of your age. How old are you now, twelve? Do you have your periods yet?'

'No,' I said, embarrassed at talking about periods with a man.

'There are tablets you can take if you have more attacks but they have quite serious side effects. I don't want to prescribe them yet. Let's see what happens shall we?'

'What is migraine? Is it dangerous? It was scary only being able to see half the book. The flashing lights weren't frightening because you can make colours come when you close your eyes and rub them.'

'No. It's not dangerous. The blood vessels that supply oxygen to the brain going into spasm is the most likely explanation.'

I nodded wisely, not too sure what spasm of the blood vessels meant. I stayed at home the next day but by the following morning I was fine.

Two weeks later, at the end of the year, Miss Jones read out our exam results. I'd come top. I always came top and I was worried that my mother would moan about having to go to Prize Day yet again. I felt like saying she needn't bother but I knew I'd feel ashamed if all the other mothers and fathers were there. My father never came. He thought prize days were for mothers not fathers.

For the prize day concert, I played the Chopin Prelude in B minor and collected the leather-bound volume of Shakespeare I had chosen from the headmistress's list.

Next morning, I saw flashing lights again, had an awful headache and was horribly sick. I couldn't bear the daylight so I drew the blackout curtains and went to bed.

It only lasted a day but that set the pattern for Prize Days. I was fine while I was revising for exams or when I took them but as soon as Prize Day was over I'd be struck down again. The doctor had made me too scared to take any pills so I never went back, but I never had more than two or three attacks a year and they were soon over. They went on until I left school at 17 and then they stopped.

We never did perform *The Wizard of Oz*. Miss Rawlings decided it would be better for us to do a shortened version of *Midsummer Night's Dream*.

My cat, Rupert, spent ages licking and cleaning his fur, paying particular attention to his nether regions, one leg stuck straight up in the air. One day I noticed that he was scratching at his ears and shaking his head as if there was something stuck there. I looked in his ears. They were filled with nasty-looking black stuff.

'No good asking me,' my mother said. 'None of our other cats ever had anything like that. Maybe he'll have to be put down.'

'Don't say that. You can't mean it. I'll take him to the RSPCA as soon as I get home from school.'

I ran all the way home when the school bell went. I wrapped Rupert in an old towel and put him in the bottom of my school bag. He mewed quietly, but I told him to hush. I wasn't sure whether you were allowed to take a sick cat on the bus, but he was well hidden.

There was only one person in the RSPCA waiting room – a wheezy old man with a white and tan bulldog that wheezed in sympathy. He wasn't in the surgery for long, and then it was my turn.

It wasn't the same vet I'd seen when Hannah and I brought Tabby. He was much younger – good-looking enough to be a film star.

'It's his ears,' I said. 'I hope it's not serious. I couldn't bear for him to be put down.'

'Let's have a look then.'

The vet examined his ears and then smiled.

'It's nothing serious, Miss er . . .'

'Waterman. Abby Waterman. He's called Rupert.'

'Hullo, Abby. I'm Paul, Paul Taverner. Your cat's got Canker. I'll clean out this muck and give you some ointment to put in his ears.'

'But what is it? Is it bad?'

'No, it's not dangerous. It's very common. Several kinds of animals get Canker. Their ear wax gets infected, usually by ear mites, and it turns black like this. Their ears get very itchy. Sometimes they scratch so much the skin gets sore and infected.'

'How much will the ointment cost?'

'It's free. You can make a donation if you like, but it's not expected from young girls like you.'

I didn't like him calling me a young girl. At fourteen surely, I was a young lady.

Next day I told Phyllis about the good-looking vet, and that I was going to see him in a week.

'He's like a film star,' I said. 'Just like Stewart Grainger, tall with dark curly hair and deep blue eyes.'

'I'll come with you, if you like, when you go again,' Phyllis said.

'No thanks. He's not for sharing.'

At first, Rupert's ears didn't seem much better, but a week later he'd stopped scratching and there was very little black stuff left.

I put on my pleated tartan skirt and new white Broderie Anglaise blouse, and tied my hair back with a dark blue ribbon. My black patent leather shoes were a bit tight but I managed to squeeze them on.

There were several people in the waiting room. Then a woman and a little girl with a puppy came in. I was a bit cross and upset when Paul called them all in first. Finally, when only Rupert and I were left, he came out.

'Come on in, Abby,' he said. 'Let's see how good a nurse you've been.'

He smelled of something nice, spicy.

'Bring him into the operating room. I can see better there.'

He looked at Rupert's ears.

'Well done. I see you've been taking good care of him.'

He scratched Rupert under the chin and made him purr.

'Aren't you a lucky cat having such a nice girl looking after you? I think Abby deserves a kiss, don't you?'

He put his arm around my shoulders and held me against him. He kissed me on the lips. It was warm and lovely, so I kissed him back.

'What a sweet girl you are. Carry on with the ointment and I'll see Rupert in a week.'

Phyllis didn't ask whether I'd been back to see the vet again and I wasn't sure I wanted to talk about it. Of course, he was much older than me, but lots of girls in films had older boyfriends.

By the next week. Rupert's ears were fine. I half wanted to go back and half didn't, but then I decided I would go. I put on some of Rebecca's eau-de-Cologne so I would smell nice.

Once again Paul saw me last.

'Thank Heaven, that's the lot for the day,' he said. 'I'll lock up or I'll be here all night. Come on through.'

After he looked at Rupert, he told me again what a good nurse I was. He put Rupert on the examination table and kissed and hugged me again. Then he turned me so that my back was against him.

'Give me your hand,' he said, pressing against me.

He pulled my arm behind me and I felt something warm and firm and smooth in my hand.

Once, when I was little and had a bad cold, I slept in my parent's room. All the beds had chamber pots underneath them. I saw my father's penis when he took it out to pee. I had never touched one.

I pulled my hand away. I was scared and shaky.

'I hate you. You're horrid,' I said.

I gathered Rupert up in my arms, and ran to the door. It was locked.

'Please open the door. Please,' I begged.

'Silly girl. You can go if you want to. See. I've unlocked it. The door's wide open.'

After that I'd make all sorts of excuses not to go past the vet's for any reason, not even walk down that road. I never told anyone why.

CHAPTER 7

Music studies

I had been having free piano lessons at Toynbee Hall since I came back from Dawlish. I would come in half an hour beforehand to practice and I was getting on well. The teacher said I was eligible for a scholarship to the Guildhall School of Music and gave me a form to fill in. I rushed home to tell my parents, but once again I was disappointed. The classes for children at Guildhall were held on Saturdays and my mother wouldn't let me go. Riding on the bus or playing a musical instrument were considered work and not allowed on the Sabbath.

However, Miss Simonds, who taught maths to the first years, also gave private piano lessons during the lunch hour or after school. I nagged until my parents agreed to pay for lessons at school with her and then I said I needed a piano to practise.

'You don't need it,' my mother said. 'You can go on practising at school. It will be a nine-day wonder and we can't afford it.'

My father took my side and they bought me a piano on hire

purchase – a first for them. Hire purchase had not long become respectable.

The removal men had to carry the piano all the way up to the third floor, manoeuvring it around the tight turns. It got stuck half way up and they had to spend ages freeing it.

'Bloody hell,' I heard one say. 'Don't know what this lot want with a piano. Haven't got two pennies to rub together and they buy one of these.'

We hardly ever used our parlour unless a rare visitor came to tea, so the piano went in there. It was too expensive to light the gas fire every day. In the winter, I had to keep rubbing my hands together to stay warm. I practised as soon as I got home from school, so as not to disturb my father when he came home from work. After supper, I did my homework on the kitchen table while he read the paper or listened to the radio. My mother would read one of the novels in Yiddish I got for her when I changed my books at Whitechapel library.

Miss Simmonds was a brilliant pianist. She made shivers run up and down my spine when she played Beethoven sonatas. As a child, I had no problem playing in public and she arranged for me to play on Monday mornings as the girls filed in for assembly. My sight-reading improved under her tuition and I often played pieces unseen.

My headmistress congratulated me on my playing.

'Thank you, Abigail. You must spend hours practising.'

'Oh no,' I replied, gauche as ever. 'I pick up any old thing to play.'

It was true but it didn't endear me to her.

The hall had a large organ and I asked Miss Simmonds if I could learn, remembering my beloved Mr Lawson, but nothing came of it.

By the time I was fourteen I regularly played at school concerts. It wasn't until much, much later that I developed stage nerves.

An ex-student, who'd gone on to play second violin in the London Symphony Orchestra, gave our school a cello. I put my name down to have free lessons, but I wasn't very hopeful because I was already having piano lessons. I wasn't altogether pleased when my form mistress stopped me at the end of the week and told me I had been chosen to learn the cello. We always had loads of homework and I wasn't sure I'd be able to fit in practising the cello as well as the piano.

Steve, the cello teacher, was a young man who played in a quartet just beginning to get well-known. He wore thick pebble glasses and had a bushy black beard that often contained traces of his breakfast. I took to him immediately. He had a dry sense of humour and played fabulously.

The school allowed me to take the cello home to practice. My walk through Spitalfields market lugging the heavy black case brought roars of laughter from the market porters. Their remarks varied from 'Give us a tune then, miss,' 'Can you put it under your chin?' 'I'll carry it for you for a kiss, Miss' to 'Can you put that big thing between your legs?' These and their variations followed me all the way to school.

I never got to play well, but enjoyed playing in a quartet with Sarah, Anne and Jo. Our practice room was next to the sixth form common room and the seniors would come out with their hands over their ears complaining about the noise. We played with great enthusiasm but not much musicianship and we were rarely quite in tune with each other.

Sarah had a little pitch pipe to give us an *A* but Jo, the viola player, had little sense of pitch. Sometimes even we couldn't stand the sound she was making and had to tell her to shut up. Mostly it was bearable and in the spring Steve decided we were good enough to play in our Prize Day concert.

I'd played the piano on prize day every year since the third form. That year, I'd chosen the first movement of Beethoven's Moonlight Sonata and had got it up to concert standard with time to spare.

Every time we attempted the beginner's piece our quartet would be playing, either we weren't quite in tune or one or other of us would come in a couple of beats too late and we'd all start giggling. Once we started laughing anything would set us off again. Steve was practically tearing out his hair and he threatened to cancel our performance.

We'd have been only too pleased not to have to play but we knew the programmes had been printed so there was no way our headmistress would let us back out.

My piano solo went well and it wasn't until I sat down with my cello facing the audience that I realised just how short my school skirt was. I tightened the supporting spike of my cello as quickly as I could, pulled down my skirt as far as it would go and drew my cello towards me.

Sarah gave us an *A* and for once Jo's viola was spot on. We had only played the opening bars when the audience broke into roars of laughter, with loud whistles from the boys from our companion boys' school who were sitting in the back row.

I pulled at my skirt, thinking perhaps it had ridden up and my navy school knickers were showing, but it wasn't that. Jo mouthed 'It's that song.'

When we'd practised, it was always very slowly and we hadn't realised that the opening phrase was the same as *'Give me five minutes more,'* the love song recorded by Frank Sinatra. You could hear it played constantly on the radio and only the week before a filthy version had been passed round the school.

I don't how the four of us got though the piece, but we just about did. We dared not look each other or we would have started to giggle and then we'd have been unable to stop. When we finished the piece, we managed to get up and bow. The other three scooted off the stage but, encumbered by a cello almost as tall as me, I had to get myself off amid continued laughter and whistles.

Afterwards Phyllis asked me

'How come you didn't recognise that the tune you were playing was the first few bars of that song?'

'Well,' I said, 'They say that when you listen to the masters practising they practise each part so slowly it's almost impossible to tell what piece they're playing. We certainly rehearsed very slowly so we just didn't twig.'

We all auditioned for the school choir and I joined the sopranos. My mother didn't approve of my going to St Botolph's Church, or any church, to give a concert, but she didn't forbid it.

I was always on the verge of being late, always tried to fit in one last thing before leaving, and I was hurrying along Bishopsgate when disaster struck. I felt my right garter snap – they were home-made strips of wide black elastic cobbled together by me. I looked down and was horrified to see a beige lisle stocking come creeping down below my skirt. I grabbed it and my skirt and hobbled the rest of the way to the church, sure everyone was staring at me. Before we got up to sing, we were ushered into pews and I could pull the offending stocking off. I went home like *my son John* –with one stocking off and on stocking on.

> *Diddle, diddle dumpling, my son John*
> *Went to bed with his trousers on:*
> *One shoe off, and one shoe on,*
> *Diddle, diddle, dumpling, my son John*

I joined the youth club in Brady Street when I was 13. We went away for two weeks every summer. That year, the children in our age group went apple picking in Kent, camping in a field belonging to the apple farm.

It was one of those perfect English summers – sunny but not so hot you couldn't bear it. The apples were crunchy and delicious and it was fun climbing up the short ladders to pick them, but I hated opening a cluster of apples to find a little nest of earwigs in the middle. I knew they couldn't jump and get into my ears, but they made me shudder just the same, with their evil-looking claws and dark reddish-brown carapaces.

Not only were there the little groups of earwigs when we pulled the clusters of apples apart but we were plagued by wasps. A wasp stung me on the neck. It was agony. Someone handed me a bottle of strong ammonia.

'Here. Dab it with this. It'll take the pain away.'

It did, but by next day I had a 2 centimetre circular ulcer on my neck. I dabbed at my neck so long that the ammonia damaged the skin. I was too worried to go home and tell my mother what I'd done so I volunteered to stay on and help clear up the site after everyone had gone home, hoping that by then it would be healed.

We were sitting around the campfire singing and swaying to the music. I leaned against Adrian and then we were kissing. It wasn't quite my first kiss – we always played kissing games at parties. His lips were warm and soft but then the others saw us kissing and began to clap so we stopped. Our faces were bright red with embarrassment but we hoped no-one noticed since everyone else's face was red from the fire.

The next night Adrian brought a blanket to the campfire and sat next to me again. We kissed and pulled the blanket over us. It's a cliché but I really was swept away on a tide of bliss. At fourteen I knew nothing about sex, had never been touched on my body by a boy and I suppose Adrian was inexperienced too, because all we did was kiss and cuddle. It didn't matter that there were people around us. Had we been experienced enough to have sex the fact that it was in public would have made no difference. We'd have gone ahead audience or no audience. We were completely oblivious to anyone or anything around us. It never happened again and by the third day I decided I didn't even like Adrian.

Phil, the boy who took me home from the club every night, was at the same camp. We were in different groups for apple picking and we hadn't met at the camp except to wave from a distance. On the last night, he kissed me as we left the campfire and we held hands as we walked back to his tent. Some boys in a nearby tent shouted things I couldn't hear but we ignored them. We crawled into Phil's tent and shared his sleeping bag. We kissed and cuddled and slept. Hard to believe now that we didn't make love, didn't even think of it. We were too innocent.

The following year, we went on a walking holiday in Wales. We were told to bring stout walking shoes and I saved enough pocket money to buy some stout lace-up boots. It was a dreadful mistake. They weren't worn-in and I developed awful blisters – as most of us did. We queued for a blissful soak in a bowl of hot water before drying our feet and applying plasters to the worst of them. They said you mustn't burst them but it was too tempting. We passed a sharp needle around, not bothering about sterilising it. None of us got infected, though.

The next summer we went back to Wales and chose a different route. This time I wore my old school shoes and my feet were fine That year it rained most days. We wore ex-army ground sheets to keep off the worst of the rain but I was never quite dry the whole two weeks.

I and my friends often had boils on the backs of our necks and on our bottoms. Phyllis had an infected finger nail – a wicklow. There were no antibiotics when we were children. You could make a hot bread poultice out of stale bread soaked in milk or buy a special poultice paste from the chemist. We treated ourselves with them to bring out the pus.

I had started growing hair under my arms and between my legs and I now began getting spots on my face. I would peer anxiously in the mirror before I left for school and squeeze out any zits that were ripe. Nothing seemed to help – however much I scrubbed at my face.

Then, one day there was blood on my knickers – little more than a stain. Visions of playing 'doctors and nurses' with the other children in *The Buildings*, and baring our bottoms to have our temperatures taken with matchsticks, flashed through my head. Had something got damaged permanently?

When I told my mother, she slapped my face.

'It's not my fault,' I cried. 'I didn't do anything to myself.'

'No, Abby. You're a woman now. You have to smack girls' faces their first time to stop all the blood going down below. I'll give you some rags and tomorrow I'll give you the money to go to the chemist and buy a sanitary belt and pads. You'll have a period every month now.'

I soon got used to visits from 'the curse' and 'my aunt'. But for me it was never 'the monthlies'. My periods were always irregular and I never suffered from premenstrual tension to warn me of their arrival.

Looking back now it's hard to understand how innocent we all were. I knew of girls who'd had to leave school because they were pregnant but I never knew one of them personally. Despite our Hygiene lessons, I didn't know exactly how you have sex; that men ejaculated or how babies are born. I had periods, of course, but I hadn't explored the region to see where my vagina was. I certainly couldn't imagine how a baby came out of 'somewhere down there'.

Surprisingly, my friends and I weren't that interested. If we did have boyfriends, they would have been as scared of getting us pregnant as we were, though they would have known much more about sex because of their biology.

But I wasn't the only innocent one.

Auntie Nathalie lived in the same tenements as we did, about two blocks away. She was a fat jolly lady with a thin weedy husband – fat as in enormous. She was short and almost as round as she was tall.

One day her husband Morris knocked at our door. He was in tears.

'The doctor says my Nathalie has a cancer in her belly and it's all her fault for not coming back to see him again.'

My mother made sympathetic noises.

'Has she been ill long?'

'No,' he said. 'She went to the doctor a couple of months ago because she had a bit of wind and she was constipated. He said it was nothing and to come back if it got worse. He gave her some medicine and it didn't get worse but now she's in agony. She's got this big tumour in her belly and the doctor says it's too late to operate.'

'What about getting a specialist? When my neighbour was ill she went to this doctor in Harley Street. She said he was wonderful and wrote down his phone number for me just in case I ever needed a specialist.'

None of us had our own telephone so Morris went off to the phone box at the top of Goulston Street. The doctor's secretary said he'd had a cancellation and he would be with them within the hour.

He sent Morris out while he examined Nathalie, now groaning in agony. When he'd finished, he called Morris in and asked for a bowl of water and a clean towel. Then – as all too often today – doctors washed their hands after touching patients, not before.

'Well,' he said 'better send for the ambulance straight away. You haven't got long. I reckon you'll be a proud father in no time.'

Morris promptly fainted and was revived by the specialist. He was a heart specialist, so perhaps it was just as well.

Sophie, a tiny dark-haired baby girl, was born almost as soon as Nathalie was admitted to the labour ward.

My mother called on her as soon as she got home after the obligatory 10 days' rest. I went too.

'What happened?' my mother asked. 'How come you didn't know?'

'Well, Morris and I have been trying for years and it just didn't happen. Then I thought it was the change when you know what stopped,' Nathalie looked over at me. 'All ears they are, the young ones.' Then she went on 'The doctor said the funny feelings in my stomach were wind and that I should lose weight. You know

I've tried loads of times, but I only put it on again when I stop dieting, so I didn't go back. But isn't my surprise baby beautiful? They said she was a bit premature but not to worry and that she was perfect.'

By now Rebecca had been called up into the WAAFs and amongst her uniform accessories she was issued with two bright pink cotton brassieres. We'd never seen bras before and now I and all my friends had to have them.

My mother took me to the corset shop, Yanovsky's, in White-chapel. The assistant tutted, looking at my small budding breasts.

'It's high time your mother did the right thing for you and bought you a brassiere.'

She fitted me with a pink contraption pulled so tight I felt she might pull my breasts up to my neck.

'You must have proper support,' she said. 'You don't want to have droopy breasts when you get older. Better try on a suspender belt while you're here.'

I'd always had garters to hold up my stockings. Suspender belts were new to me. They had two grips on each side to clip onto the top of my stockings.

Later we all had roll-ons – pink elasticated tubes that acted as suspender belt and corset. Some had gussets between the legs and replaced knickers as well.

I met Simon at the Youth Club. He wore baggy flannel trousers that were constantly slipping down his narrow hips. If I try to picture him in my mind's eye it is with a great fold of waistband in his right hand, yanking his trousers up yet again. He had dark straight hair and blue eyes, not handsome but pleasant looking. He was a gangly youth, a bit spotty but not as bad as some. He didn't exactly walk – he lurched.

I didn't like him very much at first. I was a couple of years younger and he seemed cold and supercilious. As we got to know each other I came to enjoy talking to him, being with him. He was very bright and set on a career in the Arts.

My best friend at the time was Sylvia, a big-busted blue-eyed beauty who all the boys including Simon hung around. I stood on the outskirts longing but not saying anything. It took me a couple of months before I fell in love with him. I remember the bliss when during a *Kiss or Tell* game at his birthday party we went outside and he kissed me but it didn't lead to anything. My love was unrequited.

I was in love with Simon for two years before he finally noticed me as a girl and asked me to the cinema. He kissed me in the back row – uninteresting wet kisses. He walked me home and as we chatted I realised I was bored to tears. I kissed him at the foot of our block of flats out of a sense of duty, but it was just as boring as in the back row of the cinema. My two-year love affair died that evening and when I saw him at the Youth Club the following week I couldn't understand what all the heartache had been about.

CHAPTER 8

Hither Green Fever Hospital

'My mum and dad gave me *Little Women* for my birthday,' Phyllis said. 'You must read it, Abby. I loved it. I cried and cried. I can't lend it to you yet – I want to read it again, but the library's bound to have a copy.'

I hurried to Whitechapel Library after school, and took out a copy. When I got home, I rushed through my homework so I could start reading my new book.

'Clear your things away, Abby,' my mother said. 'Supper's ready.'

It was 1944. I was the only one still living at home. Hannah, disappointed that she hadn't been able to train as a doctor or even a nurse and hating secretarial work, had left home to work on a farm. Rebecca was away in the WAAFs (Women's Auxiliary Air Force).

The Luftwaffe were bombing London nightly so we still slept in our designated air raid shelter in the basement of a garment factory in Middlesex Street.

'My throat hurts when I try to swallow,' I said to my mother.

'Maybe a piece of toast scratched your throat. Hurry up and get ready. We need to leave before the blackout. It's your father's turn to be on air raid warden duty, so he's gone on ahead.'

I folded up my best cardigan, and found my book of pressed flowers from the Holy Land. I hid my torch and *Little Women* inside my pyjamas. You couldn't shine a torch in the streets during the blackout, but I'd be able to use it to read under the blankets. I stuffed it all into the pillowcase in which I took my most precious things to the shelter. I also took my homework with me in case *The Buildings* were bombed. The teachers heard the excuse 'Haven't done it, Miss. We were bombed last night' so many times, they didn't believe you unless you could prove it.

I tried to remember whether I'd forgotten anything, but my head ached so much I couldn't think clearly.

'Hurry up,' my mother called. 'Are you going to be all day, Abigail?'

I followed her down the stairs and across the road to the factory. Before it was turned into a shelter, the basement was cleared of all the boxes of hangers and stands, and the cement floor hosed down with disinfectant. The council provided enough iron bunk beds for over a hundred people, and installed metal lockers in which our bedding could be left overnight.

I trailed along behind my mother, feeling worse and worse. Maybe it was our school dinner. I loved *Spotted Dick*, but perhaps I shouldn't have eaten Phyllis's, as well as my own.

I ached all over by the time we arrived. It hurt climbing down the steps to the basement.

'Mummy, I don't feel well.'

'Stop fussing, Abby. You'll be fine after a good night's sleep. And no staying up until all hours, reading under the blankets. I'll take your torch away if you do. I know you brought it.'

She undid the padlock fastening our locker, took out our blankets and pillows, and made up my bed on the top bunk. We'd been lucky to be allocated bunks near the lockers, not on the other side, near the chemical toilets. There was a horrible smell of disinfectant and pee over there.

'Your forehead's a bit hot,' my mother said, 'but you'll be better in the morning.'

My mother's hand was cool and gentle. I tried to hold it, but she shook me off.

'Go to sleep, Abby, and no reading.'

I kept waking up, disturbed by the sniffs and coughs of people sleeping all around me. My throat was on fire and my skin felt as if it was burning up. I pushed off the blankets and lifted my pyjama top. My chest was covered in a bright red rash. I waited as long as I could before I woke my mother.

'Mummy, I think I've caught something. My throat's bad and I've got a rash.'

I was terrified it might be diphtheria. I knew if you caught diphtheria and there was a skin in your throat, you'd have to have a tube put in your neck, or you'd choke to death. You might still die, even if they did that.

'It's straight to the doctor with you as soon as we've dropped off our things at home. It's Friday. I've still got all the shopping to do.'

Dr Wilson asked me to stick out my tongue and say 'Aah'. Then he listened to my chest.

'Scarlet Fever. It's going around. Best *Strawberry Tongue* I've seen for a long time. Shame we haven't got any medical students here. It's a classical sign. You'll have to go to the Fever Hospital, Abigail,'

108

Dr Wilson said. 'You can't go by bus. Scarlet Fever's too infectious. I'll phone for an ambulance. All your clothes will have to be disinfected once you get there. You can't take any books or toys with you, Abby. Before you ask, Mrs Waterman, no you can't go in the ambulance with her.'

Even if she had been allowed, I was sure my mother would have made some excuse not to go with me,

I felt better as soon as I lay down on the stretcher. The ambulance man gave me a big smile as he pulled a soft red blanket over me.

'You'll have a super time at Hither Green,' he said. 'They mainly treat toddlers and babies there. You'll be quite the King of the Castle.'

'Queen, you mean,' I said.

'Would you like me to turn on the bell?' he asked. 'Since you're a special patient.'

It was fantastic racing through London, the bell pealing away – except that it made me think about the plague, and watchmen ringing their hand bells.

'Bring out your dead. Bring out your dead.'

I'd never heard of Scarlet Fever but I didn't think it was a plague, though it must be dangerous, if I had to go into hospital. I'd come through the war so far without being bombed. I didn't want to die of a fever now.

At Hither Green hospital, a doctor examined me.

'It's Scarlet Fever all right,' he said. 'Quite a mild attack. Nurse here will take you to the ward. You'll be out of here in about ten days.'

The nurse told me to take off all my clothes and put on a white nightdress.

'Leave your clothes here,' she said. 'We'll fumigate them. Don't worry, dear. Nothing will be spoiled. You'll get them back when you leave.'

'Can my parents visit me? My father might want to come.'

'I'm sorry, love. No visitors. This is an Isolation Hospital.'

When I got to Q ward, I hated it. There were only eight proper beds. The rest were cots full of babies and toddlers – some screaming, some sitting sucking their thumbs, rocking backwards and forwards.

I sat on my bed, utterly miserable. I didn't want to spend ten days with babies. Suppose they made me change their nappies. Yuk!!

'Hullo. You're new. I'm Ellie. I've been here three days, so I'm feeling loads better. You still itchy?'

Ellie was fourteen, a pretty girl, a year and one month older than me. She was tall and thin with green eyes and a posh accent.

'They won't let you go outside for a few days, but then we can go exploring.'

Now I felt lots better about being in Q ward.

'We don't have to take any medicine – only gargles, and calamine lotion if we're itchy. The food's OK. Miles better than school dinners.'

Suddenly I felt dizzy. A nurse bustled over.

'That's enough gossiping, Ellie. You can see Abby feels poorly.'

She put her arm round my shoulders.

'Don't cry, love, or you'll get the babies started.'

'Most of them are crying already,' I sobbed.

The cool white sheets were bliss against my itchy skin. I burrowed deep into the pillow and was asleep at once. When I awoke, it was tea time. Ellie was standing by my bed holding a large sticky bun.

'Nearly missed tea, you did. I'll tell Nurse Brown you're up. I'll have your buns until your throat's better.'

The first few days passed in a round of jigsaws, all with a few pieces missing, dog-eared picture books and Ellie, smiling and teasing.

Finally, Nurse Brown said I could go outside. She brought over an assortment of clothes. The vest, knickers and socks were fine, so were the black plimsolls, but the bright red skirt was too long for me, it came down to my ankles. The blue blouse with yellow spots was too short to tuck in, while the black and white checked coat was so big, Ellie and I could have got inside together.

'You look a right "nana" in those clothes,' Ellie said.

'Looked in a mirror lately? We look like a couple of scarecrows,' I replied. 'Reckon kids who died left them behind?'

Ellie giggled.

'Yes, and their ghosts are still inside. Whoo-ooo. Come on then. I'll show you around.'

It was warm and sunny when we went out. The wards were housed in separate brick buildings each with their own garden.

'We're not allowed inside any ward except our own, Q ward,' Ellie said. 'They each have a tree that begins with the first letter of their name. O has an oak tree, P has a pear tree and W has a willow.'

'Can't think of one that begins with a Q.'

'Nor could I, until Nurse Brown told me.'

Our tree had dark green leaves and orange-yellow fruit that looked like a cross between a pear and an apple.

'We're not supposed to pick them, but let's see if we can find some in the grass.'

We poked around, but all the fruit was rotten and maggoty. Then Ellie found one that hadn't a mark on it.

'Here, smell,' she said.

It had a sweet, slightly sharp, delicious smell.

'It's a quince,' Ellie said. 'They're too sour to eat. Nurse Brown said you can make jelly with them. You can keep it if you like, but they go off quickly. Maybe because they're windfalls.'

As we walked back in the warm sunshine, I sniffed at the quince.

'Is this one of the perfumes of Arabia?' I asked.

'You're nuts,' she replied. 'Race you back to the ward.'

The quince was soon too squashy to keep, so I had to throw it away.

'Write to me,' Ellie said when she was about to be discharged. 'Promise? Cross your heart and hope to die?'

I made the Sign of the Cross, hoping that my Jewish God wasn't watching. I knew it was a terrible thing to do, so I had the fingers of my other hand crossed behind my back. That way, He would know I didn't mean it.

'I'll write as soon as I get home,' she said.

On the day before I was sent home I got her postcard with her address. Nurse Brown took it away to be disinfected. She said they'd send the card on to me, but it didn't come, so I couldn't write back.

The good thing was that when I got back home, the night-time bombing raids had stopped. Hitler was sending over *Doodlebugs* (V1 unmanned rockets) during the day, so I never had to sleep in that smelly shelter again. The rockets came over at any time of the day or night so there was no point in only taking shelter at night. We certainly didn't want to stay in a shelter all day just in case a Doodlebug came over.

But they were frightening. You didn't need to worry while you heard the drone of their engines but then their engines cut out you knew they were going to crash. It was OK if they cut out directly overhead, although the big black cross in the sky was terrifying. Once its engine stopped it would glide and crash some distance away.

Though I resented having to 'respect' my older sister – my mother was very much into respect, *'Derech eretz'* – literally The Way of the Land. It was important to obey the fifth commandment

Honour your father and your mother, so that you may live long in the land the Lord your God hath given you.

And that applied to Rebecca too.

But in her own, rather reserved way, she was good to me. She took me to the ballet so see Margot Fonteyn dance and when she went for long walks with her boyfriend, much of the time she'd take me with her. She'd offer me 2d to keep quiet for an hour. I was and am a chatterbox. I don't think I ever earned the bribe.

As a WAAF she was offered cheap place mats and tray cloths to embroider. I taught myself the stiches from a book I got from the library and made enough for a trousseau. Clothes were rationed so we had all learned to darn socks and jumpers and knit. My mother thought that sitting just reading was a waste of time so I learned to knit and read at the same time. We took our knitting everywhere – on the bus, to friends. I even saw women knitting in the cinema.

It was easy for servicemen and women to get lifts. Some weekends, when Rebecca was off duty, we would hitch a lift into the country. To our delight, once the driver of a Rolls Royce gave us a lift. Rebecca sat next to the senior officer in the back and I sat on the comfortable carpeted footrest at his feet.

I was delighted when Rebecca finally, had a GI boyfriend though

it only lasted a few months. The American servicemen had their
cheap PX stores and could not only get chocolate off ration but
nylon stockings. Until then I'd had thick lisle stockings for school
and rayon stockings for best – neither very flattering. Rebecca's new
boyfriend provided us both with much prized nylons. They had
dark seams up the back and we twisted and turned to see the backs
of our legs to make sure our seams were straight. Unfortunately,
Rebecca's boyfriend was posted abroad and her other boyfriends
were all British Airmen without access to such goodies.

Then I caught German measles and had an all-over rash when
Rebecca came home on weekend leave. We didn't know at that
time that it was good to catch German measles as a child and
develop immunity. That way you wouldn't catch it while pregnant
and damage the developing baby. For Rebecca catching it from me
would give her a few days' extra leave. She slept in my bed while
my rash was at its height but complained that I kept her awake
scratching. It was all for nothing. She didn't catch it and had to go
back to camp on time.

We had now moved into a larger flat, still in Wentworth Dwellings,
but now facing onto Wentworth Street market. Finally, I had a
proper bedroom to myself.

I would wake early to the sound of barrows being wheeled over
the cobblestones into the market. I was pleased to see one of the
fruit and vegetable stallholders unload some oranges. After the
market closed and the stallholders had left, leaving their debris to
be cleared up by the dustcarts, I looked for some orange boxes that
were clean and didn't smell too much of oranges. I made a couple
into cupboards and a plank of wood resting on the top made a desk.

My mother always had scraps of fabric left over from her sewing and I made them up into curtains for my new cupboards.

It was my job to scrub out our flat. Every Friday night when I got home from school, I filled a bucket with water heated in the kettle and using a scrubbing brush and large bar of carbolic soap I scrubbed the kitchen floor. If it was our turn, I also cleaned the steps leading down to the next floor. As our neighbour got older and more feeble, I took over her turn and scrubbed the stairs every week. When she heard the bucket handle rattle as I moved it down she'd come out and pat me on the head.

'What a lovely girl you've grown up to be, *bubbele*. Your mother must be so proud of you.'

I wished it was true and even more I wished people would stop saying that. She wasn't proud of me and never would be.

As soon as I was old enough, I joined the adult section of White-chapel library, I made my way alphabetically around the shelves. I was much taken with the French authors – Malraux, Maurois and Jean-Paul Sartre – but also English classics – Jane Austen, the Brontes, Thomas Hardy, Dickens, Mansfield, du Maurier, Orwell, Waugh and George Elliott, amongst others. After I had read all the novels I fancied, I started on plays – Shaw, Ibsen and Strindberg – and then psychoanalysis. I chose books by their size. Anything less than about 250 pages I'd get through so quickly it wouldn't be worth taking the book home. I was a bookworm. I would read almost anything – I just had to be reading.

My mother preferred to read in Yiddish, which is written in Hebrew script, though she could read English. She'd tell me to ask at the library for Yiddish novels and mostly I managed to bring her home something she liked.

My father read the newspaper which he brought home in the evening but that was only for him to read, so I never developed the habit of reading the daily newspaper.

On May 8th, 1945, it was all over. The war with Germany had ended. All the church bells were ringing and Phyllis and I joined the thousands who thronged Trafalgar Square to celebrate. I'd never been kissed so many times. Two soldiers lifted me onto their shoulders and danced around with me until I complained that I felt dizzy. As it got dark I took the bus home. Everyone was singing the old wartime songs – *It's long way to Tipperary* and *Pack up your troubles in your old kit bag* and *We'll meet again some sunny day*.

No more rocket bombs, no more news of battles but the horror of the concentration camps slowly revealed itself. Children were discouraged from watching the news in the cinemas. The images were too horrendous.

VE day was followed on August 14th by the surrender of the Japanese and new horrors emerged – the ghastly treatment of Allied prisoners of war by the Japs. We couldn't bring ourselves to care about the horrors of the atom bombs.

Food was still rationed – rationing didn't formally end until 1954 and the Black Market in food flourished. Everyone knew someone who could get a bit of extra butter or tea. Even bread and potatoes were rationed.

The worse thing for me was having to collect a newly killed chicken after school on Fridays. A woman living in one of the large ex-Huguenot houses in Spitalfields kept chickens in her back yard. If you were one of her regulars, she would illegally kill one of them for you – killing of livestock was strictly controlled. She wrapped the still-warm carcass in newspaper and I would have to walk home with it tucked under my coat, sure I'd be stopped by a policeman and taken off to jail.

There were still lots of uncleared bomb sites in the East End. It was amazing how quickly they were covered with flowering plants, especially with Rosebay Willowherb. I grew to hate its purple spikes and still do – though purple is my favourite colour.

CHAPTER 9

A Working Girl

My favourite summer job was at the *Vita Sun* café on the ground floor of the J Lyons Coventry Street Corner House in Leicester Square. From the time I was 15, I took a job every summer. I never worked at the same place twice. That would have been too boring. School children could legally work full-time in the holidays and on weekends once they reached school leaving age, which was then 15, going up to 16 in 1972.

The *Vita Sun* was one of the first self-service cafés in the UK. Many customers found the *Vita Sun* confusing. They weren't sure whether they should sit at a table and wait for the staff to bring their food, or move along the counter helping themselves. At the ubiquitous J Lyons teashops, they were used to being served by waitresses, nicknamed *Nippys* – because they *nipped* around so quickly. Distinctive in their black dresses with a white Peter Pan collar and a double row of tiny pearl buttons down the front, they wore starched white aprons and wide frilly head-bands with the J Lyons logo on the front.

The advertisement in the *Jobs Vacant* of the Evening Standard said to queue at the staff entrance in Rupert Street, and six of us were taken on to start the following Monday. We were given aprons and small white hats and shown the staff canteen on the top floor where we could eat free of charge. I was the only schoolgirl – the others were all students.

On that first day, the manager showed us around the café and told us how to load the counter. For 1/6d (7½p) you got Welsh rarebit (a cheesy mixture on toast), a pastry (a chocolate éclair or fruit tart), a pot of tea and a vanilla ice cream with chocolate sauce. We had to pull apart the white paper which wrapped the squat cylinders of vanilla icecream, place each on a stainless-steel sundae dish, pour over the thick chocolate sauce and stick in a couple of thin golden wafers. The metal teapots came with a spoonful of tea leaves already in them, and as the customer reached the end we added boiling water to them from an electric urn. The customers helped themselves to a small jug of milk – there were glass pourers of sugar on each table. They paid the cashier at the end.

The six of us soon formed a tight gang of warriors with the customers as the enemy. Welsh Rarebit was prepared in the large kitchen behind the café. The cook, a permanent member of staff, often burned it. Gossiping about what she'd been up to the night before, she let the Welsh Rarebit rotate over the heated elements twice and the surface would burn. There was a bin for spoilt food and the manager didn't seem to mind if it was full or empty, but we always made a point of putting the charred Welsh rarebit near the front of the counter. If customers asked if they could have one that was less well done, we'd say that was how they were coming in that day. If a frozen ice-cream roll dropped from our hands on to the floor as we were unwrapping it, instead of throwing it away, we would pick it up and put it in a sundae dish, again right at the front. If we were on clearing duty and the cafe was full, as it often was, we delayed clearing the tables as long as possible. Customers were left standing forlornly, balancing their trays, or be forced to clear a table for themselves. Sometimes we, especially the men, 'accidentally' flicked our wet dishcloths at the customers as we wiped the tables – when we finally got around to clearing them. It was war.

I loved being part of a gang and getting a beige wage envelope at the end of the week. It wasn't until I got back to school at the end of the summer holidays and told Phyllis all about it, that I realised just how badly we'd behaved towards the customers.

During the rest of the year I earned some pocket money cleaning the flat of a distant aunt with arthritis. Although she was a very distant relative, my mother said it was no disgrace to go out cleaning, as long as it was for family.

The next summer I decided to look for a job in a clothes factory. I knew how to use a sewing machine and thought it would be useful to learn speed dressmaking.

I took a bus to Mason's garment factory in Commercial Road and walked up the concrete steps to the red door marked 'Staff Entrance'. As I opened the door I was hit by a blast of *'Music While You Work'* – a programme of popular music, broadcast by the BBC morning and afternoon. I backed off, unable to face listening to that noise all day.

Instead I found a job in a shipping office in the City, checking shipping manifests against goods received. The women in the office were all much older than me, so they mothered me, making sure I ate all my sandwiches for lunch and took my full tea breaks.

When I was interviewed for the job, which was a permanent position, I hadn't told the personnel manager that I'd only come to work for the holidays. At the end of the month he called me into his office.

'You've done very well Abby, my dear. You put some of our older employees to shame. I've decided to give you a raise, another ten shillings a week. That will help you build up your bottom drawer.'

I blushed and told him I would be leaving to go back to school.

'You deceived me,' he said. 'I'm surprised at you. I would never have taken you on and trained you had I known you were only here temporarily. You should be ashamed of yourself. You took the job away from another girl who left school this summer and needed to start work.'

When I got outside his door I burst into tears. He was right and I was ashamed. I had been thoughtless and I was sorry.

My last holiday job while I was at school was in an office that organised sales on the *never-never*. Tally men going door-to-door round the tenements in the East End of London sold household goods and cosmetics, and their customers paid off their debts in small weekly instalments. The interest rates were extortionate. The tally men tried to call when the husbands were out at work, when their wives would be alone and more susceptible to their sales patter. Often the women were talked into buying more goods before the last lot was paid off, so they were perpetually in debt – hence the name *never-never*. My job was to check the entries in the heavy Bakelite-backed books the salesmen carried around with them, to make sure the amounts they entered agreed with the cash they brought in. There were no adding machines, so we had to do the arithmetic with pencil and paper.

Over the four weeks I worked there my addition and subtraction improved enormously.

Corduroy trousers had come into fashion that year and I decided to buy a pair with my first week's wages. C&A in Oxford Street had just the kind of blouse I was looking for and I proudly paid for it out of the money I'd earned, but I couldn't find a pair of suitable trousers. The fashion was for slightly flared trousers and they were all either too straight or too flared. If the cut was right either I didn't like the colour or they didn't fit.

My mother had long since given up making my clothes and, though I could make myself something simple like a skirt, trousers were too tricky. I asked Jackson, the black man from the fabric shop near our flats, to recommend a tailor. It was the 1940s and he was the only black person other than Prince Honolulu I had ever seen. There were no black girls at our school then. My parents always referred to him as the *schwartze*, the black man, but not in a racist way.

'There's a tailor just over the road above the baker,' he said. Some of our customers go to him.'

On the tailor's advice, I bought a length of dark maroon corduroy from one of the fabric stalls in the market. It had an unusually wide stripe, but the assistant said it would look fine when it was made up.

The tailor measured me and said the trousers would be ready by the following Friday.

'Won't I need a fitting?' I asked, with memories of standing on a chair while my mother pinned and undid and pinned again.

'A little thing like you?' he said. 'No need. Mind you call in early. *Shabbat* comes in early this time of year.'

I woke on the Friday morning impatient for the day to be over so

I could collect my trousers. Work at the Tally Office finished early, since most of the staff were Jewish and needed to be home before the Sabbath.

'For Heaven's sake, Abby. Stop looking at the clock and get some work done. It's not like you,' my supervisor said.

Three-thirty finally came. I pulled on my coat and rushed out. As I hurried home I wondered whether I should go up and collect my new blouse to try on with the trousers, but I was worried that the tailor would close before I could get there.

'There you are, my dear,' he said. 'Got them all wrapped up for you,'

He handed me a brown paper parcel.

'I think I'd better try them on, just in case.'

They fitted perfectly.

'I told you,' he said. 'No need for a fitting.'

I turned to look at myself in the mirror. There was something funny about the trousers. I turned the mirror sideways but it was just the same. The two trouser legs looked different colours.

'You've used some other material for one of the legs,' I said, near to tears.

'It's only the nap. You get that with corduroy. I told you when you brought in the fabric. I said you didn't have enough and we'd have to cut the fabric as best we could. You said it was OK.'

I knew he hadn't said any such thing, but I'd already paid him and there was nothing I could do.

I walked home. The market traders in Petticoat Lane were putting their goods away and called to me as I went by.

'Hi, Abby. Give us a smile then.'

Usually when I walked through the market I'd stop and gossip, but I wanted to get home and have a good cry.

My mother said, 'I told you so,' though she hadn't said anything to me about the fabric having a nap.

I never wore the trousers. I couldn't. They looked ridiculous – like the Pied Piper.

The other thing I spent money on was an Olympia typewriter. I decided I needed it to write up my school notes. I collected a hire purchase form from the typewriter shop near Liverpool Street Station. With the money I got from cleaning regularly and my pocket money I could afford the repayments. My mother would have made a fuss about it, so while she was having a nap I asked my father to countersign it. I bought a book on Pitman's shorthand and tried to teach myself but never got very far with it, though I did teach myself to touch-type.

I had never learned to ride a bicycle. No-one in *The Buildings* owned a bicycle. Our families were poor, just scraping by, and there was certainly no spare money for children to have luxuries like bicycles. But I did try to learn to ride one when Phyllis and I stayed at a farm in Somerset the year I turned fifteen.

When we arrived, we were offered a full cream tea – fresh toast with creamy butter and homemade blackcurrant jam. We were surprised to see that the farmer's wife left us a jug of cream to have with our tea.

'Could we have some milk instead?' I asked her.

'Oh, my dears,' she replied, laughing, 'That's what milk is like when it comes from the cow. When we sell it to the golf club we know they water it down.'

We went for long walks, mostly with their big Alsatian, Larry. One day, a real scorcher, we had a dreadful fright. As we crossed a field, Larry suddenly ran round and round in circles and jumped into the pond at the edge of the field. We stood by helpless as he sank until his nose was under water. We were terrified that he had drowned. There was no way we could pull him out and what could we possibly say to the farmer? That we had let his precious dog drown? Then Larry hauled himself out of the water, came up to us with a silly grin on his face, shook himself briskly, drenching us. We told him off, of course, but he wasn't listening. He was off chasing a rabbit that had foolishly stuck its nose out of its burrow.

On the way back, an army lorry passed us and stopped a little further on. Phyllis and I ran up.

'Can you give us a lift to Willow Bay farm?'

'Of course, Miss. Jump in.'

We hauled ourselves up the tall steps into the cab. The two young soldiers grinned at us, but their grins faded when Larry appeared and climbed up to sit at our feet. We'd brought our guardian with us. There would be no hanky-panky.

There was a well-used woman's bike in the barn and Phyllis said she'd teach me to ride. I got on alright and managed to cycle down the path from the farm to the main road, but then I rode straight into a hedge of blackberry bushes. I didn't appear to have hurt my arms or legs but my right eye was sore. I wheeled the bike back to the farm and tried bathing my eye but it only got worse. Soon my eye was bright red and I could barely open it.

The farmer drove me to the Casualty department of the local hospital where the sister quickly and efficiently removed the piece of blackberry thorn embedded in my eye.

I never tried riding a bike again

The following Easter Phyllis and I had saved enough to have a week at the seaside in Hastings. We chose a vegetarian hotel so that we wouldn't have to eat non-Kosher meat.

We were shown into a small but clean attic room and issued with a printed set of rules about not wearing muddy shoes indoors and when we could have a bath. It listed the meal times and stated that we would be provided with a packed lunch but would have a hot supper.

Breakfast was fine. We met the two middle aged couples who were also staying and accepted their offer of their spare walking map with alacrity. We were surprised to find the cornflakes already parcelled out into six bowls and just six slices of bread cut ready to be toasted, but we ate them with pleasure.

There was a packet of sandwiches near the front door with our names on and we stuffed them into the small ex-army rucksacks we had bought just before we came away. There was a large emporium in Hampstead Road that sold 'ex-army' clothes and equipment. We also had large rectangular waterproof groundsheets to wear when it rained – which it did almost as soon as we reached the gate at the end of the long drive.

We looked at each other, rain streaming down our faces, our shoulders covered in a groundsheet which came to our knees leaving our legs sticking out below.

'You look as if you're wearing nothing under that groundsheet,' Phyllis said. 'a real *nana*.'

'So, who looks more like a sodden banana?' I retorted.

'I'm hungry,' Phyllis said.

Our packets contained two delicate cheese and mustard pickle sandwiches cut into triangles and with the crust cut off. We demolished them in a couple of bites.

'I guess we're going to have to buy a bun or something to keep us going,' I said.

We stayed there five days. We walked a lot, never accepted a lift and were hungry most of the time.

As we paid our bill on the last day we turned to each other.

'Never again,' we said together.

Then we had to say 'Rabbits' – as you do when two of you say the same thing.

You couldn't take a bus or the underground on the Sabbath, but I could easily walk from Petticoat Lane to Trafalgar Square. Sometimes my father would still take me for walks in the City on Saturday afternoons but when he decided to have a nap instead I would walk to the National Gallery.

Most of their paintings were removed to caves deep in the countryside for protection during the war but I could enjoy those that were still on display. During the last years of the war, Dame Myra Hess gave free lunchtime concerts in the National Gallery. I could get a bus there lunchtime and half-term and listen enthralled.

I was fifteen, nearly sixteen, when I met Sebastian. I was queuing for gallery tickets at the New Theatre in St Martin's Lane. Ralph Richardson was playing Cyrano in Edmond Rostand's Cyrano de Bergerac.

I'd left home at 7.15am that morning. Though I was at the side entrance of the theatre by ten to eight, there were already several people in the queue. I paid three pence to hire a camp stool, and sat trying to revise my Latin vocabulary. I shivered in the chilly morning air, wishing I'd put on an extra jumper.

'It's freezing,' said the young man next to me. 'I hope the Box Office opens on time.'

'Freezing,' I echoed, turning to look at him. He was the most beautiful man I'd ever seen – dark curly hair, olive skin and soft brown eyes.

I was now in the sixth form and we had no classes until eleven.

I wished I hadn't come in school uniform. I could easily have worn my weekend clothes, gone home and changed into uniform after I bought my ticket. I tucked my feet under my stool to hide my white knee-length socks. We were supposed to wear beige lisle stockings but, for me and my friends, our white socks were a form of protest, like wearing army surplus groundsheets as raincoats when we went to the Youth Club.

I bought a 1/6d gallery ticket. I couldn't see how many tickets the young man bought, but I hoped he hadn't bought two – one for him and one for his girlfriend. Back at school, I thought about him all day and was rebuked for daydreaming.

We arrived at the door to the gallery together. He was alone.

'Hullo again. I'm Sebastian,' he said.

'I'm Abby.'

I glanced at our reflection in the mirror by the door, and thought how gorgeous he looked next to ordinary me. As we climbed the long stairs to the gallery, I tripped. He held my arm to steady me and kept hold of it until we found some seats. He was tall, so it was difficult for him to tuck his legs between the long benches. They ended up touching mine all through the performance. The play was fabulous. I prayed for Cyrano, thought that Christian was a wimp, and that Roxanne was too stupid for words.

'Care for some coffee?' Sebastian asked as we went down.

He was a music student and worked mornings as a porter in Covent Garden Market. We laughed when we caught ourselves both looking at ourselves in the mirror behind counter in the cafe. I had no idea how old Sebastian was, though I could see he was quite a bit older than me.

We went on meeting. Over the next weeks, we climbed up to the topmost gallery in the Opera House to see *Aida, Turandot, La*

Bohème and *Madame Butterfly*. I told my mother I was going to the opera with a friend. When I visited Sebastian's bedsit in Belsize Park on Saturdays I said I was going to the Youth Club. I walked all the way to Bank Station so no-one I knew saw me go into the Underground on the Sabbath.

We'd cuddle on his bed. Sebastian tried to persuade me to go further.

'It's quite safe,' he said. 'It's killing me not being able to make love to you properly. Please, Abby. I'll be very careful.'

I was too scared. What if I got pregnant? I'd have to leave school and my parents would be furious.

Then it was my birthday. Cards from my dad and sisters, but no presents of course. I decided that now I was sixteen I should give it away, get rid of it. I told my mother I needed new underwear and after school I took the bus to Marks and Spencer in Oxford Street. I bought some lacy cream camiknickers and hid them inside the petticoat I also bought.

On Saturday, when Sebastian opened the door, I whispered in his ear that I'd changed my mind and that I wanted to make love properly. He poured us large glasses of whisky to celebrate. The whisky tasted nasty and made me cough, but soon I felt warm and giggly. In the mirror on the wall opposite the bed I saw my naked back. I thought it was like the violin-shaped back of the young woman in the Velázquez painting, *The Rokeby Venus*, in the National Gallery.

Sebastian's hand reached under the pillow for something that crackled and then I couldn't, I just couldn't. Now in tears, I scrambled off the bed and pulled on my clothes.

'Don't be such a baby, Abby,' he shouted after me as I rushed out.

I phoned Sebastian from outside Aldgate East station. He said he'd fallen asleep; it was all right, not to worry. I felt too miserable for words.

'I was silly,' I cried. 'I'll skip school Monday afternoon and come over.'

'I'm rehearsing all week,' he said. 'I'll meet you at the Tate next Saturday at two.'

I waited in the entrance until the gallery closed but he didn't turn up. I phoned. There was no reply. I wrote. He didn't answer. I wrote again, phoned again and called at his house. Nothing.

By the following year, I couldn't remember what Sebastian looked like but I can still visualise that mirror on his wall and my naked back reflected in it.

Phyllis and I had saved enough money to go to Paris for ten days. We bought return tickets for the boat-train from Victoria, and we each changed £20 into French francs. We'd taken School Certificate French and felt sure we'd be able to get by.

We arrived at the Gare St. Lazare in the early evening, tired and hungry. We had decided we would stay on the Left Bank and explore the Artists' Quarter, so we got the Metro to Ste. Germaine de Prés and started looking for a cheap hotel. The second one we tried had a double room available. The concierge spoke good English and the reception area was clean and welcoming. He said we could leave our cases with him and recommended a restaurant in the next street.

It was seven thirty when we arrived at the restaurant and we worried that it would be awful, since it had only two customers. However, by the time our *steak frites* arrived, the restaurant was packed and there was a queue outside. We hadn't realised how late the French ate. We splashed out on a carafe of red wine and walked back to the hotel, replete and a bit tipsy.

The same friendly concierge showed us to our room. It was vile. The walls were hung with ancient peeling wallpaper and there was only a double bed, not the twin beds we had asked for. Having a bath was extra and had to be booked an hour beforehand. A grubby porcelain sink with taps that had never been cleaned stood in one corner. Phyllis said that the chipped oval enamel basin on a wire stand was for washing feet.

We felt like crying. It was so disappointing, especially after our lovely dinner. We tossed and turned all night, careful to make sure we never touched. Breakfast was included but that was another disappointment. We expected a full English breakfast which would see us through the day, but all we got was bitter coffee and a small stale croissant.

Luckily, we'd only booked for one night so, taking our room key with us, we went out to find somewhere better, but still on the Left Bank. Within minutes we had found a hotel that was cheaper and cleaner. This time we made sure we saw the room before we went back to collect our cases.

Continental breakfast at this hotel was also included. We decided we would have dinner in the restaurant we'd eaten at the night before and manage during the day on a bun or something. We couldn't afford two meals.

We set off to explore Paris. We didn't visit any museums or art galleries, but spent all our time wandering in and out of shops and, when the shops closed for lunch, we window gazed. I liked the look of a corset shop and fancied a lacy bra – the kind we'd seen in French films. A smiling middleaged man greeted us and found the brassiere in my size. When he followed us into the changing room intent on fitting it for me we ran out. Once outside, we could hardly walk for laughing.

We had hoped to find a bakery and buy a roll to have for lunch, but we left it too late and all the shops were shut until four. Tired and foot-weary, we got more or more bad-tempered from our hunger pangs we trudged back to our hotel. At least our room was nice and clean. We collapsed onto our beds and fell asleep at once. Dinner at the restaurant of the night before cheered us up no end. After that we made sure to have a *petit pain* or croissant mid-morning.

At the end of our week's stay I had just enough money left to buy a shirt and Phyllis wanted a silk scarf so we went up and down all the shopping streets until we found just the thing.

We'd spent no time on culture but we had thoroughly enjoyed ourselves, except for the couple of hours before the restaurant opened for dinner when we were ravenous. The second time we ate at our favourite restaurant the waiter recognised us.

'Ah. The English Demoiselles,' he said, and brought out a large basket of crusty French bread. We demolished it long before he returned with our meal.

I hated half term. At least during term time, I could usually get out of running errands by saying I had too much homework, but now I had to buy a loaf of bread and then collect my new school shoes from Wickham's Store. They were the school's outfitters and everything had to be bought there, even the navy interlock knickers we all hated so much.

I walked up the Minories kicking my toes against the uneven paving stones. I made sure I didn't step on any lines. I was always very careful about that, even in Goulston Street where the paving stones were so small. I went past the Royal Mint and up Tower Bridge Approach.

I was going to be brave today. I was going to look up at the overhead walkway while standing on the gap between the two halves of the bridge, even though looking straight up made me feel dizzy. Perhaps the siren that warns passers-by that the bridge was about to open and let a ship through, would sound off. Then I'd be let off standing on the crack or going to Wickham's. Only it didn't happen and I had to go through with the dare.

I walked around the curved bridge support and on to the straight part of the bridge, right up to the centre. A few cars and vans rumbled past and it wasn't too bad but then a big cement lorry passed and it was terrible. As I straddled the gap I could feel my feet moving up and down as it passed. I imagined the bridge giving way under me, sending me tumbling down into the river.

I felt sick. I leaned over the balustrade just in case I vomited, and watched as a tug pulled a line of coal-filled barges through the Thames just beneath me.

A hand fell on my shoulder.

'Wouldn't even think about it, Miss.'

I started and looked up at a giant of a policeman.

'I'm only looking. You didn't think . . .'

'No. No. Of course not. But run off home now. It's going to rain any minute.'

'I've got to go to Wickham's to collect my school shoes. I hate the man in the shoe department, with his fat shiny face. He's always asking the girls for a kiss and he makes me sick.'

'Don't you put up with his nonsense then, Miss. Next time he tries any of that funny business you say you'll tell a policeman. That'll stop him.'

With a pat on my shoulder he marched off.

Just then the sun came out and the Thames didn't look quite so murky, and I'd managed the dare, and I hadn't fallen in or anything.

I'd just stick out my tongue at the assistant if he asked for a kiss but it made me feel awful just thinking about his fat, greasy lips and I couldn't bear the thought of going to the shop.

By the time I got home I was utterly miserable. I didn't know what to do with myself. Looking in a mirror I drew myself. I was ugly as well as miserable.

I don't know now whether I really wanted to commit suicide or it was a call for help, but I decided that taking lots of aspirins was the answer. I bought a bottle of aspirins from Boots, the chemists, and set about swallowing them with water. After about thirty I felt too sick to go on and went to bed.

When I woke next morning, I felt sick and dizzy. I wasn't dead, but I had a loud buzzing in my ears and a dreadful headache. I told my mother that I thought I should go to a hospital. I didn't tell her about the aspirins.

I persuaded her that my buzzing and headache were something to do with migraine I'd had since I was about 13, and took myself off to the Royal Free Hospital. I can't understand how they agreed to see me, a 16-year-old, without a parent being present, but rules were different then and there wasn't the same emphasis on parental consent.

I was examined in front of students and remember the consultant demonstrating how to test the cranial nerves and how to look for changes in co-ordination by getting me to hold out my arm and then touch my nose with my finger.

He muttered something about 'fanciful young girls' and sent me off. I thought about ending it all over the years but never tried taking too many aspirins again.

CHAPTER 10

A Girl at the Boys' School

It was all so confusing, the year I had to decide which subjects to take in the sixth form. I had done quite well in my Lower School Certificate (GCSE equivalent), with five A's and 4 B's but I had no idea what I wanted to become, which career to choose. We had little in the way of careers advice. We were expected to become secretaries, nurses or teachers – and as soon as possible get married, have children and keep house.

Miss Williams became headmistress during my second year at CFS. Unlike her predecessor, who was outgoing and very popular, she was reserved and cold. Thinking about our limited lessons on 'Hygiene', I went to see her and said I wanted to train to be a teacher. It would have been fine if I had left it at that, but I said that, as girls were so ignorant, I wanted to teach sex education. She blushed as she told me I'd have plenty of time to decide once I'd finished my training.

My mother warned me against becoming a teacher.

'Do you want to be a dried-up old spinster like them? They never get married.'

She didn't know that there had been a bar against marriage for women teachers but not, of course, for male teachers. The male teachers' union strongly supported the bar. Women had to resign if they wanted to marry or, as some did, they kept their marriage secret. The marriage bar wasn't removed until 1935 and it would have affected several of our teachers.

I didn't want to be a spinster, an old maid, on the shelf, an old biddy or a maiden aunt. I was not yet 16 and the pressure was already on to get married. OK, so I decided I wouldn't become a teacher.

Hannah was now living on a Kibbutz. I thought perhaps if I became a doctor it would somehow make up for her disappointment at not being able to study medicine. I still felt partly responsible for her leaving school at fourteen.

Not all service men and women had been demobbed so there was still a post WW2 shortage of teachers, especially in the sciences. Some schools combined sixth form classes. Our school shared teachers with our brother school. If I decided to study medicine, I would need to take biology, physics and chemistry in my Higher Schools Certificate (A levels). We had a chemistry teacher at the girls' school but I would go to the Central Foundation School for Boys for Physics and Biology. The boys came to us for Arts subjects.

Having to take physics and biology at the boys' school wasn't the best reason for deciding to study medicine, but it was a factor. I was sure amongst the 500 or so boys there had to be some dishy ones.

I was the only girl taking lessons at the boys' school that year. On my first day, I arrived at the end of their morning break. Checking that my blazer was pulled down, my striped red and green school tie on straight and my beige lisle stockings pulled up and free from wrinkles, I pushed open the door to the playground.

At our school, we queued one behind the other to go back after break, but the boys lined up side by side. All 500 stood facing my path to the science block. The scruffiest, spottiest, first years at the front kept up a muted barrage of personal remarks and wolf whistles, until a master strode over and knocked two of their heads together. On the way up to the laboratories on the top floor, I had to hold my breath because of the smell from the loos on each landing.

The physics master, Mr Parker, tried his best with me, but I found physics baffling and it took me months to catch up with the boys. They'd been playing with electrical sets and motors for years.

Mr Matthews, who taught botany and zoology, was a brilliant teacher. A little man with a high voice, he sported a three-piece tweed suit, a striped tie and highly polished brown brogue shoes.

We started with invertebrate zoology – amoebae, paramecia, worms and crustaceans – and in botany, flowering plants. His lessons were fascinating and it was easy to get A's for my homework.

He explained that disadvantageous characteristics may continue to be inherited and not die out, if they were associated with a characteristic that conferred an evolutionary advantage. He wasn't usually a jokey sort of person, but he giggled when he explained it to us.

'You see,' he said. 'When I met my wife, she had a little yapping dachshund that always tried to nip me in the ankle. I loved the future Mrs Matthews very much but if I wanted to marry her, I had to accept the dog too. It's like that with linked inheritance. Sometimes a beneficial mutation is linked to one that is irrelevant or even harmful, such as resistance to malaria being inherited with the predisposition to sickle cell anaemia.'

Chemistry at the girls' school was fine too. Miss King was a bit out of touch with the latest ideas but she took a lot of care, making sure that we got through the required syllabus.

I did well in the end of year exams and came top in all three subjects. The headmaster had to arrange for the endowed prizes at the boys' school for Biology and Physics to go to me.

When we came back after the summer holidays, it was to find that Mr Matthews was no longer teaching biology. Instead we had Mr O'Connor. Burly and red-faced and wearing a baggy mustard-coloured checked suit, he exuded a strong smell of aftershave, peppermints and alcohol. He told us he had failed his exams as a medical student but had an M.A. in education, regaling us with stories of being accosted by prostitutes at King's Cross on his arrival from Dublin.

He said that animal anatomy was exactly like human anatomy, though clearly it wasn't. His idea of teaching was to read passages from our biology textbook for us to copy, so I followed the passage in my textbook and refused to write any of it down.

I was called out of my chemistry practical at the girls' school. My headmistress wanted to see me. I waited outside her office, wondering why.

'Come in,' Miss Williams called. 'Sit down. I've had disturbing complaints about you from the boys' school, Abby. Apparently, you have been disrupting the biology lessons and the others are copying you.'

The others were five pimply boys and they were such spineless creatures, probably they were copying me.

'Mr O'Connor says you refuse to take notes in class and that you cause problems in biology practicals.'

I was too embarrassed to tell Miss Williams about what he did during biology practicals. Our school blouses were always cut too short and they rode up out of our skirts if we stretched or leaned forward. Mr O'Connor would wait until the boys were at the other side of the room and put his hand on my bare back. It was sickening. When I glared at him, he pretended he'd done nothing. When I tripped over a box someone had left in front of the bench, I saw him trying to look up my skirt.

I was seventeen and to me Miss Williams was a dried-up old spinster. What could she know about lecherous men? I didn't tell her about how he used to creep up behind me and make any excuse to touch my bare back. It wasn't my fault, but I was too ashamed to talk about it. She'd never understand, but I could at least explain about the note taking.

'He dictates from our biology textbook, *Grove and Newell*. What's the point? Last week I brought in my copy and had it open under the desk. Honestly, Miss Williams, he read out Chapter Four, word for word.'

She looked uncomfortable.

'Yes, well . . . Just be tactful and at least pretend to be listening. You can be very difficult, you know.'

No. I didn't know. And it wasn't being difficult refusing to take dictation from a textbook you've got in front of you.

'I don't want to hear any more reports like this, Abby. We were so pleased with you in your first year, especially when you came top in the exams and they had to give you prizes meant for the boys. It's just six months until Higher School Certificate. Just stay out of trouble.'

*

It was in my second term that the good-looking English teacher at the boys' school decided that, since they had a girl pupil in the boys' school, when they put on Act II of *Romeo and Juliet*, a boy could play the Nurse but they'd ask me to play Juliet. The boy playing Romeo was a very good actor but I didn't find him attractive. It was all terribly disappointing. I'd had such high hopes of finding a boyfriend in our brother school.

We did a dress rehearsal in front of the fifth form. I decided the English teacher really was too old, though I'd enjoyed being close to him when he put my makeup on for me. Then, right in the middle of the front row of the boys watching us, was the most gorgeous boy. His long blond hair was swept across his forehead and he had fabulous green eyes.

I couldn't think of an excuse to talk to him but one day I managed to be at the gate when he came out. I smiled at him and he smiled back.

'I'm Peter,' he said. 'I thought you were fantastic in Romeo and Juliet. I asked the others what you were doing in our school. What's it like being the only girl?'

'It's OK. Bit smelly on the stairs up to the science labs.'

'I wonder. Would you like to go to the cinema some time or just go for a walk?'

We met on Saturday afternoons in the walkway on the north side of the Thames near Blackfriars Bridge. There was no-one around in the City at weekends and we had the flat area by the railings to ourselves.

I enjoyed the kissing and petting at first, but Peter wanted to touch me and I wouldn't let him. One day I stood him up. He waited for me outside school the next Monday but I walked on. When he caught me up I ignored the tears in his eyes and was really mean. It was time to end it.

'It's over Peter. You're just too young for me. I don't know how I ever got started, going out with a fifth former.'

My father went to the synagogue every Saturday but my mother had her own versions of the Jewish laws. She said that women don't have to go on Saturdays, only on the High Holydays and they also didn't have to go to funerals.

Although you weren't allowed to cook on the Sabbath, you could leave a hotpot of potatoes and chicken slowly cooking on a low gas overnight. The fourth commandment bade you keep the Sabbath and *neither thou, nor thy maidservant, nor thy manservant, nor the stranger within thy gates* could break it. My mother said it was allowable to get a *Sabbath Goy* (non-Jew) to light the fire for you on a wintry Saturday, provided you told them to do it well beforehand and not on the Sabbath. I had no sympathy with this way of thinking.

I stopped believing in a personal God. Although my parents were orthodox Jews, little was spoken at home about God – it was forbidden to say His proper name out loud. You referred to him as *Ha Shem* – the name. Any discussion of religion was about Jewish practices – whether something was or was not allowed; whether it would be permissible to eat in a restaurant or in a certain friend's house and whether the food would be Kosher.

What I read of psycho-analysis – Freud, Jung and Adler – made me decide belief in a personal God was incompatible with rational thought, even though it wasn't explicitly stated in any of their writing.

I could share my thoughts with no-one – certainly with not my orthodox parents. My best friend, Phyllis, came from a firmly atheist, communist family and would just laugh. Sophie's family, on the other hand, was so orthodox it would offend her feelings, even hinting that I was now an atheist.

It hurt, challenging my belief in God. It hurt a lot. I had a real physical pain in my chest. I turned over and over in bed, unable to sleep and felt weepy all the time.

'Lots of people must have gone through this pain over the centuries,' I thought. 'Why couldn't one of them have taken on this pain and dealt with it once and for all, for everyone to come?'

Although I no longer believed in God, I still followed all the Jewish laws – didn't do my homework on Saturdays, didn't take a bus on the Sabbath and even fasted on the Day of Atonement. I was never tempted to eat non-Kosher food. For me, pork and bacon and shellfish were dirty, unspeakable things and I wouldn't dream of having a forbidden milk pudding or a cup of tea after a meal containing meat. While my intellect told me I was being inconsistent, I couldn't help myself – my orthodox upbringing was so strong.

Things had never been good at home with my mother, and I felt I had no-one to turn to. My father was kindly but distant, and never contradicted my mother, at least as far as her attitude to me was concerned. Now I didn't even have a paternal God to rely on when things were bad for me. I was used to making bargains with Him – if you let me pass this exam I'll go to synagogue every Saturday for a month, maybe two months or, if it was a big wish like 'Please let my mother love me, even a little bit,' I'd promise to go every Saturday for a year.

Finally, the pain of disbelief settled to a dull ache, but I still couldn't give up my orthodox practices. It was many years before I could ignore the Jewish High Holydays. Even then I felt I was letting my people down and ought to be showing solidarity with other Jews.

When I grew up in the East End of London, the district was essentially a Jewish one. It had two large synagogues and seven smaller ones.

The large synagogue our family attended, The Great Synagogue, was for Ashkenazi Jews – those originating in Eastern Europe. The other large synagogue, in Bevis Marks, was for Sephardic Jews who came originally from Spain and Portugal. Such was the gap between the original Iberian immigrants, who were well established and often by now wealthy, and the newly arrived often impoverished Jews from Russia and Poland, that I have never set foot in Bevis Marks *shul*.

The Great Synagogue in Duke's place was bombed in 1942 but in its time, it was magnificent, with huge electrified chandeliers, originally candle-lit, and long stained-glass windows depicting the twelve tribes of Israel. There was a large carpeted central stage for the cantor and rabbi and a dais leading up to the curtained alcove, the *Holy Ark,* where the ancient hand-written books of the *Torah* – the Old Testament – were kept.

The service on the night before the Day of Atonement, *Erev Yom Kippur,* was magic. People came from far and wide to hear the *Kol Nidrei* service sung by the famous cantor, Koussevitzky. My family had always belonged to Duke's Place Synagogue so we had reserved seats, but outsiders crammed the gangways full to overflowing to hear the ancient melodies sung in his rich tenor voice. We all had tears in our eyes as he sang.

As the sun set, the ram's horn, the *Shofar,* was blown three times to announce the beginning of *Yom Kippur.* Neither food nor water would pass the lips of Orthodox Jews until sunset of the next day. Young children, pregnant woman and people too ill to fast were excused but I now fasted with the rest of the family. We had a special Holyday meal before going to synagogue.

143

I was wearing my new cerise wool dress, its tight waist and full skirt making me look soft and petite. My mother had bought it for me for the Jewish New Year, ten days before. Mostly I wore hand-me-downs from my older sisters but this year we made a special trip to C&As in Oxford Street and found a dress even my mother approved of.

Now, mid-day on the Day of Atonement, half way into the fast, everyone's breath smelt. The older and more Orthodox Jews had been at the Synagogue since first light, and were tired and sweaty. The service was in Hebrew and mainly consisted of muttered prayers rather than the haunting melodies of *Kol Nidrei*. My prayer book had a side-by-side English translation but I'd read it all before. I was bored.

I looked over at David in the fourth row on the right and nodded towards the exit. In orthodox synagogues men and women are segregated. In the original building, women sat upstairs under the coloured light that streamed through the stained-glass windows. They peered through the ornate gilded rails to nod and smile at their men below. Now the services were held in a concrete single storey hut, built on the previous site. The women sat in the middle and the men at right angles on either side. It was much easier to pass messages.

David mouthed 'Yes'.

'Just going for a walk to Tower Hill,' I told my mother and slipped out.

While the older Jews stayed in the synagogue praying and chant-ing all day, young people made their way to the nearest running water – the River Thames near Tower Bridge – to wash away their sins. You were supposed to say a prayer, but for David and me it was an excuse to get some fresh air.

It was one of those warm September days – just enough of a chill in the air to warn you that winter wasn't far away. The sun glinted off the river and for once the Thames looked gay and sparkly. Just as we arrived a bell clanged, the entry was roped off and the bridge slowly opened to let a tall ship pass. I had seen the bridge open lots of times; had stood on the join where the two halves met while a lorry rumbled by; felt a frisson of fear as my feet moved up and down out of time with each other – but it was as exciting as ever. I narrowed my eyes and imagined running up the bridge just as it was opening and sliding down again just before it opened completely.

Large black canons, captured in battle, stood along the walkway on the north side of the river between it and the Tower of London. Screaming children climbed over them, running from one to another. David and I were too old for that sort of thing but we both wished we weren't.

We turned to go back.

'Is your sister . . . ?' David asked.

'No. It's all right. There'll be no-one at home.'

Petticoat Lane was deserted. Even the non-Orthodox shop keepers and stall holders wouldn't open on this most holy of days. I tensed as we reached the entrance to my block with its overwhelming smell of cat pee and rotting food, though David was even poorer than me so I shouldn't have felt so ashamed. Where he lived was worse.

He kissed me, ignoring the smell.

'Let's go upstairs,' I said, pulling him after me.

The front door led straight into the kitchen, which also served as our living room. David sat on the only armchair and pulled me onto his lap.

I didn't love David, not like the boy I'd fallen in love with at the

Youth Club, but I loved the feeling of comfort from being kissed and stroked and made much of.

The armchair was a utility design with a hard seat and flat wooden arms. The back could be lowered to convert it into a narrow single bed. It was fiendishly uncomfortable and after a few minutes David pushed me off and stood up.

'This chair is killing me. Can't we go into one of the other rooms?'

I wasn't sure about taking him into my bedroom with its iron bedstead and furniture made from orange boxes salvaged from Petticoat Lane market, but I held David's hand and started to turn the handle. David pulled away and reached for his back pocket.

'I've tested them, blown them up and filled them with water. They're quite safe.'

I froze. This wasn't what I wanted. I was scared and shivery. It was Sebastian all over again.

He wiped away the tears that had begun to run down my cheeks.

'It's OK Abby. It's alright, it really it is. Don't cry, please don't. I'm a bit scared myself. I couldn't bear it if I got you pregnant like that girl, Anna. You'd have to leave school and everything.' He tried a smile. 'Anyhow, you're such a swot you probably wouldn't know how to look after a baby.'

I cried properly now. Cried with relief, cried because I felt unloved and unwanted at home, cried because I really liked David, wanted him to go on kissing and cuddling me but didn't want to go the whole way, not now, not with him.

We stood a while longer kissing and holding and feeling for bare skin under our clothes.

David kissed me one more time.

'It's time to go back' he said. 'They'll be starting the evening service. We'll try again next Yom Kippur. Maybe you'll say 'yes' then.'

I reached up, ran my finger along his lips and kissed him.

'It's a promise,' I said, but I wasn't quite sure I meant it.

Sam, who lived in North London, visited our Youth Club during my final year at school.

'I stay with my grandfather in Cable Street from Friday evening to Saturday night,' he told me. 'My parents insist that I walk to St Margaret's for my Saturday morning lectures, though of course it's just as forbidden to go to college on the Sabbath as it is to use public transport. It's boring. My grandfather falls asleep as soon as we've eaten and there's nothing I can do in the dark once the Friday night candles have burnt down.'

I asked my mother if Sam could come over after supper on Friday nights and she insisted that he ate with us. An orthodox Jewish boy who was training to be a dentist was worth cultivating.

He was a keen photographer. On Saturday afternoons, he collected me and we walked to Fleet Street. At that time, in 1949, both sides of Fleet Street were lined by newspaper offices and printing works, their windows full of photos of the latest news. He insisted on looking at every one, commenting on the quality and composition.

We were friends, but no more than that. I looked forward to his visits, though the pilgrimages to Fleet Street got boring after the first couple of windows.

His uncle was leader of the second violins at the Royal Opera House, Covent Garden. Now and again he gave Sam a pair of complimentary tickets in the stalls. I'd go in school uniform and sit there amongst all the women in evening dress and men in black tie and tails, feeling as if I was thumbing my nose at the wealthy people who'd had to pay for their tickets.

My applications for medical school at the beginning of my second year in the sixth form hadn't gone well. Neither my headmistress nor the careers mistress seemed to know anything about the process. I had to find out everything for myself.

I had no idea how slim my chances were. I had nothing in my favour. I came from a school in the East End of London and I was competing with girls who had been to Roedean or Cheltenham Ladies College. Some had parents on the staff. In addition, there was a quota of only 10% for women entrants, as well as a secret, even smaller, quota for Jews.

First time round I didn't apply to the Royal Free Hospital for Women because it only took women students and I'd had enough of being in an all-girls school. I applied to St Mary's, University College, St Margaret's and King's College. I didn't apply to the London Hospital in Whitechapel, not wanting to go to medical school so near home. It would have seemed too much like being back at school.

I didn't apply outside London. If I got a place in London, I'd live at home and could get a London County Council grant to cover my fees and a small living allowance. I had few clothes, other than my school uniform, and medical textbooks were very expensive. If I went to medical school away from home, I wouldn't have enough money to buy clothes and pay for books as well as lodgings.

I heard first from St Mary's. I was asked to come up the following Saturday for a short examination, from which a list would be made of students to be interviewed. I told my headmistress that my parents would not want me to take an exam on a Saturday and asked her to contact the medical school to make other arrangements. After two weeks, I'd heard nothing so I went to see her.

'What happened about St Mary's?' I asked.

'Haven't you heard from them?'

'No.' I said. 'What did they say when you spoke to them?'

'I thought you were going to phone them,' she said, 'but never mind, there are plenty of other medical schools.'

I was furious with myself. Why had I said anything to her? How stupid to give up the chance of a place at medical school because I was so indoctrinated about not travelling on the Sabbath.

I was then offered an interview at St Margaret's. Two of the other candidates were from Roedean, the private girls' school on the South coast. They had posh accents and wore tailored suits and high-heeled shoes. I was in my school uniform and wore clumpy lace-ups.

'Daddy said I was to go to Harrods and get a decent outfit for my interview,' one of them said. 'Of course, I just had to splash out on a new party dress.'

Her friend sniggered in sympathy.

At my interview the chairman of the committee, the senior tutor, grew redder by the minute as I said what I thought about religion and science being incompatible. I can't remember how the subject came up. Perhaps they had mentioned something about my being Jewish. Finally, he dismissed me abruptly,

By the time I had an interview at Kings, I had saved enough money to buy a new coat and shoes, but I was turned down there as well.

However, at the end of my first year in the sixth form I had every hope of doing well enough in my Higher Schools Examination to get a State Scholarship. This would guarantee me a place at a Medical School.

But my Higher Schools results were disappointing – 2 Bs and 2 Cs – nothing like good enough for a State Scholarship.

Mr O'Connor's teaching had been useless. There was no way I was going back to school to re-sit. I couldn't bear the thought of another year with him trying to touch me. My school uniform was too tight and I knew my mother would grumble if she had to buy a new set.

'Why don't you apply to St Margaret's Dental School?' Sam said, when I told him about my poor Higher School certificate results. 'It's next best to medicine.'

I rang St Margaret's dental school, had an interview with the Dean and he accepted me on the spot. As we ended up a small class of only fifteen, I suspect he was so pleased to have another candidate that he didn't question my motives too closely. Getting a London County Council grant was straightforward and in October 1949 I started at St Margaret's.

Dentistry was a strange choice for me. Although I could sew and had taught myself to touch-type, I was quite cack-handed. Nothing I did with my hands came naturally. All through my subsequent careers I would have to think carefully about anything practical. I'd have to tell my hands how to move – right a bit, left a bit.

I once dissected the nervous system of a crayfish and drew a careful diagram of my dissection. Then, trying to remove a stray piece of shell, I managed to get my forceps under the spinal cord and yanked the whole thing out, destroying the whole morning's work.

CHAPTER 11

St Margaret's Hospital Dental School

I was just 18 when I first dissected a human body. We'd had our first lecture on the anatomy of the thorax and now we were to start on our dissection.

Just inside the dissecting room there were tall mahogany shelves packed with rows of sealed glass jars containing preserved human organs. Most of the specimens were bleached white by formalin; others, injected with embalming fluid, were a dusky red.

Paul, the brash student from Manchester, picked up a pot containing a white specimen the size of a fist. He turned it upside down to see the label.

'It's a spleen,' he said, giving the jar a shake.

Little white fragments detached themselves from the surface and floated down.

'What do you think of my snowstorm, Abby?' he asked.

'Stupid prat,' I muttered under my breath.

He picked up another specimen and gathered the male students around him. I tried to see what he was holding, but I couldn't see over their heads. They sniggered and made way for me. Paul held out the jar. It contained a large erect penis. I blushed bright red and backed away.

'That got you. Curiosity killed the cat,' he said.

Wearing our new white coats and clutching our rolls of dissecting instruments and manuals we waited, nervous and excited, in the subdued light of the basement corridor. The double doors of the dissecting room were locked and the portholes were filled with opaque wired glass. As we tried to peep through the gap between them, a cadaverous man in a brown laboratory coat came out of an adjoining room.

'I'm George, the technician in charge,' he said. 'If you want anything, you have to go through me. Remember: no smoking, no fooling around and show respect.'

He unlocked the doors and we filed in. An antiseptic smell, a mixture of carbolic and formalin, lay heavy in the air.

'Pay attention, you dental students. You are to work in groups of four,' George said. 'Your tables are over there, under the window.'

'But there are fifteen of us,' Paul protested.

'Well, one group will have to manage with three students. Try to include one of the ladies. She'll keep things nice and tidy for you.'

The men tittered while we three women grimaced.

Long metal tables filled the high-ceilinged room. On each, there was a body covered with a grey linen sheet. It was still, cathedral like. We spoke in whispers.

I went to the furthest table with my new friends, William and Oliver. I had sat next to them in our first psychology lecture. We'd giggled together at the professor's interpretation of the underlying sexual message in everything, even in nursery rhymes. After that, we always sat together at lectures and in the refectory.

William was tall and thin, his wispy blond hair beginning to bald. Oliver was the opposite – short and tubby, with horn-rimmed glasses. He was the clown of the year, already in demand for his impersonations of our professors.

Standing by our table, we each waited for one of the others to begin. I wanted to show I wasn't a wimp and peeled back the grey sheet. I recoiled at the sight of the emaciated body of an elderly woman.

Dr Taylor, the anatomy lecturer, breezed in.

'Well, don't stand around. Make a median incision from the suprasternal notch to the pubic symphysis and turn back the skin flaps. Cut through the rib cage on either side of the sternum and lift out the breast plate.'

'I'm not going first,' William said. 'I'm sure I'll cut something I shouldn't.'

'Well it won't be fatal,' said Oliver.

'Stop it, you two,' I said. 'I'll start.'

'I'll hold the dissecting manual for you,' William said, with a sigh of relief.

Over the next few weeks, the three of us got used to dissecting as a team, got used to the smell permeating our clothes. It remained in our nostrils even when we were away from St Margaret's.

It was hard to keep up the gruelling pace set by Dr Taylor. Copying the medical students, we started to bring our sandwiches into the dissecting room so we could catch up. We waited until George went off for lunch, then one of us would go on dissecting while the other two ate.

Dr Taylor was demonstrating surface anatomy. He pointed to Paul, the student who had embarrassed me on our first day in the dissecting room.

'Take off your shirt. You can be our model today.'

Paul pulled off his shirt, blushing deep red.

'And your vest,' Dr Taylor ordered.

Paul shivered in the chilly air of the lecture room.

'Learning surface anatomy may seem a bore to you dental students, but it's vital to know where the internal organs are in relation to the overlying skin.'

He drew the outline of the heart and lungs on Paul's chest and told him to lower his trousers to just below his waist. It was great seeing that show-off embarrassed.

Dr Taylor asked each of us to point to the areas that overlay Paul's heart, his liver, his spleen and kidneys.

'It could be a matter of life and death for a doctor to know his surface anatomy. A patient with trouble breathing after an accident, because air or blood has leaked into his pleural cavity, would need a chest drain inserted into the right area fast. Someone with liver disease might need a biopsy taken with a hollow needle pushed through the overlying skin. As dental surgeons, you will need to know as much about the heart and lungs as do doctors. To listen to the heart, you need to locate the apex of the left ventricle, which lies below the left nipple, and the right ventricle which lies behind the right second intercostal space.'

William nudged me.

'So that's why doctors listen to your heart there. I always wondered why not in the middle of your chest.'

'You will carry out extractions and minor surgical procedures on patients under general anaesthesia,' Dr Taylor continued, annoyed at the interruption. 'You must be prepared to deal with any emergency if a patient collapses in your dental chair.'

'That's a thought,' William whispered. 'Hate the idea of a patient dying on me.'

We also had lectures on Dental Anatomy – the development, shape and function of the teeth and jaws. When teeth are extracted at the Dental School because they are loose due to periodontal disease, or for other reasons, but free of decay, they are cleaned and kept for teaching dental anatomy or used to practice putting fillings in them. Despite the cleaning they got they still had a musty organic smell and none of us really liked handling them.

After the Thorax, we started dissecting the Head and Neck. Now we were finally studying subjects with more relevance for us.

Dr Taylor stopped me as we were filing out from his lecture on the anatomy of the head and neck.

'My wife and I would like you to come to dinner sometime next week, Abby. Would Wednesday do?'

'Where? What time?' I stammered, surprised to be singled out. I knew I looked young for my age. Perhaps he felt sorry for me. Or maybe I would find he was alone when I got there. There were whispers about the physiology professor and how it was better not to get caught alone with him in the medical school library, once the chief librarian had gone home.

'Is 7.30 OK?' he asked, holding out a card with his address.

I bought a bouquet of flowers from the stall outside Belsize Park underground station. I was too early, so I walked around a bit, took a deep breath and rang the bell exactly on time.

Much to my relief, Mrs Taylor, a small pretty woman wearing a navy and white striped butcher's apron, opened the door.

'Come on in, Abby. John has been telling me what a bright young student you are. Dinner will be ready in a couple of minutes. He's just finishing up. Will you have a glass of sherry? *Tio Pepe* alright?'

I'd never tasted sherry but I didn't like to say no. I was used to sweet *Kiddush* wine. The sherry was sour and made my mouth purse up.

Dr Taylor came in.

'Hello, Abby. Sorry to keep you waiting.'

His wife brought in a big bowl of salad and a dish of new potatoes. She put a slice of cold meat on my plate. This was the first time I tried eating non-Kosher (*traife*) meat. Though I no longer believed in the Jewish religion, I found it hard to give up the observances like not eating forbidden food. I'd prepared myself to eat *traife* meat, but this was a longitudinal slice of tongue, looking just like the illustration in *Gray's Anatomy* and the tongue we had been dissecting that week. The sherry was bad enough, but this was worse.

I took some salad and a couple of potatoes and managed to finish the meat though it was difficult downing the last few mouthfuls. Dessert was a delicious-looking trifle but, still feeling queasy, I asked for a very small portion.

He didn't invite me again and I don't know why he asked me to dinner in the first place.

It wasn't then considered inappropriate for teaching staff to socialise with students. It was quite acceptable for Dr Taylor to ask me to dinner with his wife and I said 'yes' when Steven Mackintosh, the biochemistry lecturer came over during a practical.

'Fancy coming out for a meal after we've cleared up, Abby? There's a very good Greek restaurant in Charlotte Street.'

'Well, er, yes. I'll have to phone home.'

I was still living at home and my mother would be anxious if I came home late.

I checked to see I had enough money to pay and waited in the students' common room for Steven to pick me up. He was a tall ginger-haired man with the trace of a Scottish accent and sparkling green eyes.

'Who else is coming?' I asked.

'Ah no, lass. It's just you and me,' he said, tucking his hand under my arm.

The meal was delicious. *Meze* to start with – Greek bread, olives, *taramasalata*, *tzatziki* and sticks of carrot and celery, then *moussaka* and salad, followed by thick Greek coffee and *baklava*. I looked in my purse, worried I might not have enough to pay my share of the bill.

'Put your purse away, Abby. This is on me.'

He saw me to the Underground and planted a chaste kiss on my lips.

'It's been lovely. You're a sweet girl. Maybe the cinema next time.'

It was a film next and a more impassioned kiss and then another meal, this time at the Angus steak house. I thought I might be falling in love.

As we left, Steven said 'Are you free this weekend? I know a lovely pub near Brighton we could stay at.'

I blushed and stammered

'No. Not really, I don't think . . . I mean I haven't . . .'

'It's OK. My wife is off at a conference.'

'Your wife?'

I burst into tears. 'But you said . . .'

'You should never say 'no' to a married man, Abby. He can just go home and make love to his wife if he's in the mood for sex.'

I couldn't believe how he had deceived me.

I was still hurting, when William asked if I'd like to come to St James's Park the following Sunday.

It was one of those sunny but cool spring days, the breeze making waves in the great carpets of daffodils and narcissi. We walked around the lake to see the pelicans and peeked through the railings outside the guards' barracks, hoping to see them on parade. Back in the park, William led me to a shady clearing.

'This is my favourite spot,' he said. 'I come here to read and get away from Oliver.'

As we lay side by side in the long cool grass I sniffed. I could smell dissecting room preservative. I sniffed at my hands, my blouse and my handkerchief. Nothing.

'What's the matter?' William asked.

'I can smell dead bodies.'

'Come here then,' he said, 'and smell me instead. I'm alive. Feel my heart beating.'

He pulled my hand under his shirt and I stroked his soft warm skin. As we kissed, a park attendant hurried over.

'Now then, now then, you two. None of that here.'

We got up to leave – William to go to the room he shared with Oliver in the Hall of Residence, and me to go home.

We met up a few times at the end of the day to see a film or go for a drink, but William had a girlfriend back in Exeter, and as he was a *goy* (a non-Jew) nothing could come of our relationship.

My mother waited up for me whenever I came home late.

'I hope you're not going out with one of those *goyim* from that college. It would kill me if you married out.'

By the end of term, it was over. No need to go on lying to my mother.

By the spring term I knew I didn't want to become a dentist. I had only applied to study dentistry as a second best. I asked for an appointment with the senior tutor to ask if I could change courses and study medicine. I received a brief note stating that no, I couldn't see him and no, I couldn't change courses,

I wrote to all the London medical schools once more, applying to study medicine. I had a refusal practically by return from all of them except from the Royal Free Hospital, which was then staffed by women and only accepted female students. After a couple of months, I had a refusal letter from them too. I wrote back saying that it was unfair to take so long to answer my application if they weren't going to interview me. I was offered an interview ten days later.

I now knew how to dress – a neat navy-blue suit and white silk blouse – rather than wearing school uniform as I had for my first interviews for Medical School the year before, and I was much more confident. Within a week I had a letter of acceptance for the clinical course, provided I completed the second part of my medical degree – Bachelor of Medicine and Bachelor of Surgery (MBBS) at St Margaret's. The 2nd MBBS exam consisted of anatomy, physiology and biochemistry. It would mean working hard to catch up with the medical students but I only needed to stay on another six months at St Margaret's Hospital Medical School.

I wrote to the senior tutor again and once again got a curt note of refusal. He refused to allow me to stay on at St Margaret's and swap to the medical course, even for six months.

It was devastating. How could I go back to the Royal Free and ask if they would let me complete my 2nd MBBS there? Surely, they would write to St Margaret's and ask why they had refused to allow me to stay on and he would give them some story about how unsuitable I was.

I was sure it was because I had offended his religious views when I had my interview to study medicine at St Margaret's the year before. At that interview for some inexplicable reason I said that science and religion were incompatible. I later discovered that he was a lay preacher.

In retrospect, when the senior tutor refused to let me stay on to complete my 2nd MBBS, I should have asked the Royal Free if they would take me. Maybe, as women, they would have understood that I was being treated unfairly, but at the time I was in despair. I found it hard to think clearly and there was no-one to ask for advice.

It was hopeless. I'd had such high hopes that finally I would be studying medicine but if I left the dental school now I would lose my London County Council grant and maybe never get another chance to go to University.

I had mucked up my interview to study medicine at St Margaret's the year before and now I'd have to stick it out and qualify as a dentist.

CHAPTER 12

Real Patients at Last

In our second year, we moved into the Prosthetics Department where we learned how to make full and partial dentures. One of the most difficult things in the world is to make a full set of dentures. I think that if you can do that, you can do anything.

Patients came for treatment to a dental school partly because treatment was free but also, since the consultants and lecturers were highly qualified, they felt they would get better treatment than in private practice. Often, they didn't realise that, though we were closely supervised, they were being treated by students.

I was lucky with my first patient. He was a lovely old man who kept calling me 'Little Lady'. He'd had all his teeth out long before so his jaws were well healed. I selected a suitable metal tray that would fit into his mouth, mixed the impression material and gingerly inserted it so that his upper gums and palate were covered. Some people find having anything on their palate makes them gag, and for a junior dental student that can be a nightmare. My patient sat there stolidly while I took impressions of his upper and lower jaws.

I poured plaster of Paris into the impression made by his dental ridges, and now had a set of models on which to make a trial set of dentures. The teeth themselves came ready-made in matching sets, but we made the acrylic denture plate in which they were embedded. I moulded a sheet of wax to fit the models and carefully inserted a set of teeth into them.

My patient came to try the temporary set, for fit, for appearance, and to establish the correct position for his upper and lower dentures to make contact – the bite. This needed to be correct for him to be able to chew his food.

'Good morning, Little Lady. How are we today?'

I explained that the dentures were only set in wax and that he had to bite very carefully.

'I've had false teeth before, Little Lady. I know exactly what to do, don't you worry your little head.'

My fears were well founded. I slipped in the trial dentures, he clamped down hard and all the front teeth splayed out. The trial dentures were too distorted to be rescued so I had to remake them. I watched with envy as my friend William effortlessly made his trial sets. I would never be as good.

I remade the dentures and cast them in acrylic. My patient was delighted. He handed me a box of Black Magic chocolates tied up with a large red bow.

'Best set I ever had,' he said, planting a kiss on my cheek.

My next patient was a woman who clearly thought she was slumming it, having her dentures made in a dental school rather than in Harley Street. She gagged as soon the impression tray was anywhere near her, though in the end I managed to get some impressions.

162

I thought I had done very well as I fitted her new dentures.

'Well they're comfortable enough, I must say, but couldn't you have made the teeth more regular? And I'm sure they're too dark. They make me look old.'

'Raddled old cow,' I thought.

I had explained at length that teeth get darker as we age and that absolutely regular teeth look artificial, like white tombstones, but she persisted.

'You'll have to make me a better set,' she said.

Sensing trouble, the prosthetics demonstrator came over.

'Congratulations on your new dentures. They make you look twenty years younger. Hasn't our Miss Waterman done well?'

She fluttered her eyelashes.

'Well, I suppose so, if you really think I look younger,' she simpered.

I found making partial dentures, in which only a few teeth are replaced, even more difficult. Having to bend and solder wire and steel bands to shape was a nightmare.

I just about scraped through our end-of-year prosthetics practical exam.

In our third year, we learned how to do fillings, how to carry out extractions and perform minor oral surgery. We practiced cutting neat cavities and filling extracted teeth mounted in plaster blocks fixed to a metal head with opening and closing jaws – *A Phantom Head*. On these we learned how to drill out caries (decay), mix fillings and pack them into the cavities. Mostly we used amalgam – a mixture of mercury and metal powder – but we also learned how to cast gold fillings. Several of us also carved brooches or buttons out of wax and used the same technique as jewellers use – the 'lost wax' method – and cast them in gold.

I bought a pattern and a length of blue fabric in John Lewis to make myself a jacket with just one button at the neck. Having bought some gold at the bullion merchant in Hatton Garden, I carved a button with a leaf design in wax and cast it in gold. It was a proud day when I wore my jacket for the first time.

We were next shown how to give local anaesthetic injections for fillings and how to extract teeth under general anaesthesia in the surgical extraction room – 'the gas room'- which was presided over by the stern sister-in-charge. Even the consultants were wary of her and everyone watched their language. She sent out students who dared to swear over a difficult extraction. Autoclaves, pressure chambers used to sterilise medical equipment, were not yet in widespread use, so the gas room was full of the sound of sterilisers constantly bubbling away.

Patients were anaesthetised with a mixture of nitrous oxide – 'laughing gas' – and air.

'Nitrous oxide was first used for dental extraction in 1844,' the consultant anaesthetist told us.

He beckoned William over, sat him in the dental chair and showed us how to place a mask over a patient's face.

'As the patients are partly deprived of oxygen, some develop a blue tinge. You mustn't let them get so short of oxygen that they start jactitating – thrashing around in the chair.'

Later we saw him testing that the gas was running by taking a couple of deep breaths. Behind his back we gossiped about Victorian laughing-gas parties and wondered whether he was an addict.

Next day William snuck into the gas extraction room at lunch time and took a few puffs. He said he hated it. Everything got very loud and he felt disconnected in a most unpleasant way. None of the rest of us wanted to try it. We had no idea that sniffing nitrous oxide from balloons would become a craze.

The best thing about our third year was having lectures on Medicine, Surgery and Pathology. We didn't examine patients but we were given a very good overview of the most common conditions. I found it all enthralling and read much more than was required to pass our end of year exams.

In our medicine lectures, we were taught about the infectious diseases that could affect the mouth and jaws.

'If you work with children you might see Koplik's Spots, small white spots on the inside of the mouth in a child who seems otherwise well. These are characteristic of measles and are quite difficult to see. The Strawberry Tongue of scarlet fever, on the other hand, is quite obvious. The tongue is bright red and the papillae stand out, looking just like the seeds on a strawberry. You are unlikely to see a primary syphilitic sore, a chancre, on the lips or tongue. They occur, of course, much more commonly on the genitals.'

We sniggered when he went on to say 'However, there is a report in the literature of seven women catching syphilis during a kissing game from a man with a chancre on his lip, so beware.'

He showed us slides of chancres in the mouth, and of Hutchinson's incisors in a young boy. Having notched front teeth was one of the stigmata of congenital syphilis.

'You should all go down to Piccadilly Circus and look at the newspaper seller, though not all together and don't stare,' our lecturer said. 'He's got the classical sunken saddle nose and bossing of the frontal ridge of his forehead. These are some of the other signs of congenital syphilis caught from the mother *in utero*.'

My new patient for fillings was a young woman in her early twenties.

'I hate these notches on the tips of my front teeth. Can you grind them straight?'

I got quite excited, thinking that I might be looking at a case of congenital syphilis, but then she said:

'We all get them, you know. They tell us not to keep opening Kirby grips with our front teeth when we're doing perms, but what can you do? You're holding on to a roll of hair in one hand and want to clip it in place. You have to use your teeth, don't you?'

I was fascinated by pathology. It was a great whodunit. Not forensic pathology – I wasn't interested in solving murders – but in discovering the nature of disease as it presented day by day.

As a pathologist, you would first examine the specimen as it came from the operating theatre and extract as much information as possible from just looking at it and feeling it. Was the lesion hard or soft, did it have smooth regular margins like a benign tumour, or did it extend crab-like into the surrounding tissues – a cancer? Did it have a central cavity and a greenish colour like tuberculosis, or contain fluid, like a cyst?

You would cut 5mm small slices to be fixed in formalin, embedded in wax, stained, sectioned thinly and mounted for viewing under the microscope. Were the cells regular in shape and arrangement and benign, or higgledy-piggledy, all sizes and shapes, going in all directions like a malignant tumour? When you carried out special stains on the sections were there the characteristic rod-like organisms of TB or the curly spirochaetes of syphilis?

I came first in our pathology exam and was awarded a special prize – any book of my choice. I chose Rupert Willis's *Principles of*

Pathology which had only recently been published. A brilliant and well researched book, it remained my standby in the years to come. I almost had it by heart. Most disease processes could affect the tissues around the mouth and jaws, so there was ample scope for diagnosis and research. I could specialise in Oral Pathology.

It happened while I was a student in the Conservation room – just a few twinges at first and then the pain got worse and worse. I had no choice but to make an appointment to see the new professor, though I would have preferred to go to almost anyone else. He'd already made quite clear what he thought about women dental students. I was disconcerted when he examined me in front of the other students in my year, rather than in private as I'd expected.

'Where's the pain, Miss Waterman?' he asked.

I pointed to my lower right second premolar.

'Patient complains of pain in lower right second premolar,' he dictated. 'On examination: small occlusal filling,'

He turned to his nurse.

'I'll take some X-rays. Get them developed straight away, will you.'

The nurse was back in minutes holding the wet x-rays clipped to a wire frame.

'Don't you know better than to drip all over my white coat? Where were you trained?'

She was near to tears. He'd bumped into her, not the other way around. I knew she'd been trained at Guy's Hospital – the premier dental school. She was highly regarded by everyone.

'Let's see,' he said. 'Come over to the X-ray box, you lot. Not you, Miss Waterman. You stay where you are.'

The students trailed behind him to the other side of the room.

'As I expected – the tooth is caries-free with a small well-fitting amalgam filling. No evidence of an apical lesion. Another hysterical young woman.'

He came back to the dental chair.

'There is no obvious cause for your apparent pain, Miss Waterman. No need to make another appointment. You can run along now. I'm sure you've plenty of reading to catch up on.'

I was seething. I wanted to say I was in no way hysterical, and I really did have toothache, but I couldn't afford to argue with him. He was our examiner in our end of year exams.

A few days later, the pain had almost gone. It seemed to be one of those sporadic toothaches that subside on their own.

My favourite patient was in the chair, and we were discussing the performance of *Aida* I'd seen the night before. Then the toothache hit again. The pain was unbelievable. It filled my whole head. It was so bad it made me feel sick and dizzy.

'Look. I'm terribly sorry,' I said, holding my jaw. 'I can't go on. I've got the most awful toothache.'

To do him justice, he did try not to laugh, but he couldn't help himself. He sniggered and then laughed until tears came.

'I'm sorry, truly sorry, my dear. I know I shouldn't laugh.'

The worst of the pain passed and I put a temporary filling in his tooth – between his smothered giggles.

As before, the toothache went away and I couldn't face another visit to my professor.

Joshua was the dental house surgeon on duty when my toothache recurred. When he removed the small innocent-looking filling in my tooth, he found an exposed and inflamed nerve.

'I'll take out the nerve and put in a root filling.'

He filled a syringe with a cartridge of local anaesthetic and injected my inferior dental nerve.

'Whoever put in the filling drilled too deep and hit the nerve. The cavity was a tiny occlusal one and there was no reason to drill so deep. Your dentist must have capped the exposure and it's taken some time to blow up. I'll do an immediate root filling.'

I knew who had messed up my tooth. My parents went to a well respected local woman dentist but I'd met a good-looking dental student at a party who offered to do my teeth. I remembered the fuss when that filling was done and that someone senior and several students had gathered round to watch some special procedure.

I hadn't really noticed Joshua very much before then. Maybe he hadn't noticed me much either. He was in the year ahead of me and the years tended to stick together. He was tall and good-looking, but much quieter than the other men in his year – two were ex-servicemen, noisy and full of themselves. I was intrigued.

Before the weekend I had another problem. None of my wisdom teeth – my third molars – had erupted. Occasionally the flap of gum over where the bottom ones were coming through got inflamed. By Saturday, the right one was very sore and I could hardly open my mouth.

All weekend I rinsed with hot salt water and by Monday it wasn't too bad. I went to see the dental sub-dean, who dealt with extractions and minor oral surgery.

'I'll get some x-rays taken, but I'm pretty sure they'll have to come out,' he said. 'They'll go on giving trouble and they'll never be much use.'

The x-rays showed that both of my lower wisdom teeth were coming through crooked and were impacted against the second molar in front. The upper wisdom teeth were there but way below the surface of the bone. They'd probably never erupt.

'I'd rather you let this inflammation settle down and then I'll extract them under local,' he said.

We were all scared of the rather dour Scotsman. He was a good surgeon and very knowledgeable, but he was scathing if you couldn't answer his questions on some aspect of dental surgery.

'Are you training to be a dental surgeon or a vet?' he would say. 'If you're going to be treating human patients you'll need to know a bit more about local anaesthetics and the distribution of the nerves supplying the teeth and jaws.'

While the discomfited student flushed bright red, the rest of us sniggered, hoping he wouldn't pick on us next.

His nurse made me an appointment for nine o'clock the following Monday. I hesitated before plucking up enough courage to knock on the door of the surgical suite. At least he didn't allow my fellow students in to watch.

'Sit yourself down,' he said. His nurse draped a large plastic apron over me. The injection he gave me worked almost at once.

'My tongue is numb,' I lisped.

'I'll just test it with a probe,' he said.

Within moments, with hardly any wriggling or tugging, he showed me my wisdom tooth.

I rinsed with difficulty. I couldn't feel that side of my mouth or tongue.

'This should heal well,' he said. 'Make an appointment for three weeks' time and we'll have the other one out.'

I had the other wisdom tooth extracted just as easily and by now he seemed much more human and less scary. I didn't care much for his parting:

'Now you be a good girlie and make sure you learn some dental surgery. Your lot seem to be particularly gormless.'

I don't know which was worse – being called 'girlie' or 'gormless.'

One surgical room was kept for extractions under local anaesthetic. I had been struggling to get out an upper right second molar for half an hour. My patient was still game but I was exhausted. The tooth just wouldn't move.

Joshua was again the house surgeon on duty.

He called me aside.

'I think you need some help, don't you? You've been at this long enough. Just put in a bit more local.'

I nodded, ashamed and relieved at the same time. Joshua picked up a heavier pair of forceps and loosened the resistant tooth.

'You've certainly got strong roots,' he said to the patient. 'Miss Waterman here has had a tough time with this tooth of yours. I can hardly move it. She can take over now.'

I could now feel movement and after a bit more manoeuvring the tooth yielded and came out.

'No wonder it was so hard to extract,' I said as my patient rinsed away the blood. 'Look it's got four roots, instead of three, and they're all twisted.'

I gave him a tissue to wipe the blood from around his lips.

'Take care you don't bite your lip now. It will be numb for some time yet.'

'Thank you, my dear,' he said. 'Maybe I should have warned you. The last dentist took well over an hour to take my tooth out, and he was a big chap, built like a boxer. I didn't want to put you off.'

I felt like saying 'Thanks for nothing' but just smiled and filled out the patient's dental record.

As Joshua was leaving, he said:

'Upper first molars like that can be very tough to get out, but next time call a house surgeon much earlier.'

I muttered 'Stuck up pig' under my breath and got the extraction room ready for my next patient.

Joshua came up to me that evening as I was leaving.

'They're showing *Les Enfants du Paradis* at the Academy in Oxford Street. Do you fancy coming? Or I might be able to get tickets for the opera.'

'I can't manage tonight,' I said, thinking of my greasy hair and how I'd meant to wash it the night before. 'Not the opera. The film sounds good.'

'How about Friday?'

'Thursday would be better,' I said.

'Fine. I'll meet you at the Academy at seven.'

I had mixed feelings about it. He was rather aloof and a bit given to sarcastic remarks when he supervised the junior students. We liked calling him over, though, when we ran into difficulty. He always seemed able to sort out our problems.

Thursday dragged by. I had put my new shirt-waister dress in my locker, together with my black patent leather court shoes, so that I could change as soon as I finished my last patient.

But calamity struck. My last patient had a difficult to reach cavity at the back of his mouth. I removed the decay bit by bit, taking care not to go too deep and damage the nerve. By the time I came to fill his tooth it was getting late and I was already wound-up about meeting Joshua. It was a huge cavity that went over the side of the tooth and I had to fit a stainless-steel band around it while I put in the amalgam. The filling broke as I removed the band.

The house surgeon in the conservation room came over.

'Clearing-up time, Abby,' he said. 'Come on. The store keeper wants to get home and we have to close up now.'

'I've just pulled out half the filling with the matrix band.' I was almost in tears. 'I'll just get some more mercury and amalgam from the store.'

'I'm afraid you won't. The storekeeper has already locked up. Just put in a temporary filling,'

My patient didn't seem to mind at all.

'You know I'm always pleased to come and see a nice young lady like you.'

I made him another appointment but I felt awful and not at all like going out with anyone, let alone with someone I hardly knew.

As we queued for tickets, I told Joshua about the broken filling.

'Things like that happen,' he said. 'If the cavity was large and near the nerve, the patient was probably better off with a temporary dressing. It would allow the pulp to form a bridge of reactionary dentine.'

But it wasn't a great evening. I was still too upset about the filling I had ruined. Joshua insisted on seeing me home. I was always ashamed of living in Petticoat Lane. The smell of the market refuse still hung around and the stink of the feral cats that lived off the refuse from the poultry and fish stalls was all pervasive.

I was glad to say goodbye at the entrance to our block of flats with a brief kiss, no more than a touch of lips and a muttered 'Thanks.'

Sam, who had persuaded me to study dentistry, asked if I'd like to be a paid assistant at a Summer School in Shropshire. He'd done it before and liked it and he'd already persuaded Joshua to come.

The week before we broke up for the August summer holiday, Sam told me he wouldn't be coming. I wasn't sure I wanted to go just with Joshua but I had nothing else planned, had no money saved and at least I would be paid.

The organisers had taken over a small boarding school and accepted about thirty boys and girls between the ages of ten and thirteen. The food was good and the activities were things I enjoyed – going on long rambles with the children, timing races, refereeing games of netball, and watching old Laurel and Hardy or Charlie Chaplin films in the evenings.

The weather was clear and sunny most of the time, though the evenings were chilly. One evening, when we weren't on duty, Joshua asked if I'd like to walk down to the village pub. He had a pint of bitter and I had some shandy. As we got back to our gate, he pulled me to him and kissed me hard. It was so unexpected that at first I didn't respond, and then I did. I broke away.

'I'm cold,' I said. 'Let's get back.'

The next night and all the remaining ten nights I went back to his room after the girls in the dormitory I supervised were fast asleep.

Back in London I wasn't sure whether we were an item or not. Sometimes Joshua seemed interested and sometimes not. There was still compulsory conscription for men at 18. Students could defer until after finals, but once they qualified, they had to join one of the Armed Services. Soon Joshua was called up for his National Service and posted to the Canal Zone in Egypt – then under British Martial Law.

My weekends were empty. I went to the cinema with a couple of the other students and the brother of someone I knew from my Youth Club days but none of it was serious.

I met an American art student who was lodging with a distant relative just around the corner in Old Castle Street. He badgered me to go away with him for a weekend. I got as far as asking Sam to cover for me if I told my parents I was staying with him. But then I didn't go through with it. I wasn't in love and it wasn't safe. I could get pregnant and ruin my life.

I was lonely. I missed Joshua. He teased me and kidded me along, but he cared for me. It was going to be a long two years before he finished his National Service.

The most comforting person was Aunt Jenny. She was married to my father's youngest brother, Nathan. Jenny was thirty by the time the local marriage maker introduced her to Nathan. My parents hadn't approved of their marriage. They thought she was an elderly spinster, after his money.

Like my mother, years before, she thought she was marrying a rich man, son of the Waterman printers. She knew my paternal grandparents had a large house with servants and silver plate and everything that goes with that life style, but, she didn't know that divided between the sons, little was left for each of them. When she discovered her mistake, it made no difference to her. She still wanted to marry my Uncle Nathan.

Jenny and Nathan never had children, though Jenny would have loved some. They finally went to a doctor for advice. My mother said that the doctor told them they had been using the wrong orifice, they were such *nudniks* (idiots). His advice didn't help, and my aunt never got pregnant.

Uncle Nathan helped out in local shops from time to time. When war broke out he became a full time Air Raid Warden and then stayed in work until he retired – first as a mortuary attendant at the London Hospital, a job he loved, and then as a porter at the Old Bailey.

I didn't see Aunt Jenny very often when I was little, but, once I was old enough to take a bus to her flat on my own, I went to see her at least once a month. I loved visiting her. She had a real bath with taps you could turn on yourself. The first thing I would do was to have a long luxurious soak.

I can't remember a time when I couldn't sew. My mother had a treadle-operated Singer sewing machine and she allowed me to use it by the time I was 11 or 12 but my Aunt Jenny taught me how to speed up and finish things off professionally. She showed me how to fell the hem of a dress, so that the stitches were invisible on the outside. She paid me a shilling for each hem. Sometimes I finished five or six in one visit. It wasn't until years later that she told me that she only got half a crown – two shillings and sixpence – for making up the whole dress. I would never have taken money from her as a present, but it was different if I earned it.

She was everything my mother wasn't – warm, loving and generous – a little dumpling of a woman with twinkling blue eyes and light brown frizzy hair. By the time I was thirteen, I was already taller than her.

'Well,' Aunt Jenny said. 'I was on holiday in France with my mother when the First World War broke out. We were trapped in Paris and the family that took us in was very poor. They shared their food with us but there was never enough to eat, so I never grew properly.'

Uncle Nathan died of a heart attack soon after he turned sixty, and Aunt Jenny bought a little terraced house in Southend-on-Sea. Every few months I would take the train and visit her.

One Sunday she handed me a cut-glass biscuit barrel. It was one of my happiest memories of her house – the biscuit barrel standing on a white lace doyley, full of homemade shortbread biscuits.

'I want to give you this,' she said.

'Oh, no,' I said. 'Keep it. You still use it.'

'Take it, please. I'd like to give you this with a warm hand.'

She wrapped the jar in newspaper and carefully lowered it into a carrier bag for me.

The following year, she had her cataracts removed. It was before you got replacement internal lenses, so afterwards she had to wear thick pebble-glass spectacles. They made her look like an inquisitive owl.

Then the doctors discovered that Aunt Jenny had diabetes. She tried going on a diet, but for dear, plump Aunt Jenny it was hopeless. They tried prescribing tablets and then insulin, but within a year, things took a turn for the worse. The circulation in her left foot started to fail. I went to see her in hospital.

'Aren't you pleased I gave you my biscuit barrel? At least you'll have something to remember me by.'

I tried not to cry. Sweet Aunt Jenny – so kind and loving.

'They want to cut off my foot,' she said. 'What do you think? What shall I do? I don't think I could bear it.'

I squeezed Aunt Jenny's hands. It was strange to see them still, unmoving. She had always been so busy – cooking, sewing, cleaning.

She was nearly blind from her diabetes and I couldn't imagine how she would cope with only one foot, alone in her little two up and two down cottage. I had mixed feelings when she died soon after, before she could have her foot amputated, though I knew how much I would miss her.

She left me £500 in her will at a time when that was a lot of money, but I valued the cut glass biscuit barrel far more.

CHAPTER 13

Dentistry Finals

I took dentistry finals in 1953. Even though when I'd taken them I was always sure I'd failed, I enjoyed preparing for exams.

First, you buy copies of exam papers from previous years and swap with other students for those you don't have. Then you draw out a neat revision timetable and embellish it. You're careful to leave a couple of weeks at the end for last minute cramming.

The first week it goes fine. You get everything done and you are even a bit ahead. The second week you go to the theatre or see a film and then you're behind. The next week it's hard to settle down because you're behind and the timetable doesn't work. You spend hours redrawing the timetable. You fall further and further behind and finally instead of the textbooks you meant to read, you rush out to buy *Aids to Medicine, An Idiot's Guide to Surgery*, and *20 Things You Must Know About Common Drugs*. Now there isn't even time to read these crammers. You go over old questions trying to predict what will come up. You work long past midnight and get up at five in the morning. At last you begin to understand the subject and you wish you had started revising much earlier.

Our aim was to get a university degree, Bachelor in Dental Surgery (BDS), but most students took the exam for a Licentiate in Dental Surgery of the Royal College of Surgeons (LDS RCS) as well, as an insurance policy. The LDS examinations were taken a few months earlier than BDS, so successful students had a qualification before taking their degree. They could start working as a Dental House Surgeon and have that extra confidence when they came to sit BDS.

I arranged to revise with Keith, another student in my year. It was a mistake. He completely undermined my confidence, always wanting to discuss esoteric topics that I knew nothing about, while stopping me when I started to ask him anything he was shaky on. It should have meant I looked up subjects I didn't know much about but all that happened was that I sat the exam convinced I didn't know enough to pass.

The written paper was straightforward, though I felt I hadn't done as well as I should. The practical dental exam was next. Patients requiring fillings were paid a small fee to act as guinea pigs for us.

I was used to doing well in exams and meeting examiners in vivas who had seen my written papers and were already well disposed towards me. The LDS examiner barely acknowledged me, pointed out a woman patient and told me not to mess about but to get on with it. I had learned to be good at the technique of dentistry but I wasn't a natural. For me it required a lot of thought and care and I was badly shaken by the examiner's attitude before I had even started.

The cavity I had to prepare extended over the side of the tooth but it should have been quite easy. To my dismay, I saw that I had slightly drilled the side of the neighbouring sound tooth. It would have made no difference to the patient – later in practice I would find that it was sometimes a necessary procedure when the teeth are closely packed together. In a final exam, it was a disaster and meant certain failure. The examiner came over just as I finished removing all the caries and noticed at once what I had done. I managed to complete putting in an amalgam filling but I knew it was hopeless.

In the afternoon, I had an oral examination on Orthodontics and I did badly. I was still shaken from the morning's fiasco.

The College of Surgeons produced the results within days. We had to go in person to the College in Lincoln's Inn Fields to get our results.

An official stood at the bottom of the grand red-carpeted staircase and called out the candidates' names one by one. We had to walk to the foot of the staircase and be told either 'I am happy to tell you, you have passed,' and proceed up the staircase for drinks with the examiners; or, 'I am sorry to tell you that you have failed,' when you would have to walk away in front of everyone.

Until I heard the actual words, I had hoped against hope that somehow, I had passed, but I hadn't. I had failed. Not only had I failed, but all the other students of my year from St Margaret's had passed, even the students who were so cack-handed that you wouldn't let them loose on your cat.

I went home devastated. My father patted me awkwardly on my shoulder.

'Well, you'd better work harder next time,' my mother muttered.

I went for a long walk in the City of London. It was after banking hours and deserted. I met no-one. I had never failed an exam before. My degree finals were in only six weeks' time. I couldn't face any more exams. I just couldn't.

The sub-dean of the Dental School called me into his office next day. To my surprise he put his arm around my shoulders and told me not to worry.

Word had reached him about my horrible examiner.

'You had bad luck getting Professor Brown. I'm sure you'll do well in your degree finals.'

I was a little comforted but I couldn't bear to stay around while everyone else was celebrating.

I had already taken and passed Part I of my BDS degree with honours in Medicine, Surgery and Pathology. Part II was in Dental Surgery and Orthodontics. I had to sit the exams only six weeks after I failed LDS.

It was the summer of 1953, the Coronation Year. London was full of people celebrating. Masses of people including my parents had bought television sets to watch the Coronation. I sat alone in my bedroom revising.

The written exam in Dental Surgery was a breeze. All the questions I thought would come up did. Even the practical went well. The examiner was a charming elderly professor and my patient was a cockney woman who called me 'Ducks'. This time nothing went wrong. My viva was more like a polite discussion of interesting cases than a rigorous exam.

Coming out of the viva, I tried to avoid the others but someone started discussing some of the topics his examiner had raised and I realised I'd forgotten one aspect. I'd thought my viva had gone well, but now I thought maybe the examiners were so relaxed in my viva because I had failed, and they felt it wasn't worth asking me lots of questions.

Getting the results was a different kind of torture from getting our LDS results. Students at London University had to go to the railings outside Senate House to look for their name on one of the many lists pinned up there. I am short, just over five feet, so I had difficulty seeing the list for the degree in Dental Surgery. When I finally found the pass list I couldn't see my name. I was frantic.

Then the others were banging me on the back and saying, 'Well done' and 'We knew you had it in you.' I hadn't seen my name because it was on the separate list of students who had got Honours. I not only had three honours in Part I but I had also got honours in Dental Surgery. Mine was the best result in the University.

Once I got my degree I decided to re-sit the LDS exam. This time everything went smoothly and I climbed the red-carpeted staircase at the College of Surgeons to the applause of my friends.

Now I can study Medicine, I thought.

With four distinctions in my dentistry finals, I thought getting accepted to study medicine would be a formality. I was wrong.

I had to go through the full selection procedure. If this wasn't bad enough, Paul said he'd been *invited* to apply to medical school. He didn't even want to study medicine. Maybe they had invited him because he was a man or perhaps he was just winding me up.

Before my interview with the entrance committee, I had to take an intelligence test. In retrospect, maybe it was part of a study correlating IQ and later performance, but at the time I was hurt and angry. Wasn't getting the best results in the university evidence enough of my IQ?

Following my interview, a letter arrived informing me I could start that October. I was given credit for my dissection of the head and neck and thorax, and I would attend anatomy, physiology and biochemistry lectures with the second-year medical students. I would dissect the abdomen and lower limb with them.

I'd had a London County Council scholarship at dental school, so I couldn't get another grant from them. I applied for the Hilda Martindale Fellowship, a bursary given only to women students, and had a pleasant interview with the committee at Bedford College in Regent's Park. They offered me a scholarship sufficient to pay my fees and contribute towards my living expenses, but I would need a part-time job to make up the balance for clothes and books.

After finals, I was appointed as a dental house surgeon at St Margaret's. Unlike doctors, dentists were not required to take a house job before going out into NHS or private practice. However, those of us who intended to follow an academic career, always took one or more six-month posts as a dental houseman.

It was a quiet, unremarkable six months. Sister in the surgical extraction room seemed less of an ogre and it was fun taking over from six-foot male students who were struggling to extract a tooth. The secret was, of course, that they had loosened the tooth, their hand got tired and there was little left for me to do.

It was much easier supervising restorative dental surgery – filling teeth – than carrying it out. I was surprised at how good some of the junior students were, even in their first clinical year. Unlike me, they clearly had a natural aptitude.

I still had a couple of months before starting my medical training so I applied for a six-week locum appointment with Dr Alton, an NHS dentist.

Wearing my navy interview suit and smart Cuban-heeled shoes, it was with some trepidation that I took the tube to Ladbroke Grove. There was a world of difference between working in a commercial dental practice, and being a dental student in a teaching hospital. As students, we had as much time as we needed to complete our fillings and an experienced demonstrator was always on hand if we got into difficulty. In general practice, I'd be working to a tight appointment schedule, and have to make all my own decisions.

There was still a lot of prejudice against women in the professions. Maybe Dr Alton would rather wait and find a male assistant.

A smiling grey-haired woman met me at the door.

'Come in. Come in,' she said. 'You must be Miss Waterman. My husband is expecting you. I'm Celia Alton.'

She ushered me into their front room, a room stuffed with armchairs and couches, a rich Indian carpet on the floor, lots of knick-knacks on the occasional tables and rows of framed photographs on the walls.

Dr Alton, a short Indian man in a long white coat, came in, hands outstretched.

'So pleased to meet you, my dear. My doctor tells me I should take it easy for a bit, so you are here to help me.'

He took me into his spotlessly clean but rather old-fashioned dental surgery. Proudly he opened all the drawers and cupboards. It was well-equipped, despite its appearance.

'I qualified in medicine in the UK and was in the British Medical Corps in the First World War,' he told me, 'but I had severe asthma. After several major attacks, my colleagues advised me to re-train as a dentist when I was demobilised. They thought it would be less stressful, but of course they were quite wrong. We too have lots of crises, even if they're not usually life-threatening. Now I'm told it's time for me to have a little break.'

We went back into the living room. Mrs Alton brought in tea and home-made Indian sweets.

'I have a terrible sweet tooth,' he said 'but luckily I'm not prone to caries. When would you like to start? It's Monday today. How about Wednesday? You must be about my size. Celia, my dear, could you bring a white coat for Miss Waterman to try on? May I call you Abigail?'

'Everyone calls me Abby. Abigail sounds a bit stuffy.'

The white coat Mrs Alton brought fitted perfectly. I started work as an NHS dentist two days later.

The practice was situated on the ground floor of his large semi-detached Victorian house. There was a second parlour where the patients waited.

Dr and Mrs Alton were unbelievably kind and welcoming. He and his wife had no children and treated me as if I were their daughter. They insisted on providing me with lunch – a different kind of curry each day.

At St Margaret's, I'd been taught to give a local anaesthetic for all but the smallest filling. His patients were amazed.

'Yes please,' they'd say when I asked if they'd like an injection. 'Dr Alton never gives me an injection.'

I looked at some of the huge fillings he'd excavated without a local anaesthetic and thought he must have managed it either with love or his hypnotic personality. I would never have dared.

In those days, dentists were allowed to administer general anaesthetics to their patients and carry out their extractions while working on their own. They could also give anaesthetics for other dentists. On the few occasions when there was too much inflammation for a local anaesthetic to work, Dr Alton anaesthetised the patient for me. He reduced the supply of oxygen it to the point where the patients went blue. I almost expected them to start jactitating but they were all fine and full of praise for him when they woke up.

It was fantastic to be given £20 for my first week's wages, after earning £6 a week as a dental house surgeon.

I was sorry to leave the practice at the end of my six weeks. But now I could realise my dream. I would be Dr Abby Waterman, a pathologist specialising in Oral Pathology.

CHAPTER 14

At Medical School

I had dissected the thorax and the head and neck as a dental student, but I hadn't yet dissected an arm. A week before term began, George, the dissecting-room technician, who had been at St Margaret's forever, brought out a right arm and directed me to a small side room. I propped up my manual in front of me, unrolled my instruments, and began.

As I made my first incision, I was thinking about the ghost story my sister, Hannah, used to frighten me with.

A man lost his arm in a riding accident and had a golden arm made to replace it. He made his family swear on the family bible that when he died they would bury the arm with him. In the dead of night, not even a week after the he was buried, his son-in-law dug up his coffin and stole the golden arm. Two nights later he awoke choking, icy fingers around his neck. A disembodied voice cried 'Give me back my golden arm. Give me back my golden arm.' He suffered a heart attack and died.

187

I looked at the arm I was dissecting and shuddered. Then I thought: how stupid – a 22year old dental surgeon studying to be a doctor, frightened by a ghost story?

Then, as I freed the blood vessels in the crook of the elbow, I nicked an artery. Thin red blood came pulsing out. The arm was alive. Too shocked to go on, it took several moments before I realised it was only embalming fluid and not blood at all.

It was lonely and scary in that cold little side room, so I was pleased when a junior surgeon, about to take his higher surgical examinations, came to do some anatomy revision. We got along fine, once he accepted that I didn't want to go out with him for a drink, for dinner, nor for a bit of sex.

We were talking about our careers. He hooted when he heard I was a dentist.

'How could you do a filthy job like that, messing about in people's dirty, smelly mouths?'

'A damn sight better than working on the other end,' I retorted.

'Not at all,' he said, offended. 'Rectal surgery is fascinating.'

It turned out that he was training to be a gastrointestinal surgeon at St Marks Hospital for the Fistula and Other Diseases of the Rectum.

I needed a part-time job during term-time to make up my grant allowance, so I applied to the dental department of the London County Council. After they'd received references from the Dean and Sub-dean of St Margaret's, they offered me two evenings a week at a school clinic near Old Street.

A pretty fair-haired nurse about my own age met me at the door.

'I'm Ellen, your nurse, Miss Waterman. I'll show you around. We don't have any little ones in the evening, and the older children are really quite well behaved.'

'Do call me Abby,' I said. 'Nice to see a friendly face. All the dental nurses I remember from school were old dragons, and we heard terrible things about school dentists. They sounded like real sadists. I didn't have much caries as a child. For the few fillings I needed I went to Guy's Hospital. I thought there would be lots of handsome dental students there, but with my luck, I never met one.'

She laughed and said, 'Not me neither.'

Ellen was right. The children, eleven and twelve-year olds and young teenagers behaved very well. Our new patients were surprised to be greeted by two smiling young women, instead of a couple of old biddies. Ellen and I got on well. After a couple of months, I asked her if she'd come and work for me, if I ever had my own dental practice. She gave me a hug.

'Like a shot,' she said. 'When do we start?'

In our first two years, medical students at St Margaret's had long holidays at Christmas, Easter and in the summer. My first Christmas back at medical school I asked the LCC to find me a full-time locum appointment for four weeks. My textbooks had turned out to be more expensive than I'd expected and my grant wasn't going as far as I'd hoped.

I was sent to a dental clinic in West Ham. The children were a delight to treat but they were incredibly poor, much poorer that I had ever been. When I asked one boy to take off his school blazer, worried that something might drip onto it, he refused at first. When I persuaded him to take it off, he was only wearing a thin sleeveless vest underneath. It was a bitterly cold winter. He must have been freezing.

'I only have the one school shirt,' he said. 'So I have to look after it. My mum washes it after school on Fridays, so it's ready to wear on Monday. I'm not allowed to wear it in the school holidays.'

I passed a clothes shop on the way to the Underground. The clothes in the windows were cheap and poorly made. They were bad bargains and would soon fall apart at the seams. Another trap for the poor.

Although my family was very poor and lived in a cold-water tenement in the East End of London, my mother was a dress-maker and she'd always made me new clothes to wear for the Jewish New Year. I was never in the position of not having a change of clothes.

I had long since learned how to use my medical books and not rely on remembering what the lecturers taught, so my 2nd MBBS results that July were good. The senior tutor who had refused to allow me to swap from dentistry to medicine at the end of my first year stopped me on the stairs.

'You did well in your 2nd MBBS exams, Abby. If you had been able to take your exams with the medical students in the spring, we could have offered you a chance to take a research BSc degree. Looks as if we should have offered you a place to do medicine first time around.'

I wanted to say 'Yes, and was it just because I offended your religious beliefs that you turned me down?' but I just nodded and pushed past him. I was never very good at quick retorts. I am more of an *'Esprit d'escalier'* person – I don't know what I should have replied until I am on my way out.

I was now with medical students who had either done an inter-calated BSc at St Margaret's or who had been at Oxford or Cambridge. There they had spent three years instead of eighteen months on their pre-clinical studies and they started their clinical studies already with an undergraduate degree. For the first time, I met privileged young people, young men and women who had been to major Public Schools – Harrow, Eton, Rugby, Roedean or Cheltenham Ladies College. They talked about choosing where to do their clinical studies, unlike those of us from disadvantaged backgrounds who were glad to be accepted by any medical school.

They were talking about the poor.

'Father says it's no use providing the poor with baths. They only use them to keep coal in.'

How we'd have loved to have our own bath. One of my friends lived in a tenement that had a bath. It was in their tiny kitchen and they kept it covered with a flat board – their only surface for preparing food. Like ours, their kitchen only had a cold tap. They would have had to remove the board, boil kettles, and send everyone out of the kitchen, which doubled as a living room, while they had a bath. It was easier to go to the Public Baths in Goulston Street.

For the first time, I realised just how poor my family was. When you're poor but all your friends are as poor or poorer, it seems normal, but these students were all so much wealthier than me.

My first patient on the wards would have known how I was feeling.

We stood outside the Bristow female medical ward, stethoscopes hanging nonchalantly out of our pockets, about to start our clinical attachments to the medical, surgical and obstetric firms.

Through the leaded windows in the double doors, we could see Sister's desk, and the nurses in their blue and white striped dresses busying themselves about the patients. We hesitated, uncertain whether to go in or wait for our senior registrar.

Dr Evans, a tall red-haired man, strode up.

'Well, what are you all standing about for, like a load of twits? You've been taught how to take a medical history and carry out a full physical examination. Get inside and collect your notes. We'll meet in Sister's office in three quarters of an hour.'

He handed each of us a buff-coloured folder. My patient was Mrs Mary Roberts.

Sister looked up.

'One of my nurses will take you to your patients. I don't want you students making a nuisance of yourselves. No coming in before eight in the morning, lunchtimes or during patients' visiting hours.'

A nurse led me to a side room and deposited me by the bedside of the most enormous woman I had ever seen.

'Our Mary's quite a character. You may need some help when you come to examine her,' she told me.

'Good morning, Mrs Roberts,' I said. 'I'm your new student, Abby Waterman.'

'Don't be nervous, girl. I won't bite you,' Mrs Roberts wheezed. 'Call me Mary. No-one calls me Mrs Roberts here.'

I pulled up a chair, sat down by her bed, and looked through the thick sheaf of notes. She'd been in and out of hospital many times.

The first two fingers of Mary's podgy right hand were stained brown.

'You may well look, dearie. They say it's because of the ciggies that I'm like this.'

She coughed wetly, and spat into the sputum cup by her bed.

'I've given them up loads of times, but they settle my nerves, they do.'

I wrote out a summary of Mary's long medical history, and drew the curtains ready to examine her. The male students had to get a nurse to chaperone them if their patient was in a side room. Being a woman, that didn't apply to me.

With a lot of struggling on my part, and heavy breathing on hers, I managed to wrestle her nightdress off. I stared with horror at her enormous breasts. The apex of the heart is under the left breast, but each breast looked as if it weighed several pounds. How on earth would I get a stethoscope underneath? When we were shown how to listen to the heart, we'd had a slim, elderly man to practise on.

Mary smiled at me.

'They usually get a nurse to help, dear.'

I hurried out, but all the nurses looked busy. Finally, I saw a nurse with a red belt, a staff nurse.

'Of course,' she said. 'Just give me five minutes to finish up, and I'll send someone over.'

I told Mary to cover herself, and meanwhile looked at her swollen hands and feet. When I pressed the flesh of her ankles, my fingers left a dent which didn't fill again for some time. She was having trouble catching her breath and her neck veins were engorged.

'Superficial examination suggests the diagnosis of right-sided heart failure,' I wrote.

A junior nurse bustled in, her starched apron crackling against her dress.

'I've been sent over to give you a hand.'

She tried not to grin as she lifted a huge left breast with both hands, while I struggled to get the bell of my stethoscope underneath. The skin was red and sore from being constantly warm and damp. There was a strong smell of caked talcum powder.

By the time I'd completed my examination of Mary's cardiovascular, respiratory and nervous systems, I was exhausted. The notes said she weighed seventeen stone, but it felt as if she weighed a ton.

'I don't really get on with the stuff they're giving me,' she said. 'The heart pills make me feel sick, and I have to have a wee every few minutes because of the water tablets. But you should have seen me when I came in. More like a barrage balloon, I was.'

A deep rumbling laugh turned into a coughing fit. When she'd got her breath back, she said:

'What wouldn't I give for a tub of jellied eels? The hospital food is all mush.'

Tubby Isaacs Jellied Eel stall stood at the corner of Goulston Street and Aldgate. The red-faced, cheerful stallholder in his signature straw boater, white coat and black bow tie, used to call after me on my way home from St Margaret's.

'Lovely jellied eels, miss. Cockles and mussels, Alive Oh,' he'd shout, knowing I would make a face. Eels and shellfish are forbidden to Jews.

I felt sick at the thought of those grey slices of eel on his stall. I couldn't imagine anyone wanting to eat the disgusting things, even if they weren't Jewish.

Over the next few weeks, I watched Mary's vast bulk shrink, as the digoxin and diuretic pills began to work. One day, as I was checking her over, she started to cry.

'They're going to put me in the geriatric ward at St Mildred's,' she sobbed. 'They say I can't manage on my own. I live on the fourth floor, and there's no lift. I can't get my breath, even to go as far as the lavatory.'

'Couldn't you stay with one of your children?'

'I haven't heard from any of my kids in years. None of them's ever been to see me in hospital. Two of the boys are inside, and I wouldn't want to live with any of the others, even if they offered, which they wouldn't.'

On my way home from Aldgate East station that night, I went up to Tubby Isaacs stall. I cringed at the sight of those mounds of cockles and whelks and other seafood I didn't want to identify. To one side there was an enamel bowl full of clear jelly containing slices of jellied eel.

'I'll have a tub of jellied eels,' I said, breathing through my mouth.

I hid the tub behind my books, away from my mother's prying eyes, and thought about Mary in a geriatric ward. If she was lucky, it would be clean and cheerful, like the one at St Margaret's, but that was only for short-term admissions. I'd visited a miserable urine-smelling long-stay ward, when my great aunt had her stroke. It was ghastly.

When I arrived next morning, Mary was dressed and waiting for the ambulance to take her to St Mildred's. Her eyes were red and swollen. She clutched my hand.

'I never thought it would come to this.'

'This should cheer you up a bit,' I said, and handed her the tub from *Tubby Isaacs. Jellied Eels, Established 1919.*

A smile lit up her face.

'You're a lovely girl, you know,' she said. 'You'll go far, mark my words. You've got a heart of gold, you have, and there's not many of them around.'

'Here's your next case, Abby,' Dr Evans said. 'Mrs Ponsonby-Smith in bed 14.'

Wearing a pink turban and a matching lacy bed jacket, my new patient was deep in a luridly coloured *Mills and Boone*. I expected to meet a sickly-sweet woman with an upper crust voice to match her double-barrelled name, but when she put down her book and held out her hand, she had a North Country accent.

'You must be Dr Waterman. Sister said you would be coming.'

Her hand was limp, although she was clearly trying to grip mine.

'I'm a medical student, not a doctor,' I said. 'Please call me Abby.'

'Why don't you call me Katharine?'

I sat down by her bedside and checked her details – name, age and past medical history. We were taught it wasn't safe to take the patient's medical history for granted. You always needed to check it, particularly with patients who'd had lots of admissions. If an error crept in, subsequent students or doctors in a hurry were tempted to copy out the previous summary, errors and all.

'Tell me how it all started,' I said.

'My husband said I was going crazy. Words I didn't mean came out of my mouth. I couldn't stop them. Sometimes all that came out was 'Ah. Ah. Ah', over and over again. I told him I wasn't crazy and that there must be something wrong in my brain, but he insisted that I see a psychiatrist and he had me admitted to a psychiatric clinic off Harley Street, where the young doctor ordered a whole lot of tests. That's when they found I had cancer in my brain. They sent me straight to St Margaret's.'

She pulled off her turban. She was bald, with a large scar on the left side of her head.

'I'm not very pretty am I?' she said, dabbing at her eyes with a pink embroidered handkerchief.

I examined her heart, lungs and abdomen and went on to do a full neurological examination. As I did so, I got to appreciate that she wasn't sickly-sweet at all. The fripperies were her way of fighting back.

The weakness in her right hand was also present in her right leg. When I examined her eyes with an ophthalmoscope, I could see swelling of her optic discs. It was a bad sign. It meant that there was swelling of the underlying brain.

'They thought they'd got it all out,' she said, 'but six months ago I got these dreadful headaches and started to drop things. They're giving me radiotherapy, but I don't think it's doing much good.'

Katharine was in tears.

'My husband hardly ever comes to see me. It's that secretary of his, I'm sure.'

I had no experience of how to deal with patients with personal problems or life-threatening disease – we didn't have any teaching in those aspects of patient care. As a dentist, I'd seen plenty of patients in pain but this was different. It was incurable. I tried hard to think of something comforting to say, but I couldn't. I concentrated on examining her cranial nerves to stop my eyes filling too.

There was little change in her condition from day to day, but I visited her each morning to chat.

By now Joshua had been demobbed from the army. He was back living with his parents and working as an assistant in a dental practice at the Angel, Islington. I was still living at home, though I had been thinking of moving into St Margaret's Hall of Residence for a bit more freedom. I could just about afford it.

We met up every weekend. My parents would pointedly find some excuse to go out on Sunday afternoons so we could be alone. Since Joshua was a qualified dentist, who was also Jewish, they had high hopes that I would 'settle down.'

I still wasn't sure. He was very caring and polite – always opening doors for me and insisting on walking on the outside of the pavement – and he had a keen sense of right and wrong, much more so than me. I don't think he was sure either.

'My boyfriend and I are going to the May Ball next month,' I told Katharine. 'I bought a gorgeous dark green ball gown from Selfridges. I'm going to nip out at lunchtime to look for a shawl.'

'But you must borrow my fur cape, my dear. It's just the thing. I'll ask Sister to phone my husband.'

Two days later she took a large cardboard box from her bedside locker.

'Here,' she said. 'Open it.'

It was a soft honey-coloured cape made of lots of little furs. It was gorgeous.

'It's beautiful,' I said. 'But the ball isn't for another ten days.'

'Take it. You'll want to try it on.'

Joshua was furious.

'That's mink,' he said. 'Do you know how much it must have cost? You can't possibly wear it. Suppose it gets stolen?'

'I can and I will,' I said. 'She wants me to wear it, and I've promised I'll get the photographer at the ball to take a picture of me in it. Lots of women wear fur wraps.'

It was our first serious quarrel, but I felt it was something I had to do for my patient.

The cape looked wonderful against the dark green silk of my dress. A professional photographer had been hired for the ball, so when I brought the cape back after the weekend, I took a copy of our photograph and a bunch of tiny pink garnet roses from the hospital flower shop. They matched her turban and jacket perfectly.

In these few days, she'd got much weaker. I helped her to sit up.

'You're a sweetie, you know,' she said as she sniffed the roses. 'Haven't I been lucky to have you as my very last medical student? You can't imagine how much seeing a pretty young face every morning has meant to me.'

I managed to get a smile from her.

'Young girl, indeed,' I said. 'I'm 23, I'll have you know. Practically middle aged.'

I had completed my six months on medical wards and now I rotated to the surgical wards. On our surgical rotation, we assisted at operations as well as examining patients. We retracted the edges of incisions to give the surgeon good access, used a sucker to keep the field clear of blood and snipped the ends of suture threads.

My first consultant was Mr Simpson. I had been surprised to find that surgeons in the UK, who are of course medically qualified, aren't called 'Dr', but jealously guard their title of 'Mr, Miss or Mrs', dating back from their barber/surgeon lineage and distinguishing them from the physicians they look down on. As a dental surgeon, I was called Miss Waterman, although our American counterparts adopted the title 'Dr'.

Mr Simpson's stitching was immaculate – even my very pernickety dressmaker mother would have approved. If he removed part of a stomach, and didn't like the look of the sewn-up edges, he would undo the stitches and sew it up again. It was exhausting, holding back the edges of his incisions with a heavy steel retractor, while he re-did his stitchery.

One day he had a large bone cyst to remove from the upper jaw of a middleaged man. Cysts of the jaw were usually dealt with by oral surgeons but, before the specialisation of today, general surgeons tackled virtually any case referred to them.

I was scrubbed-up, gowned and masked, ready to assist. There was a solitary upper molar that needed to be removed.

'Abigail, this looks like your cup of tea. Sister, please bring the tray of forceps for Miss Waterman?'

I extracted the tooth to muffled applause from my fellow students. They left the theatre without waiting for Mr Simpson to complete the operation.

'Well my dear, we know who was the star today.'

Mr Simpson's ward rounds were often traumatic, for patients as well as for students. He would sweep in followed by his entourage of registrars, pre-registration housemen and medical students. When we presented our cases, he would try to trip us up on some detail of the patient's medical history or on our examination of them, some minor thing we had overlooked.

My patient was a bus conductress with a gastric ulcer. As I read out her details, I noticed that her pillow was crawling with lice. Mr Simpson noticed too.

'What can you expect from that class of person?' he said. 'She's infested with lice. This sort of women never takes a bath or washes regularly.'

I felt for her. I knew how hard it could be to keep clean in poor circumstances and remembered only too well how humiliating it was to discover that I had lice when I was a schoolgirl.

CHAPTER 15

Villefranche-sur-Mer

That summer, Josh and I decided to go on holiday to Villefranche-sur-Mer, in the South of France. It was then a small village with a tiny railway station at the top of a steep hill and just a few shops, restaurants, hotels and *pensions*. Joshua knew it from one of his hitchhiking holidays when he'd stayed in a nearby camping site. I told my mother a group of us were going.

Villefranche was skinny-dipping by moonlight in the summer-warmed sea, our bodies phosphorescent in the moonlight, and snogging on the beach to the sound of '*J'attendrai*' coming from the restaurant on the harbour wall.

Sometimes we ate at one of the cheaper restaurants, but mostly we cooked dinner on the beach. We'd brought the little meths cooker that Josh still had from his camping days. We cooked steak and sun-ripened tomatoes on the little stove, drinking the local *vin du table* in his tin camping mugs and mopping up the juices with chunks of a crusty baguette.

Buying the steak had been a near disaster. When we walked down the steep road to the harbour, we passed a butcher shop, its window full of delicious-looking meat. I asked the price of two of the bright red steaks in the window. The butcher picked up on my English accent.

'*Pardonnez-moi, Madame.* You do not require this shop. *Celui-ci. C'est la viande de cheval.*'

I'd thought the horse's head hanging outside was purely decorative, never having seen a horse-meat shop. The regular butcher shop was in the next street. We bought two large steaks, checking to be sure it was *viande de bœuf* not *viande de cheval.*

After the steak, we were too full to finish the Charentais melon we'd bought in the outdoor market, but once back at the *pension* we ate it, tipping the rinds into the waste paper basket under the washbasin in my room.

The bright morning sun woke me early. I started to swing my feet onto the floor when I saw a column of ants marching under the door towards the rinds in the waste-paper bin. I rushed across the corridor to wake Joshua.

'Joshua, wake up. Do they have driver ants in the south of France?'

'Of course not, silly.'

Half asleep, he filled my washbasin with water, dropped in the rinds and went back to bed. Back in my room, I watched the ants make a bridge across the water, climbing over each other's backs to reach the melon. I fished out the rinds with my fingertips and wrapped them in my *Paris Match* magazine. Pulling on my shirt and shorts. I ran round to the back of the hotel, and stuffed the package into one of the overfull rubbish bins. By the time I got back, the remaining ants had given up in disgust.

Next day we took the train to Nice, and the ferry to the *Ile St Marguerite*. It was ten years since the war ended, but the claustrophobic dungeons in the ancient prison, where *The Man in the Iron Mask* had been incarcerated, were an unpleasant reminder of what could so easily have happened to us, had Hitler invaded Britain.

The island was almost deserted. We swam in a small secluded cove, the water clear and deep green, and we ate the *pan-bagnats* we'd bought on the sea front in Nice – large round rolls stuffed with lettuce, tomato, peppers, onions, hard-boiled egg, olives and anchovies, smothered with a delicious *vinaigrette* dressing.

We had dinner at a fish restaurant in Nice. I ordered *sole meuniere* while Josh had white fish with *aioli* sauce, thinking the sauce was a white *béchamel* sauce, flavoured with garlic. In fact, it was cloves of raw garlic pounded with butter. In those days, garlic was hardly seen in the UK and we weren't used to it. There'd been none or hardly any in my food so I had to keep turning my head aside, to avoid the overwhelming smell of garlic wafting over me every time Joshua opened his mouth to speak.

The rest of the week flashed past in sun-drenched days. On Monday, we caught the overnight train to Calais and boarded the ferry home. As we stood at the bow, watching the ship's wake, my neighbour tapped me on the shoulder.

'Hullo, Abby love. Fancy meeting you here.'

My mother knew I was going on holiday with Josh. What she didn't know, was that the group I had told her about, was a group of two – just Josh and me.

I quickly worked out a plan. If Mrs Greenberg mentioned to my mother that she'd met us on the boat, I would say that I'd had to be back early, as I was now on the wards, and that the others didn't have to be back until the following week.

I worried for nothing. She didn't tell my mother she'd met me.

Joshua was still pale and seasick when he asked me to marry him on the ferry back from Calais. Cooking, cleaning and keeping house for someone else wasn't on my agenda and I said I'd think about it. Back in London, I said I'd rather just move in with him. Nothing about marriage attracted me, but Joshua was having none of it so I said 'Yes'. I did love him, and I didn't want to lose him. My mother was delighted. He was Jewish, even if he didn't come from an Orthodox family.

We wanted to get married when there was a chance of fine weather. As my brother-in-law was a big noise in his local synagogue, we arranged to get married there on April 29th, 1956. I would leave from my sister's home for the ceremony.

My mother no longer did any dressmaking, but Phyllis said she knew a good dressmaker. I bought a length of a silvery, lavender brocade at John Lewis for my wedding dress and a simple white bridal veil. I decided on a V-necked long-sleeved dress with a fitted bodice and just the hint of a train.

We hadn't thought about an engagement. There seemed no point. We would be getting married in just a few months, but my mother insisted that we got engaged.

'Do you want everyone to think you had to get married?'

Josh had bought me an exquisite antique silver ring with a large amethyst stone for my birthday in October. I thought that would do fine as an engagement ring. My mother was shocked.

'Never heard of such a thing. Everyone has a diamond engagement ring,' she said.

Neither of us liked the idea, but we went to Samuel's in Oxford Street, and bought a ring with a single diamond.

'Bit small, isn't it?' my mother said, when I showed it to her. And she didn't approve of my keeping my maiden name at St Margaret's.

'Never heard of such a thing,' she said again.

We had no savings to put down as a deposit on a mortgage. I was still living on my Hilda Martindale Scholarship and my earnings from two evenings' work in the LCC dental clinic. Joshua was working as a not very well paid assistant in an NHS dental surgery.

We looked through newspaper advertisements for a furnished flat near St Margaret's. Those we went to see were all too far from public transport, too tacky or too expensive. Flats were still in short supply. You often had to pay a substantial sum for what was called 'Key Money', another word for a premium. As it was illegal to charge a premium for unfurnished flats, landlords put in the minimum of furniture. The apartment could then be let as furnished and it would be legal to charge a non-refundable deposit – another way of getting 'Key Money'.

I called in at the University of London accommodation bureau.

'We've just been offered a furnished basement flat in Hampton Street just up the road from St Margaret's,' the receptionist said. 'They haven't let it before and they're not asking for a large deposit. Shall I ring and make an appointment for you?'

We went to see the basement flat two evenings later. We had hoped to rent something at four guineas a week, but the landlords were asking six.

Mrs Williams greeted us at the door of an end-of terrace Edwardian townhouse.

'Come in, come in,' she said. 'You're the couple from the student bureau? Martin is upstairs.'

She ushered us into an elegant living room on the first floor. Its full-length windows looked out onto Hampton Street.

Martin, a smiling middle-aged man, got up to shake hands.

'We used to let our basement flat to our cleaner,' he said. 'Now they have a baby, they've been offered a council flat. She moved out last week. Come down. I'll show you around.'

Although it was a basement flat, it was light and airy, with surprisingly tall ceilings. It had a separate entrance down some outside stairs and opened into a tiny kitchen. Leading directly off the kitchen was an arched cellar that extended under Hampton Street. Two more cellars led off the area at the bottom of the stairs.

There was a large living room and beyond that a short passage, with a double bedroom on the left. Further on were some extensive wine cellars. A claw-footed iron bath, with a large Ascot gas heater above it, stood in the connecting hallway, and a window in the bedroom looked out onto a small paved area below ground level. A staircase led up to the ground floor of the main house.

We loved the flat on sight. It was within a short walking distance of St Margaret's and near several Underground stations. Joshua would be able to get to his job at the Angel with ease. Their charlady had left it beautifully clean and fresh.

'Come up and have some coffee,' Martin said. 'Let's see if we can come to an agreement today, but you don't seem to be married,' he said, looking at my left hand. 'I don't think we'd let to an unmarried couple.'

'We're getting married on April 29th and it would be useful to rent the flat from April 1st so we can collect together some linen and crockery and stuff. I'm in my third year as a medical student at St Margaret's, and we're both qualified dentists. Josh is working as an assistant in an NHS dental practice, and I work at a School Clinic two evenings a week.'

'We're asking six guineas a week and a deposit of £100 in case of damage or breakages,' Martin said. 'We won't, of course, be asking for Key Money but we'll need bank references.'

We looked at each other. Neither of us liked bargaining, but six guineas would be very tight, and we worried about finding the money for a deposit.

'We were hoping to find something for four,' I said.

'Why don't we make it five?' Martin said, 'and we'll forget about a deposit.'

We got our bank managers to write references stating that we were respectable, and took over the flat on April Fools' Day.

We didn't have a formal lease and paid our landlady in cash once a month. She entered our payments into the Rent Book we bought in Woolworth's.

Joshua's mother still had the remnants of a very extensive trousseau, so we were well off for bed and table linen. We bought saucepans, crockery and cutlery at Woolworth's. It was like playing 'Mothers and Fathers'. I loved it.

We had a tea dance after the wedding ceremony and then spent the night at the Goring hotel before taking the boat train to Paris and on to St Tropez.

In 1956, St Tropez was still a village. We found nowhere to stay that we liked in the town centre, so we walked along the beach until we found a hotel on the sea front. The room was lovely, but a night's stay was so expensive we couldn't afford their continental breakfast, let alone dinner. We had brought Josh's camping stove again so we cooked in our room, even though the notice on the back of the door said it was strictly forbidden. When a maid knocked on the door just as we were making some minestrone, we pushed the camping stove, saucepan and soup into the wardrobe until she'd gone. Luckily, the soup didn't spill and nothing caught fire.

One day a small bright red sports car came tearing out of the gates.

'That girl's driving much too fast,' Josh said.

'That not a girl,' I replied. That's Bridget Bardot.'

We'd ended up in the most exclusive hotel in town.

On the way home, we stayed a few days in Paris. This time we visited the museums I'd missed when I'd stayed there with Phyllis when we were both seventeen. And this time we had more than £10 each to exist on for a week.

I was amazed and delighted to find that when you shopped for fruit and vegetables in Paris you could choose for yourself. At home in Petticoat Lane, while the produce was usually of excellent quality, heaven forbid you touched the goods. The stall holder would as soon cut your hand off.

Back in Hampton Street our landlords didn't seem to understand that once they'd let their basement flat, they didn't have automatic right of entry – unless the rent was unpaid or there was an emergency. When we took the flat, there was a polished wooden loo seat and cover, clean and in good condition. Our landlords swapped it for a thin plastic one when Josh and I were out. We didn't think we could complain. It was a petty thing after all.

One day when Josh went upstairs to pay the rent, our landlady said:

'I'm sure you won't mind, but our friends have put a few bottles of wine in the wine cellar.'

The wine cellar was, of course, part of our flat.

Josh, always quick off the mark, retorted 'As long as they don't mind us tasting a bottle now and again.'

When he came back down, we walked through the bathroom corridor to have a look. They had stacked four cases of what we were sure was very good wine on our shelves.

We were upset that they'd been through our flat again, but when we got home next day all the bottles were gone. Our landlords obviously took Josh at his word. As far as we knew, that was the last time they trespassed. At least if they did, we never found out.

The year after we got married, we decided to start our own dental practice. Ellen, my dental nurse at the school clinic said she'd be delighted to leave the LCC dental service and work for us.

'You're lovely, Abby,' she said. 'But some of the other school dentists I work for are real ogres. The kids are terrified of them and so am I. Just say the word and I'll hand in my notice.'

One night, coming back from the fish and chip shop in Marylebone Lane, we saw a 'Rooms to Let' sign above the laundry. It was on the first floor, with three good-sized rooms and a newly-refurbished bathroom. The rent was reasonable and it was within easy walking distance of our flat in Hampton Street. We took measurements, discussed room colours and started to list the dental equipment we would need.

A friend from St Margaret's dental school had a practice in Harley Street where he only worked part-time. He said Josh was welcome to rent it for a couple of sessions a week, while we waited to finalise things with the owners of the laundry.

We arranged to rent his rooms on Wednesday afternoons and Saturday mornings. Wednesday afternoons were always kept free for sports at St Margaret's, so I could work as Josh's nurse without missing lectures or clinics. Student friends and nurses formed an abundant supply of willing National Health patients. They loved being able to say they went to a Harley Street dentist – even if it was as a NHS patient. However, it wasn't an entirely happy situation – for Joshua to have a dental nurse who was constantly tempted to say, 'But wouldn't you rather . . . ?' 'Shouldn't you . . . ?'

We had planned everything for re-plumbing and decorating the flat above the laundry. Being near to, but outside, the medical area we could put up a plate with our names and qualifications to entice passers-by.

In 1957, professional people, doctors, dentists, lawyers, couldn't advertise. The Medical Area comprised Harley Street and a few of surrounding streets, including Wimpole Street, Weymouth Street and Devonshire Street and was owned by the Howard de Walden estate. You could have your name on the front door, but not your qualifications nor anything about you. Patients came by recommendation or referral from another dentist or doctor.

We phoned the laundry to fix a date, only to be told that they had let the flat as living accommodation. No warning, nothing.

We were in despair. Josh was now working part-time and his boss was looking for a full-time assistant. Ellen was ready give notice to the LCC. As a last resort, we contacted the agency run by a dental supply company.

'We've a suite of rooms in Harley Street. They're just opposite where you're renting,' the receptionist said.

We didn't know what to do. We had no idea how we could build up a practice in this area, with no way to indicate that we were there. It was one thing filling two half days but we worried about filling a whole week. There would be no plate with our names and qualifications to attract passers-by.

We arranged to meet the landlord at the second-floor rooms. As he was showing us around, Joanna, a medical student from the year above me came in.

'Hullo. What are you doing here?' I asked. '

'I live here,' she said. This is my flat. What are you doing here?'

The landlord hadn't warned her that the Howard de Walden Estate was cracking down on rooms in the medical area being used as living accommodation, as they had been during the war. He had been given notice to convert all the rooms in the house to consulting rooms, except for the attic flat, but he hadn't got around to telling his tenants. He soothed Joanna's ruffled feathers by offering her a reduced rent for the attic flat.

We still weren't sure about starting what would be an NHS practice in Harley Street, but the landlord was very persuasive. He was a medically qualified dentist, and had his own dental practice around the corner.

'Look,' he said. 'You're just starting out. How about if I reduce the rent by £50 a year and pay for the plumbing and redecoration?'

We said 'yes' on the spot, but then we had to raise a loan to pay for the equipment. Joshua's bank manager grudgingly offered us a loan of £500, but next day his letter arrived with an offer of only £250 – not enough to be useful.

My own bank account was still in my maiden name. I had opened it for my grant to study dentistry. I went to my branch of the National Westminster Bank to rectify this. I was ushered into the manager's office.

'I see you've done well, my dear. Started off with a London

County Council grant to study dentistry, and now a scholarship to study medicine, and you're working part-time while studying. The Bank is proud of you.'

I explained our dilemma. We wanted to start our own practice but Joshua's bank had let us down.

'Well, if you move your accounts here, I'm sure our bank can help you out.'

I worked as an NHS dentist in the practice Wednesday afternoons and Saturday mornings, and soon Joshua could give up his part-time job in Islington and fill the rest of the week with students, nurses and doctors.

Ellen was our nurse until she got married and moved to the country.

When I had to give up working in the practice to live in residents' quarters during my time on an Obstetric firm, and then to study for medicine finals, Josh took over my patients. I was delighted to hear that several complained:

'Oh, so I'll have to have second best now!'

CHAPTER 16

The Obstetrics Firm

My bleep went. It was my turn to go out with the Obstetric Flying Squad. Bell pealing loudly, our ambulance raced through the warm spring afternoon to a small terraced house in Kentish Town. A worried looking man greeted us at the door.

'The baby's early,' he said. 'The midwife who's been looking after my wife is on holiday and we can't get hold of anyone. Will she be alright?'

Sally, the Flying Squad midwife, calmed him down.

'Mr Pullman, is it? Nothing to worry about, my dear. Just show us up to the bedroom and go and boil the kettle, there's a good lad.'

She turned to me.

'It's always a clever idea to give the husband something to do. Gets him out from under our feet.'

Mrs Pullman, a slight woman in her 30s, was sitting in the middle of a large double bed. Her white cotton nightdress was soaked with sweat, her curly blond hair plastered to her head. She managed a smile before she grabbed my hand as a contraction took hold.

'We'll just get ourselves ready, Mrs Pullman,' Sally said, 'and we'll see how you're getting on. I'll just slip this rubber sheet under you to protect the mattress.'

We scrubbed our hands under the hot tap in their bathroom and put on aprons and sterile gloves. Back in the bedroom, Sally spread Mrs Pullman's legs apart and examined her.

'You're doing really well, dear. You're practically fully dilated. It won't be long now. I'm sure you won't mind if, Abby, our nice young student examines you.'

I could feel that the mouth of her womb was wide open. Soon we saw the baby's head appear.

The current view at St Margaret's was that a cut – an episiotomy –needed to be made in the perineum, the area between the vagina and the anus. This widened the vaginal opening to make giving birth easier. It was designed to avoid prolonged labour, which could result in a tear.

One of our registrars was opposed to routine episiotomies.

'If the Almighty had wanted to make women into cows, He would have done so,' he declared.

'Nearly there, dearie,' Sally said. 'Just give us a really good push.'

'Push, Mrs Pullman. Push,' we chanted a few times and Sally allowed me to deliver a little boy – bright red and squalling lustily.

'Never did believe in those awful episiotomies,' Sally said, too softly for Mrs Pullman to hear. 'Lucky there was no time. We midwives often manage without doing one, and we never get perineal tears.'

Sally unpacked a set of spring scales.

'Lovely boy,' she said. 'Seven pounds. The spitting image of Mr Pullman. I'll just give him a call, shall I?'

A beaming husband came in.

'Can I hold him? OK to bring my little Theresa in?'

'Of course, you can, love, but a nice cup of tea wouldn't go amiss.'

After kissing his wife and his new-born son, he went off to put the kettle on once again, Sally and I finished cleaning up Mrs Pullman and remade the bed.

A silver-backed brush, hand mirror and comb were arranged neatly on a lace runner on the chest of drawers. I passed them to Mrs Pullman.

'My mother, God rest her Soul, was in service from the time she was twelve until she married my dad. It was a hard life, but her last place was with Lady Richardson. She left the set to my mum in her will. If only my mum had lived to see her grandchildren.'

She dabbed at her eyes as Mr Pullman came in with a wide-eyed toddler. He carried a tray with cups of strong sweet tea and a plate of chocolate digestive biscuits. The little girl climbed onto the bed and snuggled up to her mother, gingerly touching her new brother's face.

Looking at a beaming Mrs Pullman sitting back in her comfortable bed, with all her familiar things around her, I wondered whether the pundits were right and that hospital delivery really was best. If an emergency arose, you would be much better off in hospital and I would prefer to have my own babies, if I ever had any, in the safety of St Margaret's. But there was a lot to be said for having a baby in your own home, in your own comfortable bed.

As students, we were only allowed to deal with single normal births – no breech births and none with complications, but I delivered an unanticipated pair of twins. Ultrasound scans were used in obstetrics for the first time in Glasgow in 1956, but they didn't come into general use until the 1970s. Before that, the presence of twins could easily be missed. This pair each weighed just under four pounds, so it was an easy birth. They were soon crying lustily, shown to the surprised and delighted parents and rushed up to the premature baby unit.

Delivering babies was great. You guided out a slippery infant, helped clean it up, weighed it and handed it to the mother like the best present in the world. As medical students, we were supposed to deliver 20 babies. I managed to deliver 26.

We all liked performing and sewing up episiotomies – it made us feel like junior surgeons. We used a pair of heavy duty surgical scissors that made a grating sound as we cut into the dense tissue. It was a quick snip made just as the baby's head crowned at the end of the second stage of labour. No anaesthetic was needed because it was done when the woman had a strong contraction. The women heard, rather than felt, the cut.

Once the afterbirth, the placenta, came out, we injected local anaesthetic around the cut and sewed up the incision using a large curved needle and black silk. Until the stitches were removed, just before the woman left hospital ten days later, it would be like sitting on a crown of thorns.

I was the youngest of three girls and my married elder sister had no children. I had never held a baby, never been interested in them. My obstetrics rotation changed all that. Joshua and I had got married when I was 24. In the 1950s, many women had their first baby much younger, but there was no question of us thinking about a family until I qualified in medicine, when I would be 28.

We'd been taught about the Stein-Leventhal syndrome and I

feared that I might have it and that there might be a problem about me getting pregnant when we did decide to start a family. Women with this condition have multiple cysts on their ovaries, few periods (oligomenorrhoea), diminished fertility and increased facial hair. Being fairly dark skinned with black hair, I always had a trace of a moustache and I had unpredictable periods, only three or four a year – great for cutting down on menstrual pains and pre-menstrual tension, but not so good if you wanted to have a baby. I would have few chances of getting pregnant, if I ovulated so rarely.

As medical students, we wouldn't have dreamt of going to another hospital for treatment. We said other teaching hospitals were no better than first aid posts, so I arranged to see my favourite gynaecologist, Ian Walton, a big, bluff Australian. I'd have preferred to be examined by a woman but there were no women consultant gynaecologists at St Margaret's. I'd have to make the best of it. After all, I had examined the groins and testes of several young men of my own age. They probably felt embarrassed too.

'OK, Abby, Ian said. 'Get your togs off, and we'll have a look-see.'

I hated having my feet in stirrups and, though he tried to be gentle, the cold vaginal speculum hurt. I hadn't liked to remind him to warm it under the hot tap beforehand.

'Your cervix looks fine and your ovaries feel normal. I'll take a cervical smear, though I'm sure it will be normal. Why don't you wait until you're ready to start a family, and have a go? You might have a pleasant surprise. It would be a big mistake to open you up at this stage.'

Nowadays women can have their ovaries examined directly as a minor procedure, inserting a laparoscope via a small abdominal incision. Before ultrasound was available and laparoscopes in routine use, it would have meant open abdominal surgery, so I did nothing. I'd worry about whether I had the syndrome when we were ready to try for a baby.

Jane, a fellow obstetric student, wasn't listening to me.

'For heaven's sake,' I said. 'What's got into you? We've got to know about pre-eclampsia in pregnancy before the clinic. You're not concentrating.'

'Well you don't have to find homes for four kittens before your landlord drowns them. I meant to get my cat spayed last time she had kittens, but it was Christmas and everything and everything. How about you taking one of them?'

'I might,' I said. 'I'll have to check with Joshua.'

Next day I told Jane it was OK.

All four were adorable little bundles, but I liked the tabby kitten best, the one that struggled hard to get away and nipped me with its tiny baby teeth.

'You're lucky, Abby, it's male. You can get it neutered free at the RSPCA.'

I lifted the little ball of fluff to my nose, and rubbed his soft fur against my skin.

'I'm going to call you Rupert, after a lovely cat I had when I was young.'

'Have you got a tray for him?' Jane asked. 'I've got a bag of cat litter you can have.'

I lifted Rupert into my basket and tucked the blanket around him.

Rupert grew into a handsome tabby, waiting for us at the top of our stairs at the end of the day and welcoming us home. We weren't sure where he went during the day but sometimes we saw him sheltering under parked cars in the street outside, rather than on our landing.

Rupert loved the old-fashioned claw-footed iron bath in the passageway from our bedroom to the cellars. The cold water tap always dripped. He would sit on the rim, dipping a careful paw under the tap and having a quick drink. Hot water came from an enormous gas-fired Ascot at the end of the bath. He didn't like the explosion when we lit it, so he would bolt off, only to return and walk around the narrow rim, looking at us quizzically as we soaked. He came perilously close to the edge, but he never fell in.

I usually got home first and one night Rupert wasn't waiting for me when I got home. He still wasn't back when Josh arrived. We searched the neighbouring streets but no Rupert. Finally, about 8 o'clock, we heard a noise outside the front door. He had dragged himself home, only just alive, a dribble of blood running down his chin. We assumed he'd been warming himself under a car and it had started off, running him over. We phoned the RSPCA, but no-one would see him before morning. They said it would have been different if he was a dog.

We stayed up with him as he grew weaker and weaker. He finally died as the sun came up. We were both in tears.

I was – and still am – a great one for reading in bed. It was approaching finals and I was reading about liver disease in my *Principles of Medicine*. A little black thing, a few millimetres long, jumped onto my book.

'I'm sure I saw something jump onto my book,' I said to Joshua.

'Rubbish. You're overtired. Give up for tonight and come to sleep.'

He yawned, turned over and was instantly asleep.

The next night the same thing happened – except that now I was onto kidney disease. Perhaps I really was tired and imaging things.

The following morning, as I got ready to leave for the 9 am ward round, I saw three or four little wriggling black things under my stockings. Memories of bedbugs in the tenement I grew up in flashed through my head, but these were black and much smaller. Then one wriggled out and jumped. They were fleas. I had fleas.

I panicked. I phoned the local council's Pest Infection Department.

'Yes. Miss,' the condescending voice said. 'Do you have a cat?'

I told him that Rupert had recently died.

'That'll be it, then,' he said. 'And do you have a carpet?'

Our landlords had left an ancient shag-pile carpet in the living room.

'The fleas must have laid their eggs in your cat's fur. Some fell into the carpet and hatched out after it died. Cat fleas prefer to live on cats, but they'll put up with humans for a temporary meal. They'll have gone for your legs because they like pale surfaces. Don't worry. They'll drop off soon. You'll only be bothered for a day or so. No. I don't need to come, and you don't need to buy an insecticide spray.'

I was in a fever of anxiety lest one decided to make its presence known during a ward round. I could just imagine what my sarcastic consultant would say when he saw a flea jump onto my white coat.

'Come with your little friends, have you Miss Waterman?'

I hoovered the carpet as soon as I got home that evening and twice a day for the rest of the week. I never saw a cat flea again and thankfully we never did have bed bugs.

According to my mother we didn't have bedbugs in our tenement in Wentworth Dwellings, even though you could see the black spots of their droppings all around their hiding places in the cracks between the wallpaper and the ceiling. In the bedroom that I finally had to myself, I would tease some out onto a piece of newspaper to prove that we had bedbugs, but my mother refused to look. The springs of my iron bedstead that were attached to the frames by tightly curled wire were a favourite hiding place for bedbugs.

Bedbugs are reddish-purple oval things – flat during the day and plump when they have fed. They only came out to bite at night. Next morning, if you squashed one you could see your blood squirting out of them.

My mother tried everything to get rid of them from our beds, although she said they didn't exist. She poured boiling water over the bed frames and washed them with methylated spirit. *Flit*, which came in a hand-operated pump was meant to kill flies, didn't kill bedbugs – or flies. We had fly-paper for those. The twists of yellow sticky paper moved slowly in the air, and gradually got covered with the black carcases of flies attracted to them.

Every spring the children who lived in our tenements came to school with 'summer spots'. They were the first bites of spring. Within weeks we stopped reacting as strongly to them, only to develop 'summer spots' again the following year.

The advent of DDT after the war changed all that. Teams of council workers toured the tenements spraying death to bedbugs. Everyone tried to pretend they'd never had any. They said they were having their flats sprayed as a precaution.

I suppose that we never had cockroaches because we didn't have central heating. Our unheated tenements saved us from them.

Part I of Finals was Pathology and Materia Medica (Pharmacology). I was finding pathology even more fascinating as a medical student as I saw the diseases I had only read about as a dental student. I was feeling quite confident when I took the exam and passed with honours in both subjects.

Part 2 was Medicine, Surgery and Obstetrics. We had written papers in each subject, as well as having patients to examine.

I found the written papers straightforward. It wasn't until I was a houseman in the Ear, Nose and Throat department that I realised I'd made a howler in my Surgery practical exam. I said that the hole behind a patient's ear might be a bullet hole, when it must have been the result of having much of his mastoid bone removed after repeated middle ear infections. However, I managed to diagnose most of the other cases in Surgery and Obstetrics correctly.

I'd always found Medicine, treatment of disease with drugs, more difficult than Surgery, treatment by operation. Perhaps it was because we'd covered more surgery in our dental course and I knew more about it before starting my medical degree.

In our Medicine practical, we had to examine and report on one long case and a couple of short ones.

'Good morning,' I said to the 60-year old man who was my long case.

'Butler's the name and butler's the profession, doctor'

I reminded him that I was a student but he ignored the interruption.

'Butler to her Majesty, I was. Got the job because I was a fighter pilot in the war. Spitfires, I flew. Got 20 Messerschmitts. Winston Churchill himself gave me the George Cross for it.'

I was already pretty sure of the diagnosis.

'What brought you to the doctor?'

'Well, lots of things. I can't stand the ringing in my ears that I got from my time as a drummer in the band of the Royal Guards.

I feel tired all the time and get short of breath. Lots of pains, first in my legs and then in my arms. Darts about all over the place.'

He was starting on an account of how he was deputy head of the Secret Service when I managed to stop him in full flow.

As I listened to his heart I heard a rushing sound and there was a dull area in the middle of his chest when I tapped it. These were signs of a swelling of his aorta – an aneurysm – in the main artery leaving the heart. His delusions of grandeur, the position of the aneurysm in the arch of his aorta and his fleeting pains were all typical of a patient with tertiary syphilis – a stage which is non-infectious but also untreatable. The damage has been done and it is irreversible.

Teaching hospitals kept a list of patients with typical conditions who were willing to be examined by students taking finals. Mr Butler kept trying to tell me what I ought to find and mostly he was wrong. Either he couldn't remember what previous students had said, or the last student was clueless. Often the pulses in the two wrists in patients with an aortic aneurysm are uneven and he told me his were, but they weren't. He did have the characteristic Argyll-Robertson pupils, small and unresponsive to light, and a foot reflex that went up instead of down, and he was right about those, but it was hard to concentrate with him going on and on.

I was now sure. His was a case of tertiary syphilis. – GPI (General Paresis of the Insane).

My other case was that of an elderly man with a hacking cough, nicotine-stained fingers and a large dull area in his chest. The diagnosis of lung cancer was obvious. I also had to examine a woman with rheumatoid arthritis who had the characteristic swelling and distortion of her fingers and wrists. That was quite straightforward too.

I had to present these cases to the examiners and then have an oral exam. It seemed unfairly difficult. They asked me to diagnose rare conditions on X-rays and asked about tropical diseases I'd only just about heard of. The questions were so obscure I felt sure I'd failed and they were just filling up the time. Even though at the end one examiner said I should take Membership – Membership of the Royal College of Physicians, the higher examination doctors need to become a consultant physician – before I forgot it all, I still thought I'd failed.

Two days later our Professor of Medicine's houseman stopped me in the corridor and whispered that I was being considered for the MBBS Gold Medal. In the event I didn't get it. I only got Honours in Pathology and Pharmacology in Part I and in Medicine in Part 2. The student from our year who did win the medal had honours in Surgery as well.

My father was delighted. My mother was unimpressed.

'I don't know why you couldn't have been satisfied with being a dentist. Studying all those years for nothing.'

CHAPTER 17

Ear, Nose and Throat House Surgeon

In 1959, when I qualified in medicine, to be registered as a doctor and work outside a hospital you had to have done two house jobs – one in surgery and one in medicine. My first post was as one of two housemen in the ENT department. As I had won the Duveen prize for Oto-Rhino-Laryngology (Diseases of the Ear, Nose and Throat) and was a dental surgeon, it was an obvious choice. Though housemen were then on call 24/7, there were two of us so we had alternate weekends off.

We had an out-patient clinic each afternoon. Housemen saw patients sent by their GP to have their tonsils and/or adenoids removed. The consultants examined more complicated cases. I went out into the crowded waiting area.

'Susie Johnson?' I called.

I waved her mother back. We were taught that children behaved better if we saw them on their own.

Susie was a friendly little ten-year-old, referred by her GP for tonsillectomy and adenoidectomy – Ts and As.

'Don't be scared,' I said. I won't hurt you.'

As I leaned forward to examine her, I was met by a most unpleasant smell – like rotten cabbage or something equally nasty. I thought maybe she had rampant caries but her teeth were practically perfect – only one small filling. The smell was coming from her nose.

I picked up the nasal speculum to look up her nostrils. The right side was clear, but the left side was blocked with something covered in mucus. It yielded slightly when I touched it. I grabbed it firmly with forceps and gently pulled. A three centimetre roll of sodden, stinking paper came out with a plop.

'How long have you had it there?' I asked

'It must have been over Christmas,' she said. 'I was fiddling with this piece of rolled up paper and somehow it got up my nose. I tried blowing my nose, and poking at it, but I couldn't get it out. Mum's always telling me off for putting things up my nose so I didn't tell her. Once I put a pussy willow up my nose. She managed to pull it out, but she was so angry, I was too scared to tell her about the paper. I just got used to it, I suppose.'

'Didn't anyone say anything?' I asked.

She smiled, shamefaced.

'My friends started to call me "Stinky". Please don't tell my Mum. I promised her I wouldn't do it again.'

I said I wouldn't say anything, but I couldn't help wondering how come the girl's family hadn't noticed. I called her mother in to tell her that she would be given a date for her operation in a week or two.

'Alright there, luvvie?' was accompanied by a powerful smell of cigarettes and alcohol. No wonder her daughter's smell had gone unnoticed.

I sympathised with the little girl with the smelly nose and an alcoholic mother. At least my mother didn't drink.

Brian Turner was lucky he snored so loudly. His new wife had issued an ultimatum – get fixed or get to sleep in the spare room. His GP referred him to St Margaret's and I admitted him one Sunday afternoon to have his adenoids removed next day. I was by now allowed to remove tonsils and adenoids under general anaesthetic in theatre. Removing adult adenoids was scrumptious – nice big adenoids I would scrape out on next day's operating list.

Much to Mr Turner's surprise I did a full medical examination as I had been taught – respiratory, alimentary and nervous systems. He was a fit looking 35-year old and couldn't understand why I was carrying out such a thorough examination.

'All this just to have my adenoids out?' he asked, as I was percussing the back of his chest. I placed the flat of my hand on his back, and moved my hand around, tapping it with the middle finger of my other hand.

'Shush,' I said. 'Take a deep breath.'

I was sure I could hear a difference between his right and left sides.

'I'll write you up for an X-ray,' I said. 'It's routine,' I lied.

Unlike now, we didn't get x-rays at once as they had to be developed by hand. Then, after taking Mr Turner's X-rays, the radiographer was called away for an emergency, so I had to hang around longer than usual for the result.

To my horror, – and satisfaction – Mr Turner had a large tuberculous cavity in his right lung. People were still dying of TB, though streptomycin was available by then. He was symptom free, except for his snoring, and he seemed otherwise healthy. He might not have seen a doctor until he had a fatal torrential haemorrhage. As a young houseman, you don't often get to save anyone's life. I had done so because I was so newly qualified and over-conscientious.

My registrar started him on streptomycin immediately and discharged him to be looked after by his GP. His enlarged adenoids would have to wait.

It was the day after Boxing Day. Everyone was feeling rather fragile, and my ENT registrar was decidedly hung over.

'Just speak very quietly,' he said. 'I'll go and sit in the surgeons' lounge.'

My bleep went.

'It's Sister in Casualty. I think you're on call for the ENT department. Can you come over, Dr Waterman?'

A very large elderly woman was sitting in Casualty, holding the hand of an equally elderly, but extremely thin, man. *Jack Sprat*, I thought.

> *Jack Sprat could eat no fat,*
> *His wife could eat no lean,*
> *And so between them both, you see,*
> *They licked the platter clean'*

It's my false teeth, you see,' she said. 'They hurt something awful and, as it was just turkey stew, I took them out to eat. No need to chew those small bits. My Doris made it with the leftovers from Christmas Day. I only had a mouthful when something stuck in my throat. I tried gargling with salt water and ate a couple of pieces of dry bread. Nothing helped. I reckon I've got a bit of turkey bone stuck in there. It's no better this morning. Haven't been able to eat a thing. Doris is a bit lazy, like. She should have been more careful, stripping the turkey bones.'

'There, there, dear,' her husband said, patting her fat little hand. 'Don't be hard on our Doris. She tries her best.'

'Can you walk over with me to the Ear, Nose and Throat department?' I asked. 'Or shall I get someone to take you in a wheelchair.'

'I'll be fine, lovey. I'll just take it nice and slow,' she said, as she waddled after me, clinging on to her husband's arm.

'Bleep the anaesthetist on call and tell theatre Sister to get the laryngoscopy stuff ready,' my registrar said, after he'd examined the patient.

He groaned and took me aside. 'Just my luck, when I thought we'd have a nice quiet morning. I'll just get some strong coffee down me.'

'Try it intravenously,' I said.

'For God's sake don't make me laugh. I think my head's going to explode.'

The turkey vertebra came out quite easily. I went to see my patient in Recovery. Her husband was sitting anxiously beside her.

'It was a bit of the neck bone of the turkey you got stuck in your throat,' I said. 'Lucky you didn't leave it any longer.'

She grabbed my left hand.

'You've been a real love. We've got a fruit and vegetable stall in the market. You come and see me when you need something. I'll see you right.'

The market was close to Hampton Street where Josh and I lived. The large Cypriot community that lived in the surrounding streets had a keen eye for quality as well as price, so it was a pleasure to shop there.

As I walked up the street looking at the various stalls I heard:

'Miss. Miss. Doctor.'

It was the turkey bone lady, standing by a stall piled high with fruit and vegetables. It all looked delicious.

I chose some apples and pears and then a bunch of bananas.

'How much is that then?' I asked, holding out a £1 note.

She waved it away.

'That's all right, Doctor. I said I'd see you right.'

'No really,' I said, embarrassed. 'I'd rather pay you.'

When she insisted, I gave in. After all it wasn't very much money.

I went back the next week and she refused payment yet again. It was impossible to go on accepting free fruit and vegetables but it was a shame. Hers was quite the best fruit and vegetable stall in the market. I'd have to shop at one of the other stalls. I did this for a couple of weeks and then she stopped me.

'I saw you buying from her opposite. Her stuff's not a patch on mine. Tell you what, if you want to pay me, come back and I'll look after you. Alright, love?'

She looked as if she was going to kiss me, so I stepped back, well out of her reach.

'Fine,' I said. 'Fine. I'll do that.'

But it wasn't fair really. My registrar had done all the work but he'd been so hung over he'd been quite rude and abrupt. The turkey bone lady had taken against him.

Josh gave me a hug when I got home.

'Just shows what a bit of TLC does.'

Mr Collins, one of the ENT consultants, and I were on our way out of theatre to get changed.

'Care to come for a spin, Abby? I took delivery of my new Ferrari last night. Do you good to get some fresh air. The other houseman can cover for you. See you outside the front door in 20 minutes?'

I nodded. Anthony Collins, then in his early 40s, was the

youngest of our four consultants. Always friendly, but not pushy, I very much enjoyed working for him and I felt our relationship might have been different if I hadn't already been married to Josh. The other consultant, whose houseman I was for the other three months, was Sir David Baines, a much more distant figure.

I folded myself into his flash new sports car and we sped off towards Westminster, down Vauxhall Bridge Road and along the Embankment. He was already speeding when we crossed Waterloo Bridge, but he must have been doing over 80 mph as he roared down Kingsway Tunnel. I was pleased we had gone out before lunch, not after I'd eaten.

'How was that then, my dear?'

I was feeling queasy as I said 'OK. I think.'

'Splendid. You can call me Tony, you know.'

It was time I learned to drive. Since I and the other ENT houseman had alternate weekends off and, as no patients were admitted on Fridays for routine surgery, we could go off at 5.30pm. There was a branch of the Royal School of Motoring (RSM) in Charing Cross Road, just before Trafalgar Square. I booked six lessons for alternate Friday evenings.

No-one in *The Buildings* in Petticoat Lane, where I was brought up, owned a bicycle let alone a car, so I never learned to ride a bike or develop any road sense. I had no idea how you drove a car or that they had gears.

To my dismay, when I got to the RSM my instructor ushered me immediately into the driving seat of a dual-control Ford. He gave me minimal instructions on how to engage the clutch and change gear, and told me to drive off. His hand rested on the wheel so he could take over at any time, but I was terrified I was going to crash into something. I drove round Trafalgar Square down Whitehall at a snail's pace.

He told me to put up my left indicator and hold out my right hand in a circular movement to indicate we were turning left. I turned into a narrow street with cars parked on both sides. I couldn't tell how near I was to the parked cars. Then there was a nasty grating sound as I scraped the offside of one of them.

'What the hell do you think you're up to?'

The driver leapt out of his car and banged on our side window, squaring up for a fight. My instructor got out of the car and held out his RSM card.

'It's all right, mate,' he said. 'We'll pay for everything and it won't affect your noclaims bonus.'

He made me drive back, up Whitehall again and round Trafalgar Square. I was still shaky when I got out, fully expecting him to tell me to cancel my remaining lessons, but he just said goodbye with a sour look on his face.

I much preferred the instructor who took me for my next five lessons and I gradually got used to the clutch and the hand signals and everything. I even managed to double declutch smoothly to get into first gear. Since I always had to drive off into the heavy traffic of Trafalgar Square, I quickly got used to driving in Central London.

We didn't own a car so I couldn't practise outside my lessons. I wasn't surprised when I failed my driving test. I was word-perfect on the Highway Code, that was the easy part, but I pulled out into a main road without waiting. That, and my general inexperience, failed me.

Joshua also failed his driving test first time, but he passed it second time. A second-hand car was advertised on our hospital notice board. I contacted Dr Phillida Burton and she drove it round to the front of the ENT department. It was a black Morris 8 Series E, an old-fashioned bull-nosed, pre-WW2 model. We paid her £150 for it and parked it in the street outside our flat. We called the car Phillida. It was such a lovely name. I could now get in a bit of practice driving with Joshua and like him passed second time.

Unfortunately, the first time I took Phillida out on my own I drove too close to a parked van as I was driving up Howland Street. The van had a narrow bumper board running along each side, about three inches deep, too low for me to see through my side window. The lorry was unscathed, but I tore off my nearside front wing. When I drove Phillida to the garage, the mechanic laughed.

'That old thing is only held together by the paint. Look it's almost rusted through.'

This was long before MOT tests.

'But is it too dangerous to drive?' I asked.

'Not dangerous, miss, but best to keep your distance next time.'

I developed a stiff neck whenever I was caught in a draught, so if the car window was open, I made sure I had a scarf around my neck. On one of my Sundays off, Joshua and I drove to Margate for the day. When we were almost out of London, I realised I had forgotten my scarf, but as it was a lovely sunny day it didn't seem worth going all the way back for it.

Next day when I woke in my room in the residents' quarters, I couldn't turn my head. When I tried, pain shot up my neck into my head and down to my shoulder.

Mr Collins had a list that Monday morning. I managed to get dressed, wincing as I pulled on my white coat. At breakfast, the other ENT houseman grinned.

'Who's got a *torticollis* then? What have you been up to on your weekend off?'

'It's not funny. I'm assisting this morning, and my neck's agony.'

I left myself plenty of time to get changed and scrubbed up. Mr Collins was clearing out the mastoid cavity of a teenager who'd had repeated chronic infections. It was a shame I hadn't seen a case like this before my surgery exam.

It was my job to suck the operating field clear of blood and pus. Mr Collins looked up.

'Abby, I can't look at you a minute longer,' he said, 'with your head on one side like that.'

'Sorry, Mr Collins. I've got the mother and father of a stiff neck. It's killing me.'

'For heaven's sake go and get some physio. Go on. Off you go then. Theatre sister can take over.'

I went up to Physiotherapy on the third floor. The receptionist tried not to grin as she read my name tag.

'Don't say "Physician heal thyself"'.

'Isabel is free. I'll give her a buzz.'

Isabel tried massaging and manipulating my neck, but I couldn't stand the pain for very long. Heat treatment didn't help either.

'If I were you, I'd take the day off, and curl up with some aspirin and a good book,' she suggested.

My mother had been a firm believer in treating a stiff neck with heated salt. I grated some rock salt from the brick we kept in our store cupboard, heated it in a small fry pan, and filled one of Joshua's socks with it. The warm compress was comforting. I went to bed and slept for a couple of hours, only to wake in worse pain than ever.

When I qualified, osteopaths and chiropractors were regarded by conventional medics as little better than witch doctors – you could almost be struck off the register for associating with them. Our landlord, Martin, was an osteopath and I was desperate. I rang his bell. His wife came to the door.

'Yes, Abby. Can I help?'

Then she noticed that my head was almost touching my right shoulder.

'It looks as if you need Martin, but I'm afraid he's in bed with 'flu. Come inside and I'll ask him what he suggests.'

She was back down almost at once.

'He says to come upstairs.'

Martin was lying back in a large double bed, a big grin on his face.

'Come on in, my dear. Just lie down beside me and I'll see what I can do.'

I was glad his wife was still in the room.

He took hold of my head and tried a few exploratory movements. Suddenly, he twisted my head to the left. It was so violent, I was afraid he'd broken my neck, but when I gingerly tried to turn my head, the pain had completely gone. I could turn my head freely.

'It's incredible. I just don't believe it. Trouble is, when I go back to work I won't be able to tell anyone at St Margaret's I got into bed with an osteopath. I might get expelled or worse.'

I admitted Alan Jenkins as an emergency at five o'clock on a Friday evening. A burly 30-year old brick-layer, he was curled up on his side moaning.

'My head's killing me and the light's too bright. Please do something.'

I examined him. His neck was stiff, a classical sign of meningitis.

'He needs an immediate lumbar puncture,' my registrar said.

It was my first lumbar puncture. Although Mr Jenkins was quite plump, I managed to pass the needle between his lower lumbar vertebrae into the space around his spinal cord without difficulty. I breathed a sigh of relief and withdrew a small amount of cerebrospinal fluid, the fluid that envelopes the brain and spinal cord. It was cloudy instead of being clear and I took it straight up to microbiology. The technician did a quick smear of the fluid. It was teaming with bacteria. There was no doubt – it was meningococcal meningitis.

I hurried back to the ward and injected penicillin directly into his cerebro-spinal fluid – but it was already too late. He lapsed into coma overnight, and died next morning.

The pathologist on duty found no surprises. Our diagnosis was right. The only abnormal findings were in his brain and spinal cord. The coverings, the meninges, were coated with a thick green layer of pus and bacteria.

I came into the post mortem room in time to hear a woman shouting:

'Burn the bugger, burn him. I hated him, and I'm glad the rotten sod is dead.'

The pathologist had been asking Alan Jenkins' wife whether she was going to arrange a church burial, or wanted him cremated. She'd made her choice abundantly clear.

Three days after treating Alan Jenkins I was headachy and feverish, so I went back to my bed in the residents' quarters. I needed to report in sick, so I phoned the Resident Medical Officer, who looked after staff. I waited several hours but, when he still didn't come I phoned my ENT registrar. He came almost as soon as I hung up.

'Hi, Abby. Sorry you're feeling so rough. The Boss has arranged for you to be admitted to the Private Wing. Sir David's quite worried about you.'

It was bliss. My room was light and airy, so different from the dingy room I had been given in residents' quarters as a junior houseman. It even had its own bathroom – no dirty ring you had to clean off the bath before you ran the water. And the food was much better than we had in the staff canteen. The nurses brought a menu each evening for me to choose my food for the next day. Nothing was soggy or overcooked and there was no burnt porridge for breakfast.

The only drawback was that I was on complete bed rest, which meant bedpans.

'Be good now, Dr Waterman. Sir David is worried you might have caught your patient's meningitis.

I laughed.

'It's just a flu-ey cold. You can see I'm getting better already. Can't I go to the loo on my own? It's not as if I'd have to walk miles.'

But bed rest it was. I held out as long I could, so I didn't have to call for a bedpan too often.

By the third day, it was quite clear that I didn't have meningitis. I rang for a nurse.

'Surely by now I can get up to go to the loo,' I said. 'It's only a couple of steps.'

She was adamant.

'Sorry. You're on bed rest until you've been cleared by the doctors.'

I'd just got settled on the uncomfortable stainless-steel bedpan, when there was a knock at the door.

Before I could say 'Keep out', Sir David came in. He obviously didn't notice that I was a good ten centimetres taller than I should have been. He asked how I was, told me I was much missed, gave me everyone's best wishes and finally a run-down on the patients on whom I'd carried out a tonsillectomy the Monday before. I was physically uncomfortable, but mentally I was in torment. At last he said goodbye. For one dreadful moment, it looked as if he might plant a kiss on my cheek and upset my precarious balance. He didn't, and I was saved the indignity of falling off a bedpan in front of the most senior surgeon at St Margaret's.

As soon as he left, I rang my bell. The nurse was giggling.

'I tried to stop him at Sister's desk, I did, but he marched right past me.'

'You could have come in with some excuse, and not left me sitting on a bedpan while he made small talk,' I said.

'I couldn't. Lady Simon bled again and we were busy with that. Anyhow, Sister says you're off bed rest. When the RMO finally turns up, he'll tell you when you can leave.'

Now that I was off bedpans, I revelled in the enforced luxury. It was great not being woken in the middle of the night to deal with some medical emergency or other, but it was only for two more days. Then back to examining ears, noses and throats and my room in residents' quarters.

CHAPTER 18

Medical House Physician

My second post as a houseman was as a house physician at the Royal Essex Hospital. I lived in residents' quarters, but as I had one weekend off in three I could go home to our flat in Hampson Street every third weekend. The rest of the time I was on call 24/7.

Josh and I started to think about having a baby. I was now 27 and in 1959 that was considered quite old to be having a first baby. I worried that I would have problems conceiving as I ovulated so infrequently, even if I didn't have the Stein-Leventhal syndrome.

We waited a couple of months before we stopped using contraception so that even if I managed to get pregnant quickly, I'd still be quite capable of working as a houseman for the remainder of my six months.

Four weeks later, I started to feel hot. My breasts were tender and I felt queasy in the morning. I thought it was probably wishful thinking, but Josh left an early morning urine sample for me at the Doctors' Laboratory in Harley Street. Pregnancy tests were then carried out using Xenopus African clawed frogs – the *Hogben* test. Female frogs were injected with the woman's urine sample and, if she was pregnant, within 10 hours, frog eggs would be seen dotting the water.

I was delighted when my test came back positive. Once I knew for sure that I was pregnant, my morning sickness vanished. Being certain cured me.

I thought how lucky I had been not to have been persuaded to sleep with any of my boyfriends before I got married. Having got pregnant so quickly, I was convinced I'd have got pregnant the first time I had sex. The Pill wasn't introduced until 1960 and it was still considered a disgrace to be an unmarried mother.

I told the sisters on the wards that I was pregnant, but assured them I would be fine working until the end of contract. The only craving I had was for tomatoes. I always had a bowl of them in my room.

Even the crabby sisters, who had seemed to resent having a woman houseman, were supportive – telling me to rest and giving me secret snacks. One sister knitted me a lovely soft white shawl, while another made me a matching set of a baby coat, hat and booties.

My Aussie friend, Ian Walton, was passing through the antenatal department at St Margaret's as I waited for my first examination.

'Well, Abby,' he said. 'You're waiting here with my patients so I guess you and that husband of yours managed it without my help. Maybe I can get you seen a bit quicker.'

'Please don't bother, Ian. I want to be treated like an ordinary patient.'

The midwife asked me what illnesses I'd had.

'I had measles, chicken pox and whooping cough. We were all vaccinated against small pox. I've two ugly scars on my arm to show for it, but we didn't have an MMR (measles, mumps, and rubella) vaccination. It wasn't introduced until 1988.'

'What about German measles?'

'I had German measles when I was 12 and scarlet fever when I was thirteen.'

She wanted to know more about the scarlet fever, because it might have led to rheumatic fever, a disease caused by the body's own immune response to the Streptococcus bacteria that causes scarlet fever. It can leave you with damaged heart valves and cause problems in pregnancy.

I remembered my bout of scarlet fever with pleasure. I wasn't very ill and I'd had a great time in the isolation hospital. It was during the Blitz and a welcome break from sleeping in the air-raid shelter. I had recovered without further complications.

At that time, medical and surgical house officers had to take turns covering for Casualty at night. The Royal Essex Hospital was in a quiet district. After the full time Casualty Registrar went off duty, the department was rarely busy.

I was bleeped by Casualty Sister my first night on call. She took me over to a young man who was mopping at the blood streaming from his forehead. He and his friends were having a fry-up in the fish and chip shop in the High Street, when they got into an argument with a couple of drunks at the next table. He smelled strongly of the Heinz tomato ketchup that one of the drunks had cracked over his head.

Head injuries bleed like crazy because there are numerous blood vessels in the scalp and the skin is so tight that the wound edges are

241

pulled apart. Once I had cleaned him up, I found that the linear cut on his forehead was quite small. I injected some local anaesthetic, sewed up the wound and arranged for him to have a tetanus shot and a penicillin injection. I sent him home with a prescription for a short course of antibiotics, and an appointment to come back to Casualty to have the stitches removed ten days later.

Three weeks later Casualty Sister bleeped me during the day.

'There's a policeman at reception waiting to see you, Dr Waterman. Can you come down now?'

My heart all but stopped. I wasn't on call. Was it Joshua? Was it my parents? I rushed over to the Casualty department. I dreaded hearing that that a family member was badly injured, in a coma or even dead.

The tall policeman towered over me.

'Dr Waterman?'

'Yes,' I said. 'Who's had an accident? Is it bad?'

'I'm so sorry,' he said. 'They should have said when they bleeped you. It's nothing to do with anyone you know. I'm here about the young man whose forehead you sewed up. The stupid idiot that did it is up before the magistrates in a couple of weeks. We'd be grateful if you would appear as an expert witness. We'll give you the date well in advance, Dr Waterman. We know you're a busy lady, and we'll make sure you don't have to hang around. There'll be a small fee, of course.'

'I'd be happy to do that, but I'll check with my consultant that it's OK with him.'

I was off the following weekend, so I collected my navy interview suit and white shirt. I took my high heeled shoes too.

The case was tried in the local Magistrate's Court three weeks later. It was all very pleasant and civilised. When I arrived, I was shown into a side room, and provided with tea and biscuits. The staff used my title in every other sentence – Dr Waterman this; Dr Waterman that – as if my status somehow rubbed off on them.

I'd never been in a Magistrate's Court. I expected the magistrates to be wearing wigs and gowns, but there were just two men and a woman in civilian clothes. A handful of people sat in the public benches. When I was ushered in, they were hearing a dangerous driving case. The man had crashed into an oncoming lorry, injuring both the lorry driver and his own passenger.

Then my case was called. I was sworn in and I read out my account of his injury. The magistrates listened very attentively, and asked for a bit of clarification on the state of the young man when he was brought in. It was fantastic being treated with such respect – and being paid a fee for attending.

I would have liked to stay to the end of the trial and find out what happened to the yob who'd smashed a bottle over my patient's head. Unfortunately, I had to get back to work.

The following day I didn't get to bed until one o'clock in the morning. A patient with a stomach ulcer had started to bleed again and by the time I'd set up a drip and got him settled down, it was gone midnight. Then I had a message to call in at the male geriatric ward. As usual, it was nothing that couldn't have waited until morning. The old men liked having a young woman doctor around. Some of them made a habit of having regular troubles with their nether regions. I swore that if I had to examine one more old man's 'old man', I'd cut it off. I looked after the geriatric ward for three of my six months and I got quite fond of them – well, some of them.

It was my turn to be on call for Casualty again. I'd only just got to sleep, after going back to the medical ward to make sure the drip was running freely, when my phone rang. I was out of bed and into my clothes before I was really awake. It was a reflex. When I went home for the weekend, and long after I finished my house job, I would be out of bed and dressed instantly if the phone rang or even if there was a loud noise during the night.

'Dr Waterman? It's Casualty. We have an injured patient you need to see.'

'Are you sure they can't just have a plaster or something?'

'You know me better than that,' Casualty Sister said. 'This patient needs stitches.'

I braved the cold, and crossed the courtyard from the residents' quarters to the main hospital. It started to pour with rain before I got to the entrance. I swore as I stepped into a deep puddle.

A boy of about 16 was sitting in a cubicle, snivelling, a green theatre towel draped over his lap. His father was sitting next to the couch.

'What's the problem?' I asked.

The teenager blushed and his father mumbled something I couldn't quite catch.

'Perhaps you'd like to wait outside,' I said to the father.

'Now tell me all about it,' I said, sitting down beside the boy.

'Isn't there a man doctor here? I don't really want to see a lady.'

I sighed.

'There's just me. Let's get on with it.'

As students, we'd been shown X-rays of weird objects in patients' rectums, objects that had been mysteriously transported there with the patient apparently not knowing quite how. At first, I thought this might be the boy's problem, but if he had something stuck up his rectum, he would hardly have been sitting down with a towel on his lap.

When I removed the towel, I saw that he had his penis out. On the upper surface was a long spiral tear.

'How did that happen?' I asked.

'I was on my bike,' he said. 'I was dying to have a pee but I couldn't see anywhere to stop and it burst. It doesn't hurt much but will it, could it . . . ?'

'No, it won't drop off, but tell me, how did it really happen?'

He stuck to his story, though it was clearly nonsense, but I couldn't think of an alternative sensible explanation.

I draped his penis in a sterile towel, injected some local anaesthetic and sewed up the tear. Once again, I ordered a tetanus injection and an injection of penicillin, and wrote a prescription for a course to take at home.

'I've used stitches that will be absorbed naturally, so you won't have to have them taken out,' I told him. 'Sister will make you an appointment to have the wound checked in ten days' time. Come back before then if you're worried, if it gets sore or anything.'

Next day I stopped the full-time Casualty Registrar, and explained what had happened the night before

'Can I ask you a favour? When you see him in 10 days, would you ask him how it happened? He wouldn't tell me, and I can't imagine how he did it.'

I confronted the Casualty Officer two weeks later when we met in the residents' dining room. He said he'd forgotten to ask.

'I'll never forgive you,' I said, sure I caught a guilty smirk as he left.

One of my elderly geriatrics died. He'd been a curmudgeonly old man but I was sorry to see him go. We were expected to attend the post-mortems on our patients, but there were no surprises. His poor old heart had finally given up. Massive coronary.

I was surprised to see what looked like two healthy young people on the other two tables.

'They look so healthy. What was the cause of death?'

'Stupid kids. Riding on a motorbike. No helmets. She was riding pillion and swinging a helmet from her hand. Makes you want to weep.'

Me too, I thought.

Just before I finished my six months at the North Middlesex, I had my most heart-breaking case.

Late one evening I admitted a young mother who was in *Status Asthmaticus* – a condition in which a patient with asthma reaches a stage where their bronchial tubes stay shut down. Her husband brought her and their two young children to the hospital in the early evening. My registrar had gone off, but I called him in. He was there in minutes. Despite everything we tried – corticosteroids and oxygen – she died early next morning.

It was down to me to tell her husband.

'I told her she should go to hospital when I got in from work, but she wanted to put the kids to bed first,' he sobbed. 'I should have made her come at once.'

I patted him awkwardly on the shoulder.

'It was such a severe attack, maybe nothing would have helped. Don't blame yourself.'

I held back my tears until I got back to my room. I cried for ages. Was there anything else I could have done? Should have done?

CHAPTER 19

Starting a Family

By the time I finished my second house job, I was five months pregnant. I was unlikely to find a part-time temporary job in medicine and I couldn't face the thought of standing all day in a dental practice.

I decided to take a cookery course instead. Only the girls in the lower streams at school did cookery and my mother had always shooed me away, especially during wartime. When we got married I could cook omelettes and minestrone and not much else, though I'd extended my range a bit since then.

'Food is rationed,' she'd say. 'Don't want you wasting good food. Time enough to learn to cook when you get married.'

My mother was a very plain cook. Her repertoire was limited to chicken soup, boiled chicken, braised beef, fried fish and sardines on toast. On Saturdays, we'd have *cholent*, potatoes and meat or chicken that had been cooking all night on a gas ring turned on very low before the Sabbath came in.

I saw an advertisement for a six-week full-time course at the Good Housekeeping Cookery School. The courses were originally designed for debutantes who needed to learn how to run a kitchen, though they might only set a foot inside one to give orders to the cook.

Most of the other students were upper crust young women who had hardly ever gone into a kitchen. One 17-year-old had never even peeled a potato. Some of the others had moved to London and got a flat of their own so they had done a bit of cooking but we were all pretty inexperienced. One student was a woman in her early thirties who had been in the ATS (Auxiliary Territorial Service) – someone more my age. We paired up and shared chores.

Before the war, the students would have cooked in the morning and learned about housework in the afternoon, though they might never have to do any housework once they were married. They were taught to use the starch-enriched water from soaking the potatoes they cooked in the morning to starch a frilly cap or a shirt; how to use gophering tongs – the tubular bladed instruments that made little tunnels in starched caps – and how to iron men's shirts. By the time I took the course, it only covered cookery.

The kitchens were in a large basement in Mayfair. There were eight Formica-topped tables for the sixteen of us. The shelves around the walls were stacked with bowls and saucepans of every shape and size and there were drawers and drawers of cooking implements. as well as several gas cookers and hobs. On Mondays, the room smelled of cleaning fluid but the rest of the week we were greeted by the gorgeous smell of the cakes we'd cooked for our tea the day before.

We were taught from scratch – how to boil an egg, how to boil potatoes, how to skin and bone a fish. It was a mixture of traditional

English cookery – roast beef, roast potatoes and Yorkshire pudding – and some more exotic dishes like *dolmas* (stuffed vine leaves), curries and the classic sole dishes *Sole Veronique,* sole with green grapes and *Sole Meniere,* sole panfried in butter.

In the mornings, we cooked a main meal for lunch and ate it – meat, fish or a vegetarian dish and two vegetables. In the afternoons we baked cakes, bread, brioches, and pastries. I adored it all, especially the chocolate éclairs. In 1960, no-one seemed to bother about pregnant women putting on too much weight and I ate for two with gusto.

I couldn't find a suitable sized alphabetised book so I bought a linen covered book and made my own index. I still have it, a few food stains on the cover and the leaves a bit faded, but the recipes as good as ever.

The teachers were all highly experienced cooks and managed their often unruly pupils with ease. At dental and medical school, there had been few women – there was still a 10% quota for us. I thoroughly enjoyed the fun of bonding and giggling and having a great time in an all-female group.

I thrived on being pregnant, though I got a bit more tired than the others. It was a lovely six weeks. I cried when they gave me an embroidered layette at the end of the course.

Now it was time to move. Our damp basement flat was not suitable for a baby. Waites, the builders, were building a small terrace of SPAN houses in Wimbledon, designed by the prize-winning Eric Lyons. Our best friends lived in a SPAN house in Blackheath and we'd have liked to move near them, but the new houses were too near the proposed M25.

It took a while to get a mortgage. Most companies were wary of houses with flat roofs because they tend to leak. In the event, of the six houses in our development only ours didn't leak, so they had been right to be cautious.

There was a small glassed-in porch, big enough to hold a pram, leading into the living room/ dining room which extended to the back of the house and had floor to ceiling windows at each end. A sliding door opened onto a small garden that had a six-foot high fence at the back to hide our washing. A small fitted kitchen came off the front of the main room and a study was partitioned off the rear. A staircase led up to two double bedrooms, a small nursery, a bathroom and separate toilet.

It was bliss. The early morning sun streamed into our rear facing bedroom, which had a small en-suite shower room. The two larger bedrooms had fitted wardrobes so we needed little furniture. We had bought a three-piece suite from Heal's for our Hampton Street flat and now bought a G-plan table, dining chairs, double bed and chest of drawers on hire purchase, though we paid cash for a white cot. It didn't seem right somehow to buy that on the *never-never*. Diana, a friend from medical school, lent me a large maroon nannie-type *Silver Cross* pram.

However, once I'd got over the pleasure of having our own home at last, I was bored, bored to tears. I had been in succession a dental student, a medical student, a Harley Street dentist and a house-man. After those demanding occupations and a full-time cookery course, I was home alone in Wimbledon, where I knew no-one. It was awful.

With only the two of us living there, the house took less than an hour to clean, but now I couldn't even do that. My blood pressure was up, my legs were swollen and I was told I must rest until the baby was born. There was a danger of pre-eclampsia – a life-threatening complication of late pregnancy.

I was delighted when David and Lilian, Josh's cousin and his wife, invited us to dinner. David greeted us with a glass of dry sherry – we weren't aware then that alcohol was bad for unborn children. Lilian is a great cook and dinner was fantastic – a clear consommé, followed by a spicy goulash with dumplings and finishing with Lilian's delicious strawberry cheesecake. We shared a couple of bottles of Hungarian wine with our meal and, while the smell of our filter coffee still lingered, we sipped the cognac we'd brought them.

As I leaned back to pull my enormous belly away from the table, a trickle of warm liquid ran down the inside of my leg.

'I think my waters have broken,' I whispered to Lilian, 'but I'm not due for two weeks.'

Lilian put her arm around my shoulders.

'Better early than late, Abby. I'll fetch you a towel. It'll soak up most of it.'

I eased myself into our old Morris car, making sure the towel was securely stuffed between my legs. I shifted uncomfortably, the amniotic fluid sticking to the shiny black seats. The car had little in the way of suspension, so there was a spirt of liquid every time we went over a bump or dipped into a pothole.

We arrived at St Margaret's in less than half an hour. The disinfectant smell that hangs around hospitals was familiar and comforting. As I was greeted at the entrance to the Maternity Department, I made up my mind I would ask to be treated like an ordinary patient, and not 'come it' because I was a doctor.

A midwife tucked me into bed.

'It's lucky for us it's your first, so it will be hours yet. We've already got three women in labour. I'll bring you some Seconal (quinalbar-bitone) to help you get to sleep.'

'I'll be asleep in no time,' I said. 'I've been like a dormouse for months.'

'Be a good girl now. We don't want to be difficult, do we?'

I gave in, and added Seconal capsules to the sherry, the wine and the cognac. I edged between the cool linen sheets and tried to get to sleep. Almost at once I felt my belly go hard. My contractions had started.

'I'll give you an injection for the pain,' the midwife said.

'But it's not really hurting,' I protested.

'Be good now.'

I turned on my side to allow her to inject the Pethidine.

That did it! I was soon as high as a kite.

I don't know many dirty songs, but I sang them all. However, I did remember lots of hymns from our Monday morning school assemblies. I started on them *forte*, ignoring the midwife's exhortation to get on with it and push. I was too sloshed to tell whether Josh was there or not.

Breaking off from a spirited rendering of '*All things bright and beautiful, all creatures great and small,*' I finally gave birth to Simon at 2am. Amazingly, I was stone cold sober the moment they put him in my arms.

'Is he alright? May I look at him?'

I unwrapped my beautiful baby boy. I couldn't have imagined the all-consuming love I felt for him. I was sure he smiled up at me as he screwed up his deep blue eyes against the light.

I very much enjoyed my time in a side ward with two kindred spirits – a ballet dancer and a health visitor. After pregnancy and childbirth our bladder control wasn't at its best and to begin with there were a few minor accidents – we had so much to laugh about.

Then the three of us were in tears. The Professor of Obstetrics had done a ward round and I heard him talking to the students about congenital heart disease. I told the others.

'It must be my Simon,' I wept. 'I think his lips look a bit blue.'

'No', the other two said. 'It must be one of our babies. As you're a doctor, they would have told you at once.'

We were crying our eyes out when the registrar came in to check on our episiotomy wounds – all three of us had had them.

He burst out laughing.

'You silly women. I'm surprised at you, Abby. Don't you think he'd have come to see you and discussed your babies with you if there was a problem. It's one of the babies in the main ward.'

We looked at each other- shame-faced.

After ten days, we were discharged. All three of us had elected for breast-feeding and had got it well-established.

As Josh drove over Westminster Bridge on our way back to Wimbledon, I suddenly felt terrified. We'd been taught how to look after sick children but had minimal training in care of new babies. Would I cope? Would I be able to continue to feed him myself?

Fortunately, we had visitors for coffee next day. William's wife had breast-fed John who was now three months old so I had a role model. We'd been taught the value of breast feeding for our baby's health but most women in the post-natal ward decided to bottle feed. Josh and William talked about old times at St Margaret's dental school while Susan and I companionably nursed our babies.

I took Simon up to St Margaret's dental school to show him off when he was three months old.

'That's it then, Abby,' the sub-dean said. 'You'll never use your qualifications now.'

But I swore to myself that I would return to medicine when my child or children were at full time school, and I did.

There was no way I could have got a part-time job in pathology at St Margaret's. The professor didn't think much of women in medicine anyhow and he would certainly not have taken on a woman who had a young baby. There were part-time medical posts available either in Health or Family Planning Clinics. Neither appealed to me. I had no wish to spend hours weighting babies, fitting diaphragms or teaching the proper way to use condoms.

We therefore planned on my having a dental practice in the small office off our living-cum-dining room. I had been registered as an NHS dentist when I worked at our practice in Harley Street and it was just a case of renewing my registration.

We bought a second-hand, but perfectly functional dental chair, a dental drill, suction apparatus, cupboards and dental equipment. By the time Simon was two months old, I was ready. I had a brass plate fixed to the top of a stout wooden post in the front lawn and waited for patients to come, which they did in a trickle, then a steady flow. At first, they were all mothers and children from the nearby council estate, but there was a police residence up the road. Soon I had a clientele of policemen too.

I worked only in the mornings, when Simon was in the garden asleep in his pram. If he woke up and cried before I was finished, none of my patients minded when I brought him in to lie on a blanket on the surgery floor. The house had underfloor heating, so it was very cosy for him.

As a dentist, I was now Miss Waterman again, not Dr Waterman. A new policeman patient looked up at me.

'You know, Miss Waterman, I'm a terrible patient.'

'Funny you should say that ...' I replied, with a grin, wanting to add 'because I'm a terrible dentist' but he looked too worried for me to joke about it.

He was right. He was a terrible patient, and fainted as soon as I gave him an injection for a filling. All 6'3" of him slid out of the dental chair onto the floor. I am only 5'1½", and my dental nurse was hardly any taller. I kept *sal volatile* capsules in my medicine cabinet and broke one under his nose. He soon came round, although he was still woozy. We never could have got him back into the dental chair while he was unconscious. Luckily that was the first and only time he fainted.

My patients waited in our living room. The more working-class parents from the council flats were very strict with their children, who would sit quietly while waiting and mostly didn't make a fuss in my dental chair. Middle class children all seemed to be born hooligans. We didn't have any antiques or real valuables for them to destroy, but it was infuriating when a small boy insisted on jumping on our pristine furniture in his muddy shoes. His mother spread her hands helplessly.

'I've tried everything. He just doesn't listen, but I don't want to inhibit him or give him an inferiority complex.'

I'd have liked to suggest a sharp slap on the bottom, but contented myself with refusing to let her make any further appointments.

'I'm afraid I really can't take on any more children. Have you tried the dentist up the road? I hear she is very good.'

Now I was working, we had a succession of nannies to look after first Simon, and then the other children as they came along.

My first 'nannie' was a 16-year-old recommended by my cleaner.

255

She said Tracy had lots of experience looking after the little ones, as she was the oldest of six children. She was a pleasant rosy cheeked girl and Simon took to her at once. She gave notice when I tried to make her have her shoes repaired, instead of throwing them away.

'I've got one mother already,' she said. 'I don't need you telling me what to do.'

The next nannie was an 18-year old young woman, whose parents had come from Pakistan. She told me her father regularly had sex with her and her younger sister.

'If we want to go to the pictures or get our pocket money, he makes us go to bed with him first.'

'Did you tell your mother?' I asked, horrified.

'She always says "Rather you than me". I've had enough of him. I'll never go home again.'

After she left to train as a hairdresser, we had a series of au-pairs. We had a wonderful cleaner who stayed with us for the next thirty-two years, so all the heavy housework was done by her. We just needed a babysitter and someone to make the children their tea and help keep their rooms tidy.

Most were 17 or 18-year olds who went to English classes in the afternoon. In contrast, Greta was a 30-year old bank clerk from Switzerland. She mothered me, making me cups of tea when I came home tired, and telling me to rest. She couldn't be persuaded to stay on permanently after her six months with us, but we kept in touch for years after she returned home to get married.

I would have liked to get pregnant again quickly after Simon's birth. I didn't want to have an only child and I was keen to get back to medicine and start a career in Oral Pathology. After trying for a year to get pregnant, I saw a woman gynaecologist who said that my Fallopian tubes were blocked. She cleared them by blowing them through with a mixture of nitrogen and air. Within weeks I was pregnant again.

I started having contractions ten days before I was due and Josh drove me to the maternity hospital. Unfortunately, mine were the Braxton-Hicks type, which are just trial contractions. It was embarrassing. I was a doctor who couldn't tell whether I was in labour or not. I begged the midwife to let me leave that evening, but she said it was against hospital policy and I must stay overnight.

Ten days later my contractions started in earnest. Once again Josh drove me to the maternity hospital, Simon strapped in the back. This time, I insisted on sitting in the car park until my contractions were really strong, before we hurried up to the labour ward. Simon had been invited to a birthday party, so Joshua left to take him there, thinking he would have plenty of time to get back before the baby was born.

Before I could have my pubic hair shaved, or be given the enema that was then obligatory, I went into the second stage of labour and Bernard was soon delivered. There hadn't been time for my consultant to arrive and I much preferred being delivered by a midwife without a gaggle of students in the room.

He was a big baby, eight pounds, with blond, almost white hair and greenish-blue eyes. He cried, looked at me, nursed for a while and fell asleep.

It was a very quick, easy labour and I was soon bored, there in a side room on my own. I tried phoning Josh, but after the party he had taken Simon to the pond in Wimbledon Common to feed the ducks. Finally, Joshua arrived, a tired Simon in his arms. Having looked briefly at his new brother, Simon wandered off across the room. Next moment, there was a sound of splashing water. He had pulled up a stool and used the long lever taps to turn the water full on. He was busy washing his hair, much aggrieved when Joshua towelled him off.

Disposable nappies had now become available. Josh christened Bernard 'Golden Babe' in honour of the brand we used. From then on, he was always 'Babe.'

He and Simon first shared a small nursery – not much bigger than a box-room. When Bernard was six months old we moved them into the bigger third bedroom. The next day, and for the very first time ever, Simon scribbled on the wall of his new bedroom.

'Babe and me thought it was a good idea,' he explained.

A new family saying was born – how to describe a stupid suggestion.

I met Naomi at the Welfare Clinic. We were there to get our babies checked. Bernard was six months old and her Elizabeth was two months younger.

We had much in common. We each had a two-year-old toddler, my Simon and her Dan, as well as a young baby, who still woke for a feed every night.

We neither of us enjoyed being suburban mums. We missed the hustle and bustle of working life, though neither of us wanted to work full time and leave our babies all day with a nanny or in a crèche. Naomi was a lawyer who had been working in a busy practice. She sat on a couple of boring local charity committees and I had my part-time dental practice that I didn't find very exciting either.

On fine days, we met up and took our children for a walk on Wimbledon Common, pushing our *Silver Cross* prams with their tall wheels and bouncy springs. Simon and Dan, in toddler seats clipped on the top, happily prattled to each other as we walked towards the windmill in the centre of the common.

It was gorgeous being out in the fresh air in adult company. We moaned about the time it took to get our toddlers dressed and how our babies always demanded a feed or a nappy change just before we were ready to set out.

It was a sunny autumn afternoon, the leaves a rich medley of green and red and orange. It hadn't rained for days, so the ground was dry underfoot, rather than muddy, as it often was. We went into the café in the centre of the Common and ordered cream teas. After having had two children, we were both plumper than we liked, but the smell of fresh baking was irresistible. The toddlers had fallen asleep on the way, so we had a peaceful half hour discussing the books we snatched a few odd moments to read and about how hard it was to stay on the career ladder, if you took time off to have a family. We avoided talking about what we were going to cook for dinner, potty training or what our cleaners had got up to.

Naomi's baby was stirring, so we got up to walk home. It had turned cold, and we hurried along the path towards Wimbledon Parkside.

As the traffic on Parkside came into view, I noticed a young man on the left of the path standing in some tall bushes to which he had attached cut-outs of Page 3 busty nudes. When I pointed him out to Naomi he unzipped his trousers and began to masturbate.

We were married women with children. Naomi had dealt with flashers and rapists in court. I was a doctor who had worked in a Venereal Diseases clinic and had looked after a male geriatric ward, where the old men had constant problems with their private parts. I should have been able to cope with the sight of a man masturbating in public, but instead I felt terrible, violated.

We hurried towards Parkside and out of the Common. We didn't speak until we crossed the road, and then only to say goodbye. We never went back there. And we didn't consider reporting him to the police. We'd have been ashamed to admit how upset we'd been.

Now I knew why exhibitionism was a crime.

CHAPTER 20

John Dobbie Toyshop

Although Josh was now working full time in our practice in Harley Street and I had my part-time dental practice in Wimbledon, we were heavily overdrawn. We had a large mortgage and when I found I couldn't have my baby at St Margaret's, since I was no longer in their catchment area, I had opted to have my baby in the private wing of Queen Charlotte's Hospital – an expensive option.

The only good toyshop in London that sold sturdy wooden toys, instead of cheap fragile rubbish, was Abbatt's in Wigmore Street. We would go there on Saturday mornings to shop for new toys. Getting two children dressed and loaded into the car and trying to park in Central London was a nightmare. Joshua made toys for the boys and we talked about opening our own toyshop. I would work in my practice in the morning and in the shop in the afternoon, leaving the children with a nanny. The shop would have to be within easy reach of home, so I could get back to breast-feed Bernard.

We approached a couple of estate agents in Wimbledon Village.

'Oh no,' they said. 'Shops almost never change hands in the village. The same shops have been here for years.'

However, two weeks before Christmas, an agent rang to say that a shop had come on the market. It wasn't a good time for us. Bernard was showing no sign of sleeping through the night and the winter of 1962-63 was the coldest for 150 years. The sea turned to ice around Britain – out to half a mile at Herne Bay. The Thames froze right across in places, and there were ice floes in the river at Tower Bridge. We hardly felt like venturing out, let alone look at premises.

But the little bow-fronted shop with multiple small panes of glass was irresistible – just perfect for a toy shop. We borrowed £250 from Joshua's parents and a friend guaranteed a bank loan of another £250. A local carpenter built display shelves with cupboards below and a raised display platform in the window for £250. We planned on spending the other £250 on stock.

We had to think of a name for our shop. Dentists and doctors weren't allowed to advertise so couldn't use our own name. We played with the idea of 'Ye Old Toy Shoppe' and 'The Teddy Bear's Picnic' but then, as Simon called himself 'Dobbie' we thought 'John Dobbie' sounded a good solid name.

It took Joshua two weeks to finish making a train engine on which Simon could scoot, and cost a fortune in wood and other materials – much too expensive to sell at a profit. We had to look for suppliers. We scoured toyshops, turning the toys upside down to find the name of toy manufacturers.

I phoned Escor Toys, a company that made brightly coloured sturdy wooden toys. As I got through, a piercing scream came from my adjoining dental surgery.

'Sorry. I'll phone later,' I managed, before bursting in to see Simon holding his right foot, blood pouring out. My dental chair was tipped back. Simon had managed to press down the pedal and trap his foot in the mechanism. His fourth toe was squashed and split.

How could I have not noticed that Simon had gone into my surgery? If only I hadn't been so engrossed in my phone call. Our cleaner was hanging up the washing.

'Can you stay a bit late and look after Bernard? Simon's squashed his toe. I'll take him up to Casualty.'

I wound a large crepe bandage around a gauze swab, wrapped Simon in his favourite blanket and put him into the car. There was only one hospital I trusted. I drove up to St Margaret's in the centre of London.

Robin Scott was the consultant in Casualty. He'd been in my year at medical school, a bit of a tearaway, much too fond of going to the pub and getting sloshed.

'Hullo, Abby,' he said. 'What have we here?'

'It's my little boy, Simon. He's squashed one of his toes.'

'Just get him registered and then I'll look at him.'

Casualty Sister remembered me. I'd spent time there both as a dental student, as a medical student, and then as an ENT house-man. It was the same sister who'd called me about the patient who swallowed a turkey bone.

'Goodness, your little boy looks just like you. What's your name young man?'

'His name is Simon but he calls himself Dobbie. Somehow he managed to release the back of my dental chair and squash his toe.'

'Dobbie hurt his foot. Naughty Dobbie touched Mummy's chair.'

Robin carefully unwrapped his foot.

'I don't think anything is broken, but pop upstairs for an X-ray just in case.'

It seemed to take forever for the X-ray to be developed. I held it up to the light to see if there was a fracture.

At that moment the radiologist, another of my contemporaries, came out.

'Thought I recognised the name. How are you Abby?'

He held up the X-ray for me to see.

'I don't see any evidence of a fracture, but you know what they call a radiologist who examines X-rays by just holding them up to the light as you just did, instead of using a viewing box?'

'OK. Tell me.'

'The defendant.'

It was funny I suppose, but I was anxious to get back home to make sure Bernard was alright. It was nearly time for a feed. My breasts were aching already.

Back in Casualty, Robin Scott dressed Simon's foot.

'I don't think it's worth sewing it up. It will only upset him. At his age, it will heal perfectly well on its own. What are you up to now, Abby?'

'I have a part-time dental practice at home.'

I didn't mention that Joshua and I were starting a toyshop. I felt guilty enough about not practising medicine.

'Well, just keep it clean and dry,' Robin said, reaching behind him for a strawberry lollipop.

'I'm not allowed,' a little voice said.

Tears came to my eyes.

'Just this once,' I said. 'Since you're a wounded soldier.'

Simon's toe healed well, though it is still odd-looking.

We opened our toyshop on Monday April 1st, 1963 two weeks before Easter. Simon was 2½ and Bernard 6 months old. We had taken on a sparky auburn-haired manageress sent by the employment agency three doors away from our shop. I was still working mornings in my dental practice and went to the shop in the afternoon.

When I was pregnant, I read Dr Spock and anything else I could find about how to look after a baby. Now I read all the Women's Pages in the newspapers. I was particularly impressed with Moira Keenan's page in the Sunday Times – sensible and down to earth – so I wrote to her saying that we'd opened an educational toyshop in Wimbledon, with good old fashioned wooden toys, books and children's furniture. She phoned to ask if she could come down the next day.

On Easter Sunday, her piece about John Dobbie appeared in the Sunday Times and then we were written up in other newspapers and the glossy magazines. We were getting well known. Most articles on toys mentioned John Dobbie.

At first, we would rush to order more of the toys they featured, but we soon realised it was a mistake. The articles drew people to our shop but they didn't necessarily buy what had been written about.

We gradually extended our range and stocked children's books, drawing and painting materials and little toys suitable to be given away at birthday parties, but gave up selling children's furniture. I looked after ordering and publicity while Joshua, who was the artistic one, arranged the shelves and window displays. There was a competition for the best window in Wimbledon Village and Josh won with a stunning display of toy sailboats in a deep blue sea.

I was worried when an article in the Daily Mail about John Dobbie mentioned my real name and that I was a doctor – a *no-no*. I contacted my insurance agency, The Medical Protection Society.

'You'll need to write a letter to the editor stating that no patients coming to see you as a result of reading the article will be accepted for treatment,' I was told – as if anyone would come to our toyshop and ask for my medical opinion! But after that I was very careful to impress upon journalists that they must not say that I was a doctor or that we were dentists.

A pushy customer tried to persuade one of our assistants to allow her to take away toys she would pay for later.

'You know,' she said, 'Mrs Dobbie is a very good friend of mine.'

We opened late on Friday nights in the weeks before Christmas and had loyal customers who came year after year. A couple buying Christmas presents for their five children were especially welcome and became our best and oldest friends. One film star's wife was a regular shopper and always chose whatever was new and exciting, so making us change our window display every time she came. She always chose the toys that were exclusive and made by craftsmen who took a long time to re-supply us.

That first Christmas the BBC asked us to take part in a program about toys. The crew set up their lights in our little bow-fronted shop and we stood in front of our shelves crammed with well-made toys that wouldn't be opened for Christmas and broken by Boxing Day.

A woman we couldn't make out behind the arc-lights asked us a series of questions about the difference between the sort of toys we sold and those available in most toy shops. They also interviewed Paul and Marjorie Abbatt of Abbatt Toys in Wigmore Street and Mr Newmark, manager of Galt toys in Carnaby Street.

When the program aired we looked fine in our shop. Both in our early 30s the background seemed quite appropriate. The manager of Galt's, only a decade older than us also looked OK standing in his shop but they had photographed the elderly Abbatts sitting in the large wooden climbing frame that dominated their ground floor. They looked ridiculous. That wasn't all. It seemed as if we were interviewed by the famous screen personality, Kenneth Hart, who we had never met. His voice had been patched in.

The worst thing was that it was all a con to make the five of us look silly. The BBC had got together a group of children from Dr Barnado's and provided them with a mixture of bright garish plastic toys as well as some unpainted wooden toys. Mostly the children grabbed the plastic toys and the voice-over pointed out how wrong we were. We never had the opportunity to tell them to come back to the children a month later and see which toys they were playing with. Most of the plastic toys would have been reduced to coloured scraps.

A neighbour, who was a graphic designer, had designed our letter heading. *John Dobbie, Good Toys and Children's Furniture* was emblazoned along the top in scarlet and the logo for *John Dobbie* was a sturdy carthorse.

We went on being written up in newspapers and magazines. Sam, who'd first persuaded me to study dentistry, was now an established photographer. He took photos of our children playing with our toys, and journalists were happy to use them to illustrate their articles

Wednesday was half-day closing in Wimbledon. As the shop was closed, it was our opportunity to visit toy wholesalers to buy cheap little toys for going home party presents. If you wanted to know what the owner was like, you could tell by the response of the person cleaning the steps as you went in. Whether they smiled or if they looked as if they would like to bite your ankles, you could predict the kind of boss there.

During the school holidays, if our au-pair was at her English class, we had to take the children with us. The owners knew what type of shop John Dobbie was, specialising in sturdy well-made toys. They would proudly point to a new range.

'This is just right for John Dobbie,' they would say, adding nervously 'but don't let the children touch.'

Obviously too fragile for us. Ours was an open-plan shop with parents and children free to wander around and touch the toys.

I was invited to join the Design Centre Committee on Toys which met in their showroom in Haymarket – the only member with young children. I would often refuse to give our label to an obviously fragile toy that the others wanted to include because it was beautiful and well-crafted. I hated that for most people the word associated with 'toy' is 'broken'.

I gave talks to mother's groups on the importance of toys in the education of young children and how they learned skills playing with good sturdy toys.

We soon outgrew our little bow-fronted shop and when a small supermarket in the main street of Wimbledon village closed down, we took on the lease.

Terence Conran had opened his *Habitat* shop in 1964 and London was full of exciting modern designs and graphics. Wanting a more exciting image, I wrote to him, asking if he would design our new shop. He assigned Rodney Fitch to our project.

We now had a large open-plan shop with shelves and cupboards made of natural pine. It was unusual to see a self-service toyshop and our customers loved it. Often women would just come in for a look around and to have a chat. On Saturdays, we had our children in the shop and grandparents would grab one of them of a suitable age and ask what toys he or she liked. Once our children are grown we forget which toys are appropriate at their various stages. We had a returns policy modelled on Marks and Spencer – their money returned if the toy was unsuitable or unwanted and in new condition. The same went for the few toys that broke within days. We would immediately withdraw our whole stock of that product from the shop, even if we couldn't ourselves return them to the manufacturer or wholesaler. We didn't want to sell toys that broke easily.

The late Colin Fulcher *(Barney Bubbles)* designed some incredible graphics for us. Now *John Dobbie* was a prancing knight and our paper bags were printed with large two-coloured, slightly sinister, butterflies. Our second shop in Putney High Street, near Putney Bridge, was again designed by the Conran Group. The shop had a ground floor, mezzanine and first floor, with offices above. When it was finally unveiled, this time in Ferrari mustard and silver, it was one of our proudest moments.

I had carried on with my part-time dental practice to begin with, going to John Dobbie in the afternoon, but a really difficult extraction finally made me decide to give up.

The children had been up all night with bad coughs and I was pretty exhausted before I began. Mrs Thomas was very stoic. I had given her enough local anaesthetic for her not to feel any pain, but my wrist was aching from trying to get her recalcitrant molar out. It finally gave up fighting and came out, but I was shattered. I still had to have a shower and go to John Dobbie.

Joshua was delighted not to have patients in our living room any more – though he was at our practice in Harley Street and never saw them.

I referred my patients to a nearby dentist who was delighted to have a fresh influx of well-trained subjects and we sold the equipment without difficulty.

Dentistry had always been an effort for me, even though I had learned to be a perfectionist. It was a great relief to give up.

For two weeks in the summers of 1962 and in 1963, the year we opened John Dobbie, we hired a large house by the sea in Cornwall, *The Captain's View* with William and his family.

William and I had stayed friends all through our training in dental school. William became a partner in a practice in Harley Street, Joshua was now working full time in our practice just up the road from William.

Josh and William had become firm friends as had Williams' wife, Susie, and I. We often had dinner together either at each other's houses or at a restaurant and went to the theatre together. When we saw the Greek comedy, Lysistrata by Aristophanes together, Susie and I were both pregnant, me with my first child, Simon, and her with her second. At the same moment we turned to each other, patted our bulging bellies and told our babies not to listen to the suggestive jokes.

The families visited each other from time to time during the year, while it became a tradition for us to go to William and Susie's for Christmas lunch. I and one or more of the other parents would fall asleep after lunch, while the children – at first one of mine and two of theirs – retired to their playroom and vanished. Susie's mother was living with them and William's mother came over on Christmas day and the grandmothers kept a wary eye out while we slept on.

The Captain's View was ideal for us. Away from the main town and only a few hundred yards from the cliff top and a stairway leading down to the sea, it had a large walled garden with a gate fastening too high for the children to reach. There was a large fully stocked kitchen and a large dining-cum-living room. On the first floor and spread along a narrow corridor where three double bedrooms, with a bathroom and separate toilet at each end.

Susie and I agreed to cook dinner on alternate nights and that we'd each sort out our own family's breakfast and lunch, but we got so well and so enjoyed each other's company that after the first few days we cooked dinner together.

The children slept together but each family had its own bathroom. Their little boy preferred ours.

'Abby's is better,' he proclaimed, 'but actually they're both the same.'

Another family saying in the making.

We took lots of cliff walks but I always had to hold on to Joshua. I could manage the walk, but I have no head for heights and needed the reassurance of Joshua's hand holding mine if we ventured too near the edge.

We were going to take a third summer holiday together but by then John Dobbie was taking a lot of effort and we felt we couldn't get away, though the families went on meeting throughout the year and of course for Christmas lunch.

CHAPTER 21

Fireworks

Like other toyshops at that time, John Dobbie sold fireworks for Guy Fawkes' day on November 5th. Whatever we didn't sell, we let off at our firework party. We stood well away from where Joshua had the fireworks safely stored in a stout wooden box and all went smoothly until he lit the Catherine Wheels and one went whizzing off sideways. Simon screamed and we thought it was with excitement, but then his screams turned into bitter sobs and he collapsed onto the ground holding his right Wellington boot. When I pulled off his boot there was a hole in his sock surrounded by burnt fabric. The firework's flight had ended inside Simon's boot, singeing his sock and burning the flesh underneath.

We rushed home and I bathed the wound as gently as I could with antiseptic, covering it with sterile gauze.

I worried whether I should take Simon to hospital but I could imagine what a nightmare Casualty would be like on Guy Fawkes' night. No-one would bother grafting such a small area and I had dressed it just as they would have done.

We never sold fireworks again and that was the last firework party we went to. The raw area healed over, but he still has a coin shaped scar on his right ankle.

Simon's wars were not over. Joshua designed a wooden sandbox for John Dobbie and we took one home. In the shape of a short wide boat, it measured 1 x 1.5 metres. Its mast was 1.5m tall and the cross dowels 20 cm apart, so that a child could easily climb it. Simon and Bernard sat for hours tipping sand through plastic sieves, in and out of buckets,

Simon loved climbing the mast, pretending to be a pirate. He loved climbing anything. When I took him to a shoe shop, as soon as I took my eye off him, he would be up one of those tall ladders on wheels all the shoe shops had.

'Be careful. He'll fall,' the worried assistant would say.

'Don't worry. He's like a monkey,' I'd reply. 'He never falls.'

The devil was listening. One sunny April day our Italian au pair rang me at John Dobbie.

'Come quickly, Mrs Waterman. Simon's fallen off the sand boat and he's hurt his head.'

A deathly pale Simon lay absolutely still on the sofa. For one awful moment, I thought he was dead, but then I saw his chest move. His right ear was full of bloody fluid. I tried to tell myself I was mistaken, and that I must look more carefully. Perhaps he'd torn his ear but I knew. I knew I was looking at cerebro-spinal fluid, and that he had fractured his skull.

'I'll have to take him to hospital. Please keep an eye on the baby until Joshua comes home.'

Casualty Sister at St Margaret's greeted me.

'What's happened, Dr Waterman? Your little boy in the wars again?'

'He was climbing. I think he has a skull fracture.'

The casualty registrar arranged an immediate X-ray.

'You're right, Abby. He's got a hairline fracture in his right temporal bone. I'll get him admitted. We'll start him on sulphonamides straight away.'

Simon was put to bed in a side room in the children's ward and I stayed the night sitting in a chair by his bedside. He woke around 2am confused and upset. I gathered him up in my arms and sat back with him in my arms. It made me feel much better to be holding him.

A nurse hurried in.

'You shouldn't be having out him of bed, mother, not with a skull fracture.'

I laid him gently back in bed.

On his round next day, the Professor of Paediatrics said Simon could go home. He was subdued for a day or two, but not apparently affected by his short stay in hospital.

Six weeks later the devil struck again. Now he was four, Simon could go to the toilet on his own, leaving me to pull the handle.

'Finished,' he called out. 'All done, Mummy.'

The water in the toilet bowl was bright red. I desperately tried to think of an explanation, other than that Simon was peeing blood. Could I have started a period and forgot to pull the handle? A quick inspection of my underwear dispelled that explanation. I flushed the toilet, and anxiously waited until he needed to pee again. There was no doubt. He was peeing blood. He had been a bit off colour for a day or two, as had Bernard. I needed to get them looked at.

Peter, a friend from St Margaret's, was now a consultant at the local teaching hospital, St Aidan's.

'I'm not sure what's going on. I'll admit them both overnight,' he said. 'There's an extra bed in the side room so you can stay the night. We'll take some blood and have a look at their urine.'

Next day Peter's face was serious.

'I'm sure Bernard's fine, it's just a mild upper respiratory infection, but as you suspected, Simon's got acute glomerulonephritis. I'll have him transferred to the paediatric ward.'

In 1964, it was taught that children who developed glomerulonephritis, which was an excessive immune reaction to a previous streptococcal infection such as a sore throat, were almost always left with kidney damage, leading later to kidney failure and early death.

When I arrived to see Simon in the main children's ward, a urine flask full of bloodstained urine was sitting on his bedside table.

The registrar and his houseman came to examine him.

'It's definitely glomerulonephritis, mother. But I wouldn't go looking up the literature. It will only confuse you.'

I was livid. Mother, indeed! The registrar knew I was a doctor and I was sure my qualifications were as good as his.

Luckily, I ignored his advice. In the medical school library, I found a recent paper stating that the outcome of acute glomerulonephritis was much better than had been previously thought. Most children recovered completely.

Next morning, I asked the houseman to arrange for me to see the consultant and he said I could see her when she came to the ward after her afternoon clinic. I waited and waited. Finally, at 6.30pm he came to the ward for his evening round. He was alone.

'Is your consultant coming over?'

'No. She's gone for the day. I've got more important things to do than make appointments for mothers to see her.'

I was distraught. The paper I had looked at was optimistic about the children in the study, but what about my Simon?

Next morning, I drove up to St Margaret's and went to see the Professor of Paediatrics.

'Of course, my dear. Just bring him up and we'll admit him. Don't worry. We'll look after your little boy.'

I drove straight back to St Aidan's and got Simon dressed.

'You'll have to sign a release form. It's your son's health you're playing with.'

I signed and left.

It was all so different at St Margaret's. The registrar came to see me as soon as Simon was settled in and he showed me the results of Simon's tests as they came through. There was no definitive treatment for Simon's condition, just bed rest, but the treatment I received as a mother was fantastic.

Simon was discharged after a week with no apparent after-effects.

I had to have another tubal insufflation before I became pregnant again. After two boys, I was hoping for a girl. The boys had slept in carry cots, but for my third baby I borrowed Susie's wicker cradle and spent hours trimming it with lace and making a cover and matching pillowcases. Pre-natal sexing was not yet available, but I could hope.

I started having labour pains in the early hours of the first day of spring and Joshua drove me and the boys to the maternity clinic in Welbeck Street. The room was like a bedroom in a country cottage, with a blazing coal fire, deep carpets and a soft feather bed. Josh took the boys off to an all-night cafe in Covent Garden for breakfast. The woman counter assistant carefully poured hot water over two teaspoons before putting them on the saucers.

'Just to sterilise them, sir. We need to make sure the kids don't catch anything,' she said – as if just pouring hot water over the spoons would do anything other than moisten the surface dirt.

My contractions stopped quite soon so, when the obstetrician did his morning round, he ruptured my membranes. Labour still didn't start, but they starved me all day in case I had to have an emergency caesarean section. I was still not in labour when the obstetrician called that evening, but soon after he left, my contractions started and Louise was born. It was wonderful to have a little girl. She was small, only six and a half pounds. I inspected her carefully from top to toe, admiring her lovely shell-like hands, shiny black hair and blue eyes.

'They'll change,' the midwife said. But they never did.

The nursing home was much less strict than St Margaret's. In the evening, I'd hide Louise under the bedclothes so the nurses wouldn't see they had forgotten to take her back to the nursery. There was none of this feeding by the clock. I fed her when she cried, but she slept a lot. She was just like a little hot water bottle beside me.

Louise was a gorgeous toddler, but she became one of those children who are constantly whining. Joshua used to tease her about it.

'Good *moaning*,' he'd say. Fortunately, she grew out of it. Perhaps she had stomach aches or something.

It was half term so the boys were at home. Simon was now seven, Bernard was five and Louise still a baby. When I got home from John Dobbie, Simon was lying on the sofa, pale and miserable.

'He hasn't wanted any lunch and now he says he has a belly ache,' our au-pair said.

'Show me where it hurts.'

'It's round my belly button.'

I felt his tummy. He flinched when I lifted my hand. My heart sank. Rebound tenderness is a classic sign of appendicitis.

'When did he have something to eat?' I asked.

'That's the trouble. He won't eat or drink anything.'

'Thank heaven for that. Give the children their tea and I'll take Simon up to St Margaret's. I think it's appendicitis. If I'm right, he'll need an operation as soon as possible.'

Once again, I drove Simon up to Casualty. The same Casualty Sister was on duty.

'Hullo, Abby, my dear. Hasn't your little boy grown? What's it this time?'

'I'm pretty sure it's appendicitis.'

Tony Marshland, another of my contemporaries, his red hair now turning silver at the temples, kissed my cheek.

'Good to see you, Abby? Sister tells me you think your little boy has appendicitis.'

After a brief examination, he looked up.

'I take it, he hasn't eaten.'

'Nothing since early morning.'

'Good, we'll get him up to surgery as soon as there's a theatre free.'

As I waited outside the operating theatre, all the possible dangers ran through my head, that Simon's appendix might have burst and so he might already have life-threatening peritonitis or that he might be sensitive to the anaesthetic and die on the table.

It seemed hours before Tony came out and pulled down his mask. He looked serious and I was sure the news was bad. Then he smiled and waved a formalin-filled jar at me.

'Just look at this, Abby,' he said.

Simon's swollen appendix looked like a bright red sausage, instead of like the pale worm it should have resembled.

'Lucky you brought him straight in. It was just about to burst.'

I stretched up to give Tony a kiss.

'Now then, you're making me all embarrassed. Such a simple operation. I'm sure you could have done it yourself. Get along now and give Joshua my best. I'm due for a check-up with him next week.'

Like so many of the staff at St Margaret's, Tony had his teeth looked after by Joshua at our practice in Harley Street.

A while after Simon fractured his skull, we noticed that he turned his head to hear. It didn't seem to worry him, but I felt his hearing should be assessed. If he had measurable deafness, we could ask that he sit near the front in class.

By now, the consultants I had worked for in the ENT department in 1959 had retired or moved elsewhere. Again, it was someone from my student year who was the consultant on duty.

I'd always liked David, but with his fair skin and straw-blond hair, he looked more like a schoolboy than a consultant.

He showed me Simon's hearing test.

'I think we should operate. I'm sure I can improve his hearing.'

My heart sank. Could I trust David? I was pregnant with Jane and easily got weepy.

'May I think about it and discuss it with Joshua?' I said, wiping away a tear.

We felt we had no alternative but to agree and Simon was again admitted to hospital.

The following day a beaming David told us that Simon's fall had dislocated the tiny bones in his ear, and that he had put in a plastic grommet.

'You'll notice the difference,' he said.

And we did, though Simon still occasionally turns his head to hear better.

I was 32 weeks pregnant and feeling very wobbly as we kissed Simon goodbye, left the children's ward and went towards the lift. I felt liquid run down my leg.

'Oh God,' I said. 'My waters have broken.'

We crossed over to the maternity wing.

'Look, Abby, you're not in labour,' the obstetric registrar said. 'It would be best if we didn't admit you. With your membranes ruptured, you're better off resting at home. Much less risk of infection. Let's see if we can't get this baby of yours a bit more mature.'

When we got home I went to bed and stayed there, except to go to the loo – no way was I going to use a bedpan. Our au pair was wonderful. She treated me as if I were made of china and very delicate. I managed to get to 34 weeks before I went into labour. I phoned for an ambulance.

Memories of the last time I was in an ambulance being taken to the fever hospital crowded in.

'How about putting on the siren?' I asked.

'Sorry, Miss. We're only allowed to use the siren in an emergency.'

'Isn't being in labour an emergency?'

'It might be if the baby was coming right away, but it isn't – or is it?'

He sounded worried.

'No, it's OK, but it's my fourth, so it could be quite quick.'

I felt the driver speed up.

By the time we drew in at the ambulance bay, my contractions were coming fast. Joshua met me in the labour ward.

I called the midwife.

'It's getting really painful. Could I have some Pethidine or even gas and air?'

'Sorry. Not safe with a premature baby.'

'At least I won't need an episiotomy.'

Having an episiotomy meant that sitting would be agony until the stitches came out.

'You know it's especially important to have an episiotomy with a premature baby, Dr Waterman. We need to make sure your baby's head isn't damaged on the way out. Your consultant is on his way.'

The contractions grew stronger and more frequent. I heard, rather than felt, the crunching sound as the midwife made the cut in my perineum.

I started to push.

'Take it easy now. Pant, don't push. We want a nice gentle birth.'

My baby slithered out and immediately began to cry.

'She's a beautiful little girl, 4½ lbs,' the midwife said. 'A good size, considering she's only 34 weeks. We'll take her straight down to the premature baby unit. You have a rest and later on you can go and see her.'

I wanted to hold her but I only caught a glimpse of her dark hair as the midwife handed her over to the paediatricians.

Mr Bateman, my consultant, had missed the birth but arrived in time to sew up my episiotomy incision.

I had a cup of strong sweet tea and then I was moved to a side room on the postnatal ward. Joshua went back to work and I fell asleep. When I awoke, I rang the bell.

'Can I go down and see my baby now?'

'Sorry. The prem unit is very busy just now. There's some emergency or other.'

I asked again in one hour, then I asked again two hours later. I got the same answer.

Around five o'clock, the Professor of Paediatrics, came in. I was surprised to see him without his usual entourage of junior doctors and medical students.

'Can I go and see my baby now?'

He looked grave.

'I think you should get your husband to come back, Abby. I'm afraid your baby's not at all well. She has Respiratory Disease of the Newborn.'

Being six weeks early, she hadn't produced enough of the detergent, surfactant, to enable her lungs to expand properly. It was a virtual death sentence in 1967.

'Is she still alive? Can I see her?'

'We're doing all we can. Better not go down now.'

Joshua had left the children with our au pair. He tried to console me.

'We have three beautiful children. Think about them.'

I couldn't. I wanted my baby.

I slept in fits and starts. When Night Sister did her last round next morning at 6am, I asked once again if I could see my baby.

'I'll ring the premature baby unit.'

She came back smiling.

'You can go down now. She's holding her own.'

Jane looked tiny in her incubator, with her funny little hat and oversize bootees. She seemed to have tubes coming out everywhere. I could see her heart beating through her ribcage as she panted away, desperately trying to get in enough air.

'You're lucky you had your baby here,' the sister said. 'Your baby's distress was picked up really quickly. She was given 100% oxygen at once.'

St Margaret's was at the forefront of research into her condition. Such a high concentration of oxygen was known to cause blindness in babies, but those with unexpanded lungs could only get in a percentage, so for them it was safe and lifesaving.

'I'm afraid you can't hold her yet.'

I had breast fed the others, and I asked if I'd be able to do the same for Jane.

'She's too immature to suckle properly, but if you express your milk we'll give it to her via her nasogastric tube. I'll give you some sterile bottles to take home when you are discharged.'

Josh brought the children to the hospital next day to meet their new sister. As they stood peering into her incubator they looked like giants to me.

'Do they hurt, all those tubes?' Simon asked.

'I don't think so,' I said.

While Jane remained at St Margaret's, I was discharged after three days. Josh left home extra early each morning so he could drop in a bottle of my breast milk on his way to work.

We drove up every other evening to see Jane and soon I was

allowed to breast feed her. Babies all lose weight after they are born, and Jane was no exception, but she soon started to gain it back again. After two weeks, the paediatric registrar came over.

'She's now regained her birth weight and seeing it's you, Abby, we'll let you take her home today.'

Jane was so tiny that I bathed her in a washbasin. Our other three children watched fascinated.

'Look,' I said. 'Her bottom's only the size of an apple.'

Simon rushed away and returned proudly with a Cox's Orange Pippin and a Bramley.

'A Bramley, Mum, don't you think?'

Then came our first family death. My mother had a massive stroke and had been in hospital virtually a vegetable for months. My sister Rebecca believed that women didn't have to go to funerals and stayed home, Hannah lived in on a kibbutz in Israel and couldn't come to the funeral and my father was in hospital recovering from an emergency hernia repair. The saddest thing about my mother's death was that I was the only one of my mother's three daughters to attend her funeral.

The mortician asked me if I wanted to see her before he closed her coffin. I was dry-eyed as I kissed her cold cheek but getting into the funeral car beside my mother's best friend, with no other members of our immediate family present, reduced me to floods of tears. It was unbearably sad that I was the only member of her family there. Rebecca, who she adored, hadn't bothered to come.

My father coped quite well after my mother's death. He stayed with us for three months and then said he'd prefer to go back to his flat and friends in Petticoat Lane, where he still lived.

He rang me to say that he was being admitted to the London Hospital for some tests, but not to worry, he was sure it was just a bit of indigestion.

I thought that he might have a coronary problem, since angina can be mistaken for indigestion, and arranged to see the houseman looking after him.

'I'm sorry, Dr Waterman,' he said, showing me my dad's barium swallow. 'As you see, his cancer is at the oesophageal-gastric junction and has pretty well closed off his oesophagus. We're hoping to take him to theatre tomorrow and put in a stent, but the outlook is pretty awful. He must have been living on slops.'

'Why didn't you tell me, Dad?'

'Don't cry, Abby. They're going to operate tomorrow and make me better.'

I didn't have the heart to tell him how dreadful his outlook was. I knew how much pain he was likely to suffer and that the stent was only a temporary measure.

I was in tears but relieved when the hospital phoned to say that my Dad had died peacefully in his sleep. Neither he nor I knew he had a heart problem, but he'd had a massive coronary and avoided a slow painful death from stomach cancer.

By now, Rebecca had died of a stroke and Hannah had suffered a fatal heart attack. I had Josh and the children, but I still felt very alone.

When I went to the hospital to collect his death certificate, I was handed the letter he'd written me the day before he died.

My darling Abby

I am writing this on a very sick bed. Yesterday Mr. Jones came to see me and said the operation would take place tomorrow . . .

He went on to tell me in detail how to deal with the contents of his flat.

> *Don't be afraid, Darling, to ask me anything. Between you and me, Darling, I think I have come to the end of my life. God bless.*

He had never called me 'Darling' when he was alive and I never knew how much he loved me until I read his last letter.

CHAPTER 22

Facing Bankruptcy

I came into our John Dobbie shop in Putney to find our book-keeper in tears.

'You'll lose your house and everything,' she sobbed. 'You've guaranteed your overdraft yourselves and it's enormous. You'll have to try to borrow from your parents or someone or you'll end up being bankrupt and disgraced.'

We realised we'd have to sell our house and buy a cheaper one. A developer had built some terrace houses in Wimbledon Village and their asking price was less than the value of our present house. It still wouldn't be enough. We'd have to get a bigger mortgage, but the company we were with refused to increase it.

We next tried a mortgage company specialising in mortgages for doctors. Foolishly, I let slip that we needed a bigger mortgage to release funds to cover the debts on John Dobbie.

'We don't lend money to be used for frivolous purposes,' he said, all prissy. 'We expect our clients to behave responsibly and use our advances to improve their property value.'

I didn't tell the next company why we were applying and they gave us a mortgage without question. I wasn't sorry to move. Our new house was nearer to John Dobbie and the development had a covered communal swimming pool that the children loved.

Although our immediate financial troubles were now over, Jane's squint made me decide it was time to sell our toyshops.

I tried keeping her hair back with clips and slides but she always had a lock of hair falling over one eye. Perhaps that was why she developed a squint. I took her to the eye department at St Margaret's.

'Hullo, Abby. How are you? What are you up to these days?' the ophthalmic surgeon asked.

'We have four children now. Jane's the youngest. She's just turned five. Simon is 12, Bernard is 10 and Louise is 6.'

'You have your hands full, I see.'

I left it at that. I was ashamed to admit that I was using my long training first as a dental surgeon and then as a doctor to run a couple of toyshops.

'She's not suitable for a patch or corrective eye exercises. I'm afraid it's surgery. I have a list next Wednesday and I can put your little girl on it.'

I made sure Jane had nothing to eat when I took her up to the theatre waiting room. She was second on the list, so I didn't have long to wait until she was called. Another mother was waiting.

'My friend's little boy needed to have his stick-out ears pinned back,' she said. 'He died under the anaesthetic. Didn't have a thing wrong with him. They should have sued the hospital.'

Just what I didn't need to hear. I already felt bad about not getting Jane treated earlier, when maybe she wouldn't have needed surgery. And I knew perfectly well that patients died under general anaesthesia.

I left the waiting room and lingered in the ladies' toilet. Luckily a squint repair doesn't take long and soon Jane was wheeled out, already coming round.

The shame of not using my qualifications persisted. Even though we were no longer badly overdrawn, we weren't making any money with our second shop in Putney. We had initially been misled by the fact that we opened two months before Christmas, a time when toyshops do their maximum business. The rest of the year was very slack. Even in January we had customers saying, 'You'll have to ask Father Christmas'. But we needed them to buy toys all the year round, as did our wealthier Wimbledon customers.

We sold the lease of our Putney shop in an attractive property deal and a year later we sold our Wimbledon shop to a couple who already had a toyshop similar to ours in Bristol.

It wasn't the last problem with Jane's eyes. I came home to see her huddled in the corner of the sofa, a duvet pulled tight around her shoulders.

'How are you feeling? Is your cold no better?' I asked.

'My eyes ache and my nose is all stuffed up.'

'Oh my God,' I said. 'How long has your left eye been swollen like that?'

I assumed the worst. One-sided eye protrusion could mean a retinoblastoma, a malignant eye tumour.

I phoned our GP.

'Abby Waterman here. Could you come and see Jane? I'm very worried about her. She has unilateral exophthalmos.'

'I'm just on my way to the theatre. You sure it can't wait until my surgery tomorrow?'

'Please come. I'm beside myself with worry.'

He was in evening dress. After examining her eyes with an ophthalmoscope, he looked in her throat and felt for enlarged glands in her neck.

'It's not what you think. It isn't a retinoblastoma. She's just got a bad cold and if you look carefully both eyes are a bit swollen.'

'I feel such an idiot.'

'Don't worry, Abby. I might have panicked if it was our little one. The car's parked just outside. If I speed a bit, we should be able to get to the theatre in time. If I'm stopped, I can always say I've been called out to an urgent case.'

One Sunday our neighbour rang our door bell. She put in perspective all we'd been taught about children with lice coming from dirty homes.

She was wearing a white polo-necked sweat shirt and tight cream jodhpurs, even though it was her daughter who went riding. Very county.

'I'm afraid we have a little problem in our house. I'm awfully sorry.'

She always pronounced a house a 'hice'. Our two daughters had endless fun asking whether we would buy them a 'hice' when they got married.

'They say my Joanna has lice.'

She pulled a nearly used-up tube of shampoo out of her back pocket.

'I've got some of the special shampoo the school nurse recommended. Not much left, I'm afraid.'

I took the proffered tube, murmured something containing a four-letter word and slammed the door. I called Louise and Jane down, combed first one head and then the other. Each time the comb was alive with small wriggling insects crawling over the teeth. I washed the combs under boiling water and set about shampooing their hair. Being a Sunday before Sunday opening was allowed, no chemist shops were open so I had to make do with one wash with the medicated shampoo for each of them and lots of combing.

Next morning, I was outside the local chemist when he pulled up the blinds.

With some embarrassment, I asked for anti-louse shampoo.

'For yourself, madam?' he asked.

'No, for my daughters,' I growled. 'Better have a couple of tooth combs while I'm about it.'

I shampooed the girls' hair again when they got home from school.

'Everyone at school's got lice,' Louise said with glee.

'It was lovely not being itchy today,' Jane said.

'Why didn't you tell me?'

'Everyone has itchy hair in my class,' Louise said.

I washed their hair every day for a week until we left for a Whitsun holiday at Ventnor on the Isle of Wight.

When we got back Bernard said his neck was itchy. When I looked, he had a bright red rash and his hair was crawling with lice. I said everyone needed to be shampooed with the medicated shampoo, even though by this time the girls were clear. To my horror, pulling a toothcomb through my own hair also yielded a crop of lice. My husband, Joshua, and elder son, Simon, had escaped, but I insisted they used the shampoo too, just to be sure.

When the holiday photos were developed, poor Bernard was

scratching in every one of them. It had never occurred to me that boys could be lousy too.

For years, we spent our summer holidays at the Camden Hurst, a large seafront hotel at MilfordonSea. With lots of activities for children, it was also very comfortable for adults.

We hated the cramped apartments that replaced it when it closed, but we fancied the idea of a weekend retreat and we still had the money from selling John Dobbie.

The builder of some small terraced houses at the edge of the village had gone bankrupt two years before, leaving the houses standing empty. We bought one of them at a knockdown price.

We drove there most Friday evenings and, with the assistance of our four children, lugged boxes of provisions and homework from the parking area twenty yards away.

Although the beach was in walking distance, it was too far to walk there with all our paraphernalia. We would drive to the car-park on the cliff-top and climb down to the beach in relays, lumbered with deckchairs, books, towels, buckets and spades. We'd often see the same elderly couple drive in, look at the sea through binoculars, get out their thermos flask and packed lunch, have a quick snooze and drive off without leaving the car once. It was difficult to stop the children sneaking up and knocking on the car windows to wake them up.

The beach was rocky and the water cold to freezing, so I rarely ventured in. However, at Christmas it became a ritual for us to paddle in the shallows in thick coats, scarves, gloves and wellies.

At the other end of the village, there was a small canal teeming with crabs. Bacon rinds tied to four lengths of string and four buckets of water to collect them in, allowed Josh and me to read peacefully all morning. We were interrupted only when the competition to collect the most crabs got too heated. When we tipped the crabs back, though their dignity might be hurt, and their appetites for bacon unassuaged, at least they didn't have hooks stuck in their jaws.

The shale beach at Kimmeridge Bay, a short drive away, was a collector's delight with fossils everywhere. The little rock pools were full of sea creatures and the children were happily exploring the shallows when Louise ran out screaming. Fierce red wheals appeared along her side and round to her back. There was a warning to be careful of incoming tides, but nothing about jellyfish. Anti-histamine cream helped, but it took hours for the wheals to vanish completely.

Our tribulations that day weren't over. When we got back to Milford – and tea, buttered crumpets and jam – we set off through the nearby building site to pick sloes from the stand of spiny Blackthorn trees, left standing when the site was originally cleared.

To make sloe gin, you wash and nick the bluish-purple sloes, pack them into a large jar, smother them with sugar and top them up with neat gin. 4-6 weeks later you have a liqueur that tastes innocent but is seriously wicked.

We didn't get to the sloe trees that day. Our accident-prone elder son, Simon, fell into a small pit and cut his knee so badly it needed stitches. It was either four hours in A&E or me revisiting my surgical skills. We always kept a suture kit in our first aid box, as well as a syringe and a tube of local anaesthetic.

'I can try to make your knee numb but I'd have to inject your skin in several places, or I can just sew it up. Three or four stitches at the most.'

'If you let me watch Dr Who.'

'It's a deal.'

I made short work of sewing up his knee and then it was Smarties all round.

Professor Richard Simmons kept me waiting, as I knew he would. It was one of his ploys to get me off balance. At ten minutes past ten he ushered out a young woman in a white dental coat, her eyes red and swollen. She looked away as she shuffled past me.

'These women dental students,' he said, holding open the door to his office. 'No stamina, but we're obliged to accept them. Come on in, Abby. Looking younger than ever, I see. What are you now, forty-five, forty-six?'

Male chauvinist prick, I thought. But I wanted a job and St Olave's had the biggest Oral Pathology department in the country.

'Forty-two,' I said between clenched teeth.

'Ah, yes. That would be about right.'

Balding head and horn-rimmed glasses, he looked prematurely aged. Like me, he had studied dentistry and then medicine. He was two or three years older than me, but as a dental student at St Margaret's he'd been a year behind me. For the past year, he'd been Professor of Oral Pathology at St Olave's. It was my bad luck not to have sold our John Dobbie toyshops a year earlier.

I first met his predecessor at my finals viva in pathology. I'd done well, got a distinction. He'd told me to come and see him if I wanted to specialise in Oral Pathology, but I was too late. He retired the year before, and it was Richard I had to deal with.

'If it's a job you want, Abby, I'm afraid I'd have to say "No", he said, not at all sorry. 'A married woman with four children and no expertise? I run a very tight research group here and Abby, you really have nothing to offer. I suggest you look in the jobs page of the British Dental Journal and see if anyone is offering re-training. I'm sure you understand.'

I said 'Yes. I suppose,' but thought 'I don't even want your stinking job.'

'And how is Joshua?' he went on, standing up to see me to the door. 'Still beavering away in Harley Street? Do give him my best.'

I was seething, but he was right. I had no expertise. I was doubly qualified and had done my regulation house jobs. I was a fully registered dentist and doctor, but I had been pregnant at the end of my post as a house physician at the Royal Essex Hospital and I had never taken further specialist training.

Tony Williams welcomed me with a big hug.

'Abby, good to see you. Hope you've come to say you're looking for a job. I'm just applying for a grant and I need an assistant.'

Tony was also doubly qualified and had joined the research group at St Margaret's, working on the types of bone disease that affect the jaws.

'I am, but I have to say my first choice was St Olave's. Prof Jones said there'd always be a job for me when I was ready.'

'Bet you didn't get much change out of Richard.'

'You're so right. Sent me off with a flea in my ear.'

'Look I won't hear from the Medical Research Council for three months but I'll let you know as soon as I hear from them.'

Now we had sold both John Dobbie toyshops, it was great having all day to myself. The children were at full time school and I could read, go up to the West End, do what I liked but I soon tired of my freedom and became increasingly crabby with the children.

'No tea until you've tidied your rooms,' I'd insist, when they came home from school, tired and hungry. I snapped at Joshua and snapped at our long-suffering cleaner.

Luckily there was a two-week Immunology Conference I could attend at Imperial College. I was horrified to discover how much catching up I had to do.

Then Tony phoned.

'I'm really sorry, Abby, but the MRC turned me down, but don't give up I've got some other ideas.'

I didn't think I could take much more of this utter boredom when Tony phoned again.

'I mentioned to Professor Payne that you were looking for a job and he remembered you from when you were an ENT houseman. Something about a patient with meningitis.'

So, Matthew Payne was a professor now. He had been the pathologist shouted at by a furious wife telling him to have her husband cremated: 'Burn the bugger. Burn him,' she'd yelled.

'He has a three-month locum vacancy for a trainee pathologist, but I'm afraid you won't like this, Abby, he said you couldn't be any worse than any of the other useless women he'd taken on.'

I was too delighted to be offended.

'When do I start?'

'February 1st. If you want the job he'll get the forms sent on to you. What do you say?'

I wasn't sure I could survive another month of boredom but finally February 1st arrived. But I was going to work in a General Pathology department not in Oral Pathology.

*

Back at St Margaret's I began by mothering the other trainee pathologists. I was 42 and they were all much younger – in their 20s. I was even older than the Reader in Histopathology, who was deputy head of department.

I brought in homemade cakes and made tea and coffee for everyone. The sink and draining board in the coffee room were always littered with dirty cups containing dregs of tea or coffee. I would wash up, but next day it was just as bad.

Then I had a revelation.

'I'm not Mummy anymore. I am Me.'

Ever since the children were born I'd been 'Mummy'. Even Joshua talked about me to the children as 'Your Mummy'. It was as if Abby no longer existed. But now, once again, I could be Dr Waterman or Abby. There was no way this Abby was going to make tea or coffee for the younger doctors and I stopped making them cakes.

Professor Payne was in process of arranging an international conference. He apportioned various tasks to the male members of staff. Delegates often took their wives and the host would organise a series of ladies' trips for when the conference was in session.

'Perhaps you could deal with the ladies' programme, my dear,' he said, turning to me.

The new Abby was having none of it.

'I am not Mummy. I am not,' I thought, but said with an innocent smile. 'I would have thought your wife would be a much more suitable person to arrange their programme.'

'You're on for post-mortems, Abby,' the deputy head said. 'It's over at St Saviour's. Just take the 367 bus.'

It was a small hospital with the mortuary in a hut in the

grounds. The PM technician, Sampson, was a miserable-looking little man.

'You're new, aren't you? Haven't seen you here before. Changing room's over there.'

I pointed to the sign 'WC.'

'Can I use the toilet or is it just for patients?'

His dour face didn't change. He didn't appreciate my sense of humour.

I changed into scrubs and pulled on a white apron. The body was that of an elderly woman who'd died of broncho-pneumonia – very straightforward with the classical signs of widespread inflammation of the lungs. But she also had a small benign brain tumour – a meningioma, fibroids in her uterus, severe narrowing of her coronary arteries and a scar in her heart from a previous heart attack, as well as multiple diverticulae in her colon – a couple of which were inflamed and ready to burst.

When I got back to St Margaret's I went to see Prof Payne and listed my findings.

'She's a catalogue of medical problems. I'm not sure what to put on the death certificate and whether there's room to list all my findings.'

'Well, my dear, in a woman of 80, if you don't find a series of abnormalities you haven't done a careful post-mortem.'

At the end of three months Professor Payne called me into his office. He had his serious face on and I expected the worst. He was going to tell me that my temporary appointment had come to an end and that I would be looking for a job again. He smiled.

'You've done well, Abby, especially considering you've been out of medicine for so long. I can extend your appointment for another 9 months.'

I felt like kissing him, but he was too reserved for that, so I gave him my best smile.

'We'll talk about it again towards the end of the year but I think you should take the pathology rotation and sit Part 1 of your membership exam.'

He was referring to the higher examination I would need to take to become a consultant – Membership of the Royal College of Pathologists (MRCPath). I would have to spend three months in each of the pathology disciplines. I had spent three months in Histopathology – looking at specimens removed at surgery and carrying out autopsies. I would also need to rotate through Microbiology (Bacteriology and Virology), Haematology (investigation of the blood) and Chemical Pathology (study of the contents of blood and other body fluids).

But I had had enough of exams and I was only interested in one branch, Histopathology. I would have to look for a job elsewhere.

I had got on well with the neuropathology professor when I introduced him at a lecture he gave at St Margaret's.

'How would you like a job in neuropathology?' Professor Payne asked me not long after. 'Mark has suggested you go there on a month's trial before your year here ends.'

It didn't work out. I missed the hurly-burly of a busy routine lab. You can take a small biopsy from most organs, and examine it under the microscope, but you can't just remove a piece of the brain without risking permanent damage. Most of the time we were looking at cells sucked up through a fine needle, needle aspirates. And there were only a few of those each day. Diagnoses of diseases of the nervous system are usually made from the presenting features, a detailed physical examination, and a variety of x-ray and scans, rather than by taking a biopsy.

In addition, because the brain is very soft, it needs to be firmed up at post-mortem by fixing it in formalin for six months before examining it under the microscope. Most patients that died at that hospital died of a disease of their brain or nervous system. The autopsies I performed were of patients who were otherwise healthy. We wouldn't know the precise diagnosis for six months. It wasn't me.

I'd cut out an advertisement from St. Justin's Cancer Hospital for a trainee pathologist who would also carry out research. The closing date had long gone by the time I knew neuropathology wasn't for me, but I phoned on the off chance.

'Well you've had a chequered history, Abby lass,' the professor said. 'Dentist, doctor, mother of four, toyshop owner. Do you think you'll stick to pathology?'

'I always meant to be a pathologist. I thought I would special-ise in Oral Pathology but it didn't work out. I had a great year at St Margaret's doing routine pathology, but I'd like to be involved in some research.'

'I'll show you around our research units and leave you to talk to my staff.'

There was a wonderful buzz about the place – masses of whirring, clanking machines. Microscopes and balances everywhere.

Two days later I was offered an appointment as junior registrar at St Justin's to start two weeks after my appointment at St Margaret's ended.

Prof Payne was unhappy about my choice.

'You know, Abby, if you want to get on in pathology you'll have to take your membership exams, better now than later.'

But I only wanted to be a self-effacing pathologist beavering away in a corner, not making waves and not going through the agony of taking more exams and thinking I'd failed.

I would be starting off with three months' research in the department of immunocytochemistry. I had no idea what that was, but my new professor handed me a leaflet.

'The focus of our research is into tumour markers. Here read this.'

Immunocytochemistry is the demonstration of the chemicals a cell produces in thin microscopic sections. Tumour markers are substances produced by cancers which may be used to diagnose them, to monitor their spread or the effect of anti-cancer treatment. Some are hormones. Others are cell components of unknown function.

I had good teachers and rapidly became expert at the technique. I spent longer than my professor would have liked on cleaning up the results.

'I think when you look down the microscope,' I said, 'whether the tissue is positive or negative for a tumour marker should be so obvious that even my cleaner would be able to read the result.'

It paid off. Soon I was speaking at international meetings and showing my results. Almost without trying, I had landed at the cutting edge of research.

I did have one nasty accident. All chemicals in laboratories are meant to be labelled, though rumour has it that some researchers are so secretive about their work that they mislabel their bottles so no-one can tell exactly how they obtained their results.

I picked up an unlabelled two-litre bottle of clear fluid. No-one was around to ask, so I unscrewed the cap and took a deep breath to see what it contained.

I couldn't breathe. I felt as if I was going to die. But slowly I was able to take short breaths. It was an unlabelled bottle of concentrated ammonia. I'm lucky to have recovered so quickly.

I worked on a variety of cancers – tumours of the testis, colon, breast and prostate. There are two main kinds of testis cancers – seminomas, which consist mainly of cells of one type with a few giant cells – and teratomas, which contain a mixture of tissues and produce substances which can be measured in the blood stream, like alpha-fetoprotein (AFP) and human chorionic gonadotropin (HCG). This is a hormone, normally secreted by the placenta. It can cause gynaecomastia, breast enlargement in men.

I was asked to give a lecture on my work to the biochemistry department at St Justin's, and was pleased to have a bunch of young men rush up to me after my lecture to ask further questions. I had spoken about the causes of breast enlargement in men, like prolactin-secreting tumours of the pituitary and certain kinds of testicular tumours. I also mentioned that smoking pot can also cause gynaecomastia. It was this that they were so eager to know more about.

You could always hear when James, a tall, dark-haired, blue-eyed oncology registrar, came into the lab. There would be roars of laughter at his off-beat jokes. I had a research project going with him.

'Coffee time, Abby?' he asked.

'How come you always arrive for coffee when it's someone's birthday and there's chocolate cake?'

'We have our little ways,' he replied.

'You must look at this slide. See how the cancer cells infiltrate the lactating breast.'

'Actually, that patient is coming to the clinic in an hour. Want to come down?'

'You know we pathologists don't like touching living flesh,' I joked. 'Alright then. I'll see you there after coffee.'

I put on a clean white coat, freshened my lipstick and brushed my hair.

'This is Dr Waterman,' James said. 'OK if she examines you? She's the doctor who reported on the biopsy we did on your breast.'

She was a pretty, slight 25-year old. A toddler clung to her skirt and she held a young baby in her arms.

'Put baby down here on the couch, my dear,' James said as we left, 'and take your top things off. I'll find some coloured bricks for your little boy.'

We waited a minute or two and went back behind the curtains.

'This is the biopsy site.' James pointed to a scar on her breast. 'But you might like to feel the other breast too.'

'May I? My hands are a bit cold, but I'll give them a quick warm under the hot tap.'

Both breasts contained hard masses almost filling them.

'Very good,' James said. 'Dr Waterman and I will have a chat outside while you get dressed.'

He opened the door for me to join him in the corridor.

'She went to see her GP while she was pregnant because she'd felt a lump in one of her breasts, but he told her it's normal to have lumpy breasts during pregnancy. By the time she went for her post-natal examination, she had cancer in both breasts. And it's spread to her bones.'

I was near to tears. For me her cancer had made a beautiful

303

slide to show at international meetings. I hadn't visualised a young woman whose body hadn't yet completely switched off producing milk for her baby, and who had a two-year old toddler.

'It's horrible to realise that she will probably be dead before the year out,' I said. 'I can't bear to think it might be me who will have to carry out her post-mortem here at St. Justin's.'

CHAPTER 23

St Justin's Cancer Hospital

With only two days left before Christmas, the pathology department at St Justin's had been quiet all day. The surgeons always put off non-urgent operations until after Christmas, so that patients could spend the holiday at home. There had been very few specimens to process and most people had gone home early to get in some last-minute shopping. By four o'clock the department was deserted. I had already got one arm in the sleeve of my coat when the phone rang. I was tempted to ignore it but, having four children, I always worried in case it was about one of them.

'Hello,' I said 'Pathology department. Dr Waterman speaking.'

'Joe here, Dr Waterman. I think you're on for post mortems. Can you come down? I'm all ready for you.'

'Oh Joe, can't it wait until the morning? I know tomorrow's Saturday and Christmas Eve, but I don't mind coming in specially. I need to get over to Hamleys and buy a present for my neighbour's new baby before they close. If I hurry I should be able make it.'

'The family would like to get this over with as soon as possible,' he said. 'It's a four-year-old. A little girl.'

All the post mortems I had carried out at St Justin's that far had been on young or middle-aged adults. It was the first PM I had to carry out on a child. If any of the other pathologists had been around I would have asked one of them to do the autopsy, someone who didn't have two young daughters of their own.

I went down to the mortuary and changed into scrubs and white rubber boots. Tearing a plastic apron from the roll, I pulled it over my head and tied it behind my back. I hesitated before pulling open the door to the PM room. It was unusual to carry out post-mortems on Friday afternoons, when everyone was ready to clear up before the weekend. The post-mortem technician got paid Friday lunch time and was usually well on the way to being pie-eyed by now.

Today Joe was sober and his face grave. He had tacked up paper chains and tinsel around the walls earlier that week. He said it livened up the place. Now he asked if I wanted them taken down.

'Leave them,' I said. 'It doesn't matter.'

A little girl with a fine auburn fuzz on her nearly bald scalp was lying on the stainless-steel autopsy table in the centre of the white-tiled room. Her ivory skin was smooth and perfect. She looked peaceful, asleep. It was hard to believe she was dead.

'You OK, Dr Waterman?' Joe asked, as I read through the notes.

'I'm fine,' I said. 'Just don't talk to me.'

I switched on the X-ray viewing box and pushed her brain scans under the retaining clips. The tumour had certainly shrunk with treatment.

I powdered my hands and pulled on the small surgical gloves that

Joe ordered specially for me. All the men had much bigger hands. I eased the gloves over my fingers until they fitted smoothly and pulled them over my cuffs.

Making a V-shaped incision around the child's neck I extended it down to the pelvis and removed her breast plate. I took out the internal organs *en bloc,* placed them on the cutting board and dissected them free from each other, handing them one by one to Joe to be weighed.

I dictated into the overhead microphone:

'The body is that of a well-nourished female child, with no external abnormalities other than a well healed posterior cranial scar. All internal organs normal and healthy,'

'Open the skull, would you please, Joe?' I said.

I normally didn't notice the sound of the electric saw or notice the sucking sound as the top of the skull was lifted off. Now I cringed. Peeling back its outer covering to reveal engorged blood vessels running over its surface, I carefully lifted out the brain with my cupped hands. I turned it over to look for the tell-tale signs of raised intra-cranial pressure. There were deep grooves where the raised pressure due to her tumour had forced her brain against the margins of the *foramen magnum* at the base of the skull.

A young woman came in, surgical booties over her trainers.

'I'm the houseman on the children's ward,' she said.

I held out the little brain towards her and pointed to a bulge in the left cortex.

'I'll leave it to fix in formalin before I examine it properly,' I said, 'but her tumour has definitely recurred. She's "coned". You can see the grooves in the cerebellar tonsils. Her hind brain has been forced through the narrow aperture of the *foramen magnum* crushing her vital centres.'

'It's heart-breaking,' she said. 'Julie tolerated her radiotherapy really well and we thought we'd got the tumour beaten. She was so looking forward to going home for Christmas.'

Now I remembered the case. I had reported on the intra-operative biopsy. The cancer was a highly malignant astrocytoma, the swirling cells a crazy travesty of the well-ordered normal tissue. At the time, I hadn't thought about the living child the specimen had come from. It was just another malignant tumour.

Joe sewed up my incision and washed the skin free of blood. The houseman followed me into the female changing area. She took off her blue overshoes and turned to me, her eyes bright with unshed tears.

'I don't know how I'm going to bear this. It's my first death on this firm. My last job was in geriatrics. You don't feel the same when an eighty-year-old dies.'

I patted her awkwardly on the shoulder. I felt like crying too.

'Goodnight,' I said as I left. Neither of us wished the other a Happy Christmas.

I showered, changed back into my outdoor clothes and stuck my head into the postmortem room to say goodnight. The floor had been scrubbed and the room was pristine. The little body was gone.

I looked at my watch. There was still time to get to Hamleys before it closed. I had no heart for shopping, but I felt I ought to make the effort.

I rode up the escalator to the soft toy department, *'I'm dreaming of a White Christmas'* loud in my ears. I forced myself to look at the rows of cuddly teddy bears but I couldn't bring myself to choose one. Struggling through the crowds, I got as far as Oxford Circus Underground before I could hold back my tears no longer.

Teaching hospitals always needed bodies for medical students to dissect and it is useful for them to have bodies donated, but pathologists have more than enough to do without having bodies bequeathed to them. St Justin's was a Cancer Hospital and not part of a medical school. There was no mechanism for us to pass bodies on to a teaching hospital.

It was another Friday afternoon and I was tired and cross.

'Joe, here. Is that Dr Waterman?'

I would dearly have loved to say 'No, Abby left half an hour ago,' but instead I said, 'What is it then?'

'Well actually, a GP wants to know the mechanism for sending a body to us. He's just signed a patient's death certificate and there's an obvious cause of death. Apparently, she's left her body to St Justin's to say thank you for the excellent care during her last days.'

'Shit,' I said, under my breath. 'Can't you put him off? Say we've got Lassa fever here or Ebola. I just wish patients wouldn't do this. What's the point of doing a post-mortem when no-one wants to know the results?'

'Yes, well,' Joe said. 'You don't have to do a full autopsy. Just make a small incision or something.'

'You know I can't do that,' I said. 'Arrange for the GP to send her in and see if she's got some hospital notes. I'll do the post-mortem first thing on Monday.'

We did sometimes use dead bodies for research – with permission from the patient or their relatives. When the physicists were first investigating the possibilities of Magnetic Resonance Imaging (MRI) they would come down to collect slices of liver with large secondary cancers to see if the tumours could be visualised with their machine.

Cancer cells are viable for about 20 minutes after death and sometimes I was called in to do a 'hot' post-mortem, so that a piece of the tumour could be put into nutrient fluid before the cells died. The pieces would be minced very small and kept at 37°C to try to establish an immortal cell line. These could be cultured and sub-cultured and used for research into how cancers grow, what stops them growing and what turns them on or off.

But there was no research you could do on a body that had been dead for days. When I read the notes, I saw that the patient's cancer was well documented. Like many old people with cancer, what she had finally died of was broncho-pneumonia – 'the old person's friend.' I looked at the patient's face after Joe had finished sewing up.

'Look how serene she looks,' I said. 'Not a bad way to go and it looks from the notes as if her pain was well controlled. Sorry to have made a fuss about it. What have we got on for tomorrow?'

It was like a honeymoon to begin with – working with Jim, a bio-chemist, and Alice, his technician.

The goal of all of us working in the field of tumour markers, was to find something specific in cancer cells that would distinguish them from normal cells. It could be used in diagnosis or to target them with chemotherapeutic drugs. A biochemist in a USA labo-ratory claimed to have raised an antibody to human milk proteins that would selectively adhere to breast cells in tissue sections.

It's easy to look down the microscope at a section of a very malignant cancer and decide that it is a tumour. The normal tissue architecture is lost, the cells are lying this way and that, they are all shapes and sizes, and lots of them would be dividing to make still more malignant cells. It is equally straightforward to recognise normal tissue. Orderly cells of the same size are arranged in groups according to their function.

However, there are biopsies in which it's difficult to decide whether the cells are malignant or benign. If we could identify a specific cancer marker, we would be able to use it on problematic slides to tell whether there is cancer or not.

Our boss had told Jim and Alice to try and raise a similar antibody to human milk proteins as that reported by the American scientist. The antibody would be raised in cuddly, long-eared rabbits who sat placidly when being injected or having blood taken.

We needed a supply of human breast milk. Altruistic women, who had more breast milk than their own babies needed, were recruited by health visitors to supply the premature baby unit. Mostly the premature baby unit needed all the milk they could get, but every now and again they would receive milk kept too long by the donor or they were dubious about it for some other reason. It could then be purified and used for experimental purposes.

Jim was on a short vacation when Alice told me the first lot of antibody was ready to be tested.

It was a *Eureka* moment when I stained sections of the first five breast cancers. The antibody had adhered to the cancer cells. The technique I used – the immunoperoxidase method – turned any cells brown that the antibody had adhered to, while the tissue between them was stained blue. it seemed that we had found a marker for breast cancer that would help in the diagnosis of difficult cases or could be linked to a cancer drug to target cancer cells.

However, when I tested pieces of normal breast tissue they turned brown too, as did sections taken from armpit skin – breast milk glands are similar in origin to the apocrine sweat glands in the axilla. Then I tested sections from a variety of tissues. The antibody bound to everything that was derived from skin or the covering of an organ – the epithelial cells. There was some specificity, but the antibody was certainly not a specific cancer marker.

I felt vindicated. Although I worked in a unit investigating tumour markers, I had always said, 'If God wanted cancer to be easy to diagnose He would have put a big C on all the cancer cells.' It would have been just too easy to find such a simple solution to diagnosing cancer in tissue sections.

I could barely wait to get into the lab each morning and get started on the next batch of tests. Every day Alice and I went up together to the third-floor canteen for coffee and discussed the day's results.

Using assays for tumour markers in the blood stream is quite different. There are low levels in the blood from normal tissues, but raised levels of substances like Prostate Specific Antigen (PSA), for example, could indicate that the patient has prostate cancer. Measuring blood levels of Human Chorionic Gonadotropin and Alphafetoprotein is essential in monitoring testis cancer.

But the presence of these markers in normal tissues, as well as in cancers, meant that they weren't useful in distinguishing malignant from benign cells where the pathologist couldn't decide based on their shape and arrangement under the microscope.

When Jim got back he said we had enough to publish a paper on our results. I wrote up my work, but Jim wanted to write the conclusion.

Then things started to turn sour. Jim wanted to put in the *Conclusion* that our antibody marked the way primitive cells matured and I felt we had no basis for that. As my friend James would say 'His conclusion was light years ahead of the data.' I just wanted to summarise our findings in the *Conclusion* but Jim insisted, and I gave in.

Though theoretically, the only people with their names on papers should be those who have contributed, it was then customary to add the name of the Head of Department. You wanted to be first on a paper or last. The first person had done the work and the last person had had the ideas and directed the research. If there were only three authors, all three would be listed. If there were more, only the first name would be given, the others would be listed as *et al* (*et alia* – the others).

Without telling me, Jim showed our professor the paper without the front page, the page where the title and authors go. He then submitted it to the Pathology Journal without my seeing the final version. It had only my name, Alice's and his. Three authors. If the paper was quoted we'd all be listed.

It was an important paper, rebutting the work from the USA and describing an entirely new antigen. When our boss received his copy of the journal and saw he hadn't been listed as an author, he was furious with me as first author, even though it wasn't my fault. After all it was he who had directed Jim and Alice to make the antibody.

I was now working in a lab where Jim and I were hardly speaking and my boss ignored me when we met in the corridor. I couldn't bring myself to tell him it wasn't my fault and that I had assumed his name would be there too.

Then a collaborator on another project phoned from the National Institutes of Health (NIH) in Bethesda, Maryland, to ask me if I'd like to spend 3 months there. I jumped at the idea. I couldn't wait to get away from St Justin's.

I loved my time in Bethesda, although I missed Joshua and the children. At first, I rented the basement of a small house a short bus ride from NIH and then I was offered a one-bedroom apartment in the visitor's block,

I gave presentations of my work on tumour makers in Buffalo, Nashville and Boston. The American system was great. Not only was my flight and stay in a five-star hotel paid for, but I received a very generous honorarium in cash. The best I had done in the UK was a £25 book token and a bottle of South African sherry.

I was surprised by New York. I'd expected sweeping well-maintained boulevards but found streets full of potholes. All the yellow cabs seemed battered. The friend I was visiting drove me to the hospital where he worked. When we drew near, he engaged the central locking.

'You know,' I said. 'We don't have central locking in the UK. Why do you need it?'

'A couple of weeks ago a young house physician was pulled out of her car and raped as she drove into the hospital car park. We all keep our cars doors locked when we drive.'

As we arrived he said, 'I'll take you to see the post-mortem suite.'

Whenever I visited a hospital during my stay in the USA, my host would take me to see the post mortem room, as if it could possibly have any interest for me. I had seen more than enough of them.

There were three healthy-looking young bodies on the slab. The girl was white and the two men were black.

'What was the cause of death?' I asked the pathologist. 'Do you have some sort of epidemic?'

'Yes. We do. Drugs and guns. The girl OD'd and the men were in a gunfight.'

When I visited Boston, I was once again taken to the PM room. I wasn't quick enough off the mark to say "No".

'At least we have no problem getting samples of normal tissues for teaching purposes,' the pathologist said pointing to another two young men, white this time, who'd died of gunshot wounds.

'Thank heaven in the UK we have to go through all sorts of formalities if we want to buy a gun. Even our police are unarmed.'

'Amazing,' he said. 'Wouldn't work here in the US, the amount of gun crime we have.'

The facilities at NIH were incredible – libraries open all hours and a supermarket in the basement – not for food, for chemicals and laboratory equipment – chemicals, measuring cylinders, beakers, retort stands. You just needed your departmental card and a trolley. I was used to waiting six weeks for a couple of test tubes.

The audio-visual department was an eye-opener. I needed an illustration for a paper I'd just written. I'd drawn out the diagram but it wasn't good enough for publication.

'We're sorry Dr Waterman but we're a bit snowed under. We can't get it done today but would late tomorrow afternoon do?'

'Tomorrow?' I spluttered.

'It's the best we can do I'm afraid.'

'No, no. I'm not complaining. Just amazed to be able to get it done so quickly. Thank you. Tomorrow will be great.'

I felt I'd be letting the side down if I told them that back at St Justin's I'd have been faced with a drawing-in of teeth and a wait of several weeks.

There were so many good things about working at NIH but I was sure I'd never get used to the guards with guns at the door of the Institute, nor that the police were so heavily armed, some with rifles. The head of department told me that if I wished, a permanent appointment could be found for me but Joshua wouldn't wish to emigrate to the States even if I would, and I certainly wouldn't want my children brought up in an armed camp.

I'd got a bus out to the local shopping mall and on the way back I was the only passenger. The driver commented on my English accent.

'I've been to good old England,' he said. 'Did the whole country in a week. Where are you staying while you're here?'

I told him I was lodging in Westlake Road.

'No problem,' he said turning off the main road. He dropped me right at the door.

'Glad to be of service, Ma'am,' he said, waving goodbye.

After six weeks at NIH I flew to London for a long weekend. On my return to Washington, I was scared when the driver of my taxi coming from the airport turned off the freeway.

'Shouldn't we be going straight on?' I asked.

'Just have to get some gas.'

I was sure that this was it – the day I'd be robbed, raped or murdered, or all three. I was wrong. After paying for the petrol he said 'Well, that turnoff is down to me. I'll switch the meter off now,' he said.

He even carried in my case for me.

I was involved in the study of a variety of cancers – of the breast, the prostate and the testis and I travelled the world presenting my research at international meetings.

At a meeting in Minneapolis, where I was presenting my work on testis cancer, I was invited to a breakfast meeting with the local cancer research team. Over industry-strength coffee and the inevitable doughnuts, we discussed alternative methods for carrying out my experiments.

'Dr Waterman, do you think you could produce comparable

results using alkaline phosphatase instead of horseradish peroxi-dase?' one of the surgeons asked.

There was a loud and sudden silence when I replied:

'I haven't tried the technique myself. You'd just have to suck it and see.'

Many Americanisms now part of UK English hadn't yet crossed the ocean; nor had the coarser connotations of my favourite expres-sions. We didn't yet talk about 'sucking people off.'

I caused a similar but even more enveloping silence while staying on holiday in the Parador Hotel in Nerja, Andalucía. Many of the government-owned Paradors are gorgeous romantic castles. This one was in an ugly factory-like building built to Franco's design, though it had an elegant interior.

I was chatting to the reception staff and trying out my Spanish. They noticed my title and asked what kind of doctor I was. Since I am a woman they asked:

'¿Es usted pediatra?' No, I was not a paediatrician.

I consulted my pocket dictionary. 'Soy patóloga.'

Most people are vague about what a pathologist actually does, other than carry out postmortems, so I thought it would be easier to talk about my research.

'Hago investigación sobre los cojones.'

Palpable and complete silence blanketed the whole of Andalucía, a deepening scarlet blush spread over the face of the woman recep-tionist and there was a smothered snort from the hall porter.

My Spanish teacher hadn't warned me that properly brought up ladies do not use the word cojones, not ever, but I think testículos sounds much worse.

CHAPTER 24

Back at St Margaret's

While I was still at NIH, I arranged to take a locum appointment at the Central London Hospital on my return. I certainly didn't want to go back to St Justin's.

A month later, I gave a presentation at a Cancer Conference in Hastings and I was surprised to see Professor Dawson, the Professor of Pathology from St Margaret's, in the audience. I'd not seen him at any of the several cancer meetings I'd attended and thought his field was diseases of the liver. I knew him by sight, but was surprised when he came up to me at the coffee break.

'Hullo, Abby,' he said. 'Enjoying the meeting? Where are you working now?'

'I'm doing a locum at the Central London. I'm not sure where I'll go next. I need to take membership before I can apply for a senior lectureship but I'll have to do more general pathology. It was great being at St Justin's but of course I pretty well only saw cancer there, and we didn't do cytology at all.'

'Have you thought of applying for the senior lectureship at St Margaret's?' he asked.

'No. I won't have membership of the Royal College of Pathologists by then. Don't you need it before you can be appointed?'

'I'd have thought it's worth you applying,' he said.

I discussed it with my professor at the Central London.

'I don't think you should apply. You won't be happy there.'

He didn't explain why, but he didn't offer me a permanent appointment either.

My interview at St Margaret's was going well. All the pathologists on the board knew me and my work on tumour markers. Then one said:

'I see, Abby, that you have four children. Who will take care of them if we offer you the post as Senior Lecturer here?'

'My eldest son is at University and he doesn't care to have me look after him.'

'Oh well,' he retorted. 'I suppose you'll be able to cope. You seem to manage most things.'

I wanted the job so I said nothing. The other two candidates who were short-listed with me were men and I knew at least one of them had a family. I wished I'd had the courage to ask if they'd questioned him about who would look after his children.

After the interview, we waited in the corridor. Professor Dawson called me into his room.

'We want to offer you an appointment as Senior Lecturer, which is an academic post. We'll make you up to an honorary NHS consultant as soon as you get your MRCPath – Membership of the Royal College of Pathologists. We will expect you to take the exam within the next six months.

I had returned to Medicine in 1973 five years before and this was minimum training time required before I could take the higher exam in pathology. It was also five years since Richard Simmons had turned me down for a post in Oral Pathology at St Olave's, saying I had no expertise and nothing to offer. When we met at an international meeting, where I was giving the keynote address, he swore he'd said no such thing – but he had.

Part 1 of the examination was in all four pathology disciplines – histopathology, biochemistry, haematology and microbiology, but you could get exemption from the examination on the basis of your research, if it was considered good enough. I submitted my research papers and got exemption from Part 1 and could probably also have got exemption from Part 2, submitting more of my research papers, but this would have been anathema to Professor Dawson. He thought everyone should take the written, oral and practical examinations, showing their expertise in routine pathology and not just in research.

After my first year back at St Margaret's, when I was just starting in general pathology, I worked at St Justin's Cancer Hospital for three years. I then spent three months as a Visiting Expert doing research at the National Institutes of Health in Washington and worked for three months as a routine pathologist at the Central London. I therefore only had a bare fifteen months' experience in general pathology. I'd seen little skin pathology other than cancer and very little of other diseases elsewhere in the body. There was a lot to catch up on.

Prof Dawson asked me to show all my reports to him initially, but he soon said I was good enough to send them out on my own and need only bring him cases I was worried about. The research committee gave me a very generous starting-up grant but for the first six months I was to concentrate on passing the exam that would allow me to be appointed as an honorary NHS consultant.

I rang a senior pathologist I knew at St Olave's.

'Abby here. Any chance you could give me some tutorials? I'm really worried about the exam.'

I went over to his office three or four times but found myself getting more and more discouraged.

'I don't think I know enough,' I said.

'No. You don't,' he replied, sounding smug.

I was so disheartened that I began to tell everyone I was going to fail. The Prof called me into his office.

'Look, Abby. You saying you don't know enough and that you're going to fail reflects on me. I signed your form to say you had completed five years of training and were competent to take the exam. You're letting me down.'

I muttered 'Sorry' and felt worse than ever.

There were two three-hour essay papers. Among the questions was one on breast cancer – a subject on which I had done research, published in medical journals and addressed international conferences, and I felt I knew enough about the other questions to pass. I went off on my own to have my sandwiches and found the afternoon paper tough but doable.

I walked to the Underground with three of the other candidates, determined not to discuss the paper, but one of the men started to talk about the question on parasitic worms. I had thought I answered it quite well but there were things he mentioned I had left out. By the time I got to Holborn Station I was sure I had failed.

I could hardly talk to Joshua and the children when I got home.

'I'm exhausted. Would you eat without me? I think I'll go straight to bed.'

When I sat up in bed next morning the room was spinning madly and I had to lie down again.

'You OK?' Josh asked.

'Not sure. Maybe it's nerves. I'm sure I failed.'

'I'm sure you haven't, but get some rest. I'll see to the children. See you tonight. I'll ring St Margaret's and say you're not well.'

I dozed off, but when I woke and tried to sit up the room was spinning around me.

I asked Joshua to phone our GP. He came within the hour.

'It's an inflammation of the inner ear, vestibular-neuronitis. It's self-limiting, so just stay in bed until it gets better.'

'Didn't you notice her nystagmus?' he said, turning to Joshua.

'I noticed her pupils were flicking from side to side but it just didn't register.'

Two days later there was a phone call from St Margaret's.

'It's Prof's secretary. We've just heard from the College of Pathologists. You've passed the paper and your practical will be held at Cambridge. Since it's held over two days, shall I book you into one of the B & B's they recommend?'

The good thing was I had been too ill to worry about the exam; the bad thing was that there was so little time to look at some slides of common conditions before going to Cambridge.

The higher examinations in the various branches of medicine were always tough, with many candidates failing who were thought to be sure passes. Cambridge had a reputation for failing candidates. Having failed all the candidates for two successive years, it had only just been put back on the list of venues.

The B&B was small and pleasant and the landlady provided

breakfast and an evening meal. I was delighted there weren't any other candidates staying there. I spent the evening revising post-mortem procedures.

My post-mortem was on a 35-year old man who'd collapsed in his office and died on arrival at Addenbrookes Hospital. He was previously fit and well with no history of coronary artery disease or any other cause of sudden death.

I was beginning to despair. I had opened his chest and abdomen and found only normal healthy organs. I had still to find a cause of death. However, when I opened the skull, blood poured out. He'd had a massive intra-cranial haemorrhage. I carefully removed the brain but other than the blood under the thinnest layer of brain covering, the arachnoid membrane, I could see no obvious source.

The Cambridge professor, an international expert in Forensic Pathology, came over, a bevy of final year medical students trailing behind him.

'I'm sure you won't mind presenting your case to the students, will you Abby, my dear?'

After reading out the patient's very limited medical history, I showed them the normal internal organs and then the brain still covered in blood.

'The most likely site of this haemorrhage is a ruptured berry aneurysm,' I said.

'But wouldn't he have had previous symptoms?' a keen-looking student asked.

'Some people with berry aneurysms have little bleeds before they have a gusher like this and an astute GP will consider the possibility in a patient with unexplained headaches. We'll have to leave the brain to fix in formalin before examining it more thoroughly. We may then see staining where there were previous small symptomless bleeds and be able to identify what is left of the aneurysm.'

As the students filed away, the student who'd asked the question winked at me.

'Just testing,' he whispered and grinned.

'Have you looked at the hindbrain?' my examiner asked. 'Just slice the pons. See those small area of haemorrhage. A very useful sign of raised intra-cranial pressure, as in this case, after a big bleed,' he said and went on to tell me about some of the cases he'd seen in his long practice.

Not entirely reassured that I'd found everything I should have, I still had to write up the case and come back next day to look at slides and specimens, and have an oral examination.

The formalin-fixed specimens in glass jars – a couple of cancers and a cirrhotic liver – were straightforward, as were the written questions on them. The exam included cytology – the examination of single cells from body fluids or aspirations from breast or other tumours. The diagnoses seemed fairly obvious except for one cancer I just couldn't identify. I described its appearance. I wrote that it was clearly malignant and I listed what it was not. What had I missed?

By the time we four candidates were called up for our oral exam our answers had been marked. On the desk in front of the examiners was a mounted specimen of a lump attached to and invading a large vein.

'The slide you couldn't diagnose was taken from this tumour. We didn't know what it was either. We had to send it out to several pathologists to find someone who'd seen something like this before. Just wanted to see what you'd all make of it.'

I felt it was unfair to include it, but I didn't think it would improve my chances of passing if I complained.

The examiners went on to ask me about my research and whether I thought it had any place in routine pathology laboratories. They then asked me how I'd go about appointing a registrar in pathology.

I walked to the station with the other candidates and found one of the examiners waiting for the same train. I tried to catch his eye to see if I could tell whether I'd passed or not, but he pointedly looked the other way. I was now convinced that they hadn't asked any real pathology questions at my viva because I'd already failed.

I was thoroughly miserable next day when I went into St Margaret's. Everyone wanted to know how it went. The Prof came in.

'I'd like to see you in my office, Abby,' he said.

He had a glum face so I feared the worst.

'Congratulations. You've not only passed but yours was one of the best papers in the country. Well done. As soon as this is official, the Board will grant you honorary consultant status and you will get a clinician's salary.'

He was such a forbidding figure that I just shook hands, but I had a big hug from my colleagues.

Demonstrating post-mortems to medical students was one of the perks of consultant status – a chance to show off and have a bit of fun at the students' expense.

The PM room had four dissecting tables in the central area with rows of stands in a semicircle above them. All year, there was a moderate audience of medical students but before finals the stands were packed. The bravest crowded the front row, while the faint-hearted stood as far back as possible, not to be grilled on the case being demonstrated. We threw the odd question to the shrinking violets at the back, while concentrating on the hardy occupants of the front row.

Only in films and TV productions are parts of the body covered for modesty. The naked eviscerated body would be stretched full length, with the internal organs arranged on the stainless-steel shelf in front of the students.

The pathologists would read out the patient's medical history and the clinical findings, holding back some clues as to the diagnosis. We then picked up the affected organs one by one, held them out in front of the students and asked what they would expect to find.

Our professor of Forensic Pathology had a robust sense of humour and would have the students roaring with laughter. The rest of us tried to make a joke or two during our presentations. Irreverent? Perhaps. But that's how we survived in such grim surroundings.

It was late evening, just after 7.30, and I was alone in the pathology department, finishing a research paper that needed to go off urgently. I ignored the first tentative knock but opened the door when it was repeated loudly.

'Yes,' I scowled at the worried-looking house surgeon in theatre greens.

'The chest surgeon has a lung tumour for you,' he said in a whisper.

'Thank him,' I said, 'but tell him it's too late. Everyone has gone home, including my lab technician.'

I was collecting lung tumours to grow in tissue culture in order to investigate their properties. Putting the specimens into culture medium was a long drawn-out process and it was late. There would be other tumours coming out and I could pass on this one.

'B-b-but he wants a frozen section,' he stammered. 'He needs to be sure what type it is.'

'Is it booked?'

'No, but he'll skin me alive for not ringing the department earlier.'

I noticed he stopped stammering when he saw me nod. I gave in.

'OK,' I said, 'but make sure it's the last time you try this on. All the labs are locked up and I'll have to get the key from security.'

With a blissful smile on his face, he went off to theatre to return a few minutes later with a sterile kidney dish covered with a theatre cloth. It contained a 4cm piece of dark grey lung tissue.

'Do you want to stay and watch? You can take the result back with you.'

'No thank you. The Boss said I was to come straight back.'

The chest surgeon was a tyrant to the juniors though a pussycat to fellow consultants. The poor houseman was obviously terrified.

I unlocked the frozen section room, put on sterile gloves and turned on the extractor hood. I picked up a sterile scalpel and made a small incision over the firm mass I could feel in the lung tissue. I expected to cut into a hard cancer mass but to my surprise, a soft pale green cheesy material oozed out. It had to be a tuberculous nodule. For a moment, I couldn't think what to do. Anywhere I put it down would be contaminated. The apparatus would have been out of commission for days while it was all being fumigated. My name would be Mud!

I couldn't put it in a formalin-filled jar, because that would kill any bacteria. The microbiologists would want to culture the TB organisms and test them for sensitivity to antibiotics. I needed to wrap the dish in a sterile cloth, dispose of my gloves and open the door without contaminating anything.

Holding the door open with my hip, I eased my way out and took the lift to the Microbiology department on the fifth floor. It requires skill to pick out tubercle bacilli in either a stained or fluorescein-treated fresh specimen, and I felt it was beyond me at that time of night. Luckily, one of the technicians was still in the department. I was right. The specimen was teaming with TB organisms.

'Bingo,' he said.

I tried to phone the chest surgeon in theatre but I was told he had sewn up the patient's incision and gone home. I was furious. Why did he ask for an urgent frozen section if he was going to close up and wait for a definitive diagnosis on a formalin-fixed specimen before proceeding? His registrar was still in the recovery room with the patient. I went storming over to him and pulled him aside.

'Why did the Boss ask for a frozen section if he was going to close up? Anyhow, it's TB, not cancer at all. You can start your patient on streptomycin straight away.'

The patient had now woken up. The young surgeon said that as a 'thank you', I could be the one to tell the patient what I had found.

'I'm Dr Waterman, the pathologist who examined the tissue from your lung.'

The patient's face fell.

'How bad is it? How long have I got? My wife's been telling me to give up smoking for the children's sake. I tried but I just can't.'

'You'll be fine,' I said. 'It's TB. You'll need to take some drugs for at least six months but you should have a normal life span, especially if you give up smoking.'

It was one of the few occasions on which I made a grown man cry. He grabbed my hand and kissed it, tears running down his face.

The registrar was smirking behind the patient's back.

'I'll get you later,' I mouthed.

'Promise?' he mouthed back.

We had six weeks holiday a year and I took two weeks in August to coincide with Josh's time off working as a part-time demonstrator at the Dental Hospital.

We were staying on the island of Hvar in a hotel by the water's edge. This was long before the bloody conflict in Yugoslavia tore the nation apart and the island was beautiful and tranquil. The service in the dining room was the usual grumpy Communist waitressing, all sour face and sling-backed white plimsolls with wedge heels. The food was better than usual – no boiled potatoes swimming in water and lots of the salty pickled cucumbers I love. Drink was cheap. We'd had tomato juice and vodka before dinner – more vodka than tomato juice, red wine with the meal and a complementary *Aquavit*-like drink afterwards. Too much to eat and too much to drink.

We fell into bed while it was still quite early and went out like a light. Then I was sitting bolt upright in bed, cold and sweating, afraid to go back to sleep. I'd had one of the dreams so many pathologists have.

In the small hours of a wintry morning, I was alone in the post-mortem room in the basement at St Margaret's. High up there was a slit-like window showing the grey overcast London sky. I was standing in front of a full-length mirror. I slipped off my surgical gown and stood naked in my surgical cap, mask and white rubber boots. I had a scalpel in my hand and prepared to make the first cut, from the notch of my chest bone down to my pubis. I opened my chest cavity and my heart came into view beating rapidly, more rapidly than it could stand. I cut into my heart, and instead of blood flowing out, little miniature hearts came tumbling out and then blood poured out, pints of blood running down my body and legs, forming a spreading lake on the dull green composite floor.

I thought I would sit and read a magazine until daylight, afraid to risk another dream like that, but I drifted off into sleep and another nightmare.

I was again in the autopsy room, this time about to carry out a post-mortem on a middle-aged man. Once again, the mortuary was deserted, no junior pathologist, no post-mortem technician. I examined the outside of the body. Then, looking for any sign of the cancer from which he had died, I felt for enlarged glands in his neck and then I lifted first his left, then his right arm, to feel in his armpits for enlarged glands. As I turned to start my dissection, it seemed as if a small smile played about his lips. I picked up my scalpel, made the first long cut and started to peel back the flesh. As I lifted out his chest plate, I thought I saw a flicker of movement in his heart, but decided it was the fluorescents overhead. Then his heart started beating, at first feebly and then more strongly. I was dissecting a living body. I panicked. Should I close up and admit what I had done? There was no way he could recover from the infection I must have introduced into his chest cavity. And what would I say to the Prof?

Then I realised why his face looked familiar. It was the 'uncle' I'd hated, the one who'd always slipped his hand under my knickers when I was a child. I hated him still and decided to cut through his aorta and make sure he was really dead. As I put my left index finger under the pulsating vessel ready to cut into it, I woke out of my nightmare.

This time I got up, had a shower and found one of the blockbuster novels I always bought in the airport bookshop before flying. It was hard to relax but soon it was daybreak and the outside world came to life.

I never had either dream again, but the rest of the week in Hvar I kept off the liquor and tried to limit how much I ate for dinner.

It was one of those cold, wet and miserable November evenings. I had taken Jane to see a re-run of *The Sound of Music* at the Leicester Square Odeon. Joshua and the other children said they couldn't face it; they would rather stay home and watch TV.

When I collected my car from the car park near the cinema, I remembered that I'd meant to ask the technicians to cut some further sections of the lung biopsy. The chest surgeon thought it was cancer, but, fortunately for the patient, it showed chronic inflammation, probably sarcoidosis. I wanted to be sure it wasn't TB. I had written the request for the stains that would pick out the bacteria, but in my hurry to leave and pick up Jane, I remembered that I hadn't taken the form to the laboratory. The technicians left long before I did, so it wouldn't have been carried out that evening, but, if I took my request round that night, they could start on it as soon as they came in next morning.

Jane didn't fancy coming back with me to St Margaret's.

'I hate hospitals,' she said. 'They smell bad.'

'I'll let you play *Pinball* on my computer,' I said, 'and you can take some photographs down my microscope.'

I parked in St Margaret's underground car park, and took Jane in through the mortuary entrance.

'Creepy,' she said. 'I don't suppose I could see a dead body?'

'Don't be silly,' I snapped, and then I was sorry. I'd spent my childhood scared of doing or saying the wrong thing, for fear of getting a sharp smack, or not being spoken to for the rest of the day.

I took her past the bank of lifts, and through a side door to the paternoster lift.

'Is this a lift for dead bodies?' Jane asked. 'It doesn't have a door.'

'No, it's for staff. The compartments take two or three people. They go round in a continuous loop. It's much quicker than waiting for a lift, especially at busy times, when the regular lifts are often full.'

At first Jane was scared of getting on the paternoster while it was moving, but, once she got on, she liked it. When we left at the second floor, she wanted to get back in again and go all the way round.

'You can get stuck, if it stops suddenly,' I said. 'Once, when I was coming up, it stopped half way between floors. I was too short to reach the ledge above, but luckily one of my colleagues was in the lobby. He grabbed my hands and pulled me up. The high-heeled court shoes I was wearing were a bit loose. One fell off and he had to climb down and got it for me. I felt a real idiot.'

'I don't care if it does stop,' Jane said. 'I could climb out on my own. Can we go all the way round? Just once. Please, Mum.'

So we did, though I insisted that once was enough.

I put in the code for my side of the pathology department, and unlocked the door of my office. I left Jane playing *Pinball* on my computer, and took the request form round to the laboratory. As I reached behind the door to switch on the light, I saw a leg on the table for surgical specimens.

'Those bloody surgeons,' I thought. 'They've done it again.'

The surgeons were always bringing specimens to be examined in sterile bags, instead of putting them into formalin-filled containers as we had asked them to do on numerous occasions. Formalin was required to preserve the specimens removed during surgery until they could be examined by a pathologist, suspicious areas sampled and sections prepared to be examined under the microscope.

One Friday afternoon, they removed a section of large bowel that contained an unusual tumour, and spent hours photographing it. Having once again bagged up the specimen in a sterile bag, they brought it round to the pathology lab. By that time the technicians had gone home, and there was noone to put the specimen into a formalin-filled container. The following Monday morning, the poor trainee pathologist on the rota had the unenviable task of dissecting a bowel that had been quietly fermenting all weekend.

'They've dumped a leg amputation,' I thought. 'Too bloody idle to find a container.'

Then the leg moved. As I pushed the door open further, I saw that the leg was attached to the body of a tall bearded man, sprawled across the specimen table. Fearing he might attack me, I slammed the door shut, raced back to my room and locked the door. I phoned Security.

After a good twenty minutes, a fat disgruntled guard, wiping biscuit crumbs from around his mouth, knocked at my door.

'What's going on then? Are you Dr Waterman?'

'Yes, I am. There's an intruder in the department. A man.'

'Let's see this intruder of yours then.'

'You stay here,' I told Jane. 'I'll lock the door. You'll be quite safe.'

'Don't leave me on my own, not if there's a scary man around.'

Jane held my hand as we walked round to the laboratory. The guard pushed open the door of the cut-up room where specimens were dissected. There was no-one there. The man had disappeared.

'Look, Dr Waterman,' he said. 'We're short staffed as it is, and I was on my tea break when you phoned. You can see there's no-one's here.'

He rang his supervisor.

'We've looked everywhere. I've been called up here on a wild goose chase.'

As he turned to leave, I noticed an open book called *Jesus is your Friend* lying face down on the floor of the laboratory. The technicians would never have gone home on Friday evening leaving a book on the floor, especially not one with a title like that. They always left the lab immaculate.

'He must be somewhere,' I said.

Still unconvinced that I had seen someone in the laboratory, the guard went round the pathology department with us once more. We looked in all the rooms that were unlocked, but found no-one.

A loud crash came from the little store cupboard leading off the cut-up room. When we opened the door, there was a gaunt grey-haired man sitting in the dark, perched on a box of specimen jars. An empty jar lay in shards at his feet. I was shocked to find that he'd managed to get into a cupboard that was next door to our sharp dissecting knives.

'I haven't done anything wrong, miss. It was an accident. I didn't touch nothing. It just fell on its own,' he said, confused and half asleep.

'Come on then, you,' the security guard said. He prodded the man along and turned towards me, adding accusingly:

'This side of the department should be locked too, Dr Waterman. It's just not safe. You know,' he went on, 'come winter, we often find dossers kipping in the boiler room. It's much warmer than a bench on the Embankment in weather like this. Haven't found anyone in your pathology department before though. I wouldn't fancy sleeping on that table myself. God only knows what you people keep on there. Dead bodies, I shouldn't wonder.'

CHAPTER 25

Illness Strikes

John Hornby, the professor of medicine, diagnosed my mild hypertension when he investigated my persistent cough – apparently a late sequel of the whooping cough I'd had as a child. I tried several different anti-hypertensive drugs before I found one I could tolerate. One gave me a cough that didn't get better for a month after I stopped taking it, and another gave me severe headaches. I finally settled for nifedipine, with a small dose of an antidiuretic.

After a year on the drugs, I started feeling tired all the time. It was an effort to walk up even a short flight of steps and I was having attacks of tachycardia – an abnormally fast heartbeat. I had a resting pulse rate of 120 instead of about 70. One attack occurred while I was lecturing the medical students on coronary artery disease and I couldn't go on. I had to make my excuses and leave.

John said I was anxious and depressed and prescribed

anti-depressants. Now, I not only felt tired all the time, but I felt sleepy and not in control of my mind. I went to see him again.

'It's no good. I feel worse than ever. I'm barely getting through the day.'

'Maybe you haven't given the drugs a chance to work. You know anti-depressants take time.'

'I think I might have myxoedema. The outer thirds of my eyebrows are quite thin and that's one of the signs of an underactive thyroid.'

'An under-active thyroid? You, Abby? You never keep still for a moment; always rushing around with some new scheme for your research. I'll measure your thyroid hormone levels but I don't think that's your problem.'

When the results came through I was surprised to see that my thyroid hormone levels were sky high. I was now in my mid-50s and an over-active thyroid may not present with bulging eyes or a swollen thyroid gland as in younger patients. I started to take the anti-thyroid drug, carbimazole.

Jane was at a summer camp with her school and Joshua, Louise and I went on holiday to Tenerife. I was tired all the time. I fell behind Josh and Louise, climbing the steep path to the restaurant.

'Wait for me,' I called.

'Come on,' Joshua said. 'We're nearly there.'

By the time I caught up with them tears were streaming down my face.

'I can't manage it, I can't.'

'I'm so sorry,' Josh said, 'but let's eat. I'm starving.'

Things gradually got better and then, for the first time since I'd started at St Margaret's, I walked up to the pathology department on the second floor. I'd always taken the lift or the paternoster and hadn't realised it was because I found stairs tiring.

'You've put on weight,' Joshua said one day. 'Your face is quite round.'

He was right. I was quite moon-faced and I'd put on several kilos. I was due for a check-up and had my thyroid levels measured before I saw the thyroid specialist again.

'That's all fine,' he said. 'Levels coming down nicely. Pulse quite steady and normal.'

'I'm putting on weight,' I said. 'Look at my face.'

'Well, it happens. Patients with an over-active thyroid get used to eating a lot because their metabolic rate is so high. Their stomachs get used to that sort of quantity. When they are treated they go on eating the same amount and so they put on weight.'

'I don't think I am eating as much as I did before.'

He clearly didn't believe me.

'Come and see me in a month and we'll see how you're doing.'

I knew I was eating less. It wasn't until I stopped taking the anti-depressants and my face returned to normal that I realised my weight gain was due to the drugs.

It was Tuesday February 1st. I was having a lovely hot shower, turning slowly and letting the water cascade over me. I squirted my new Elizabeth Arden shower gel into my hand and as I soaped myself I felt a hard lump in my left breast.

'It's the cyst filled up again,' I told myself.

I'd found a lump in my left breast two years before and, while I thought it was probably benign, I asked one of the surgeons to have a look at it.

'I think it's nothing to worry about, Abby,' he said. 'I'll just put a needle in it.'

The dark green murky fluid he drew out was revolting.

'I'll send this off for cytology, but I'm sure it's just a benign cyst. The fluid is green because at some time you must have knocked your bosom and bled into it. It could fill up again. Let me know if it does, and I'll drain it again for you.'

Three days later the cytology result came through.

'Benign breast cells. No evidence of malignancy.

But this new lump was different. It was hard and attached to the surrounding tissue, not freely moveable like the cyst. I was sure it was cancer and I was certain my cancer would be one of the rapidly progressing malignancies that would kill me in months.

Four weeks would make little difference. I was on the rota for supervising junior pathologists and I decided to do nothing until I finished my stint. We were two consultants short in the pathology department – one pathologist was off sick and another had retired and had not yet been replaced. I didn't want to worry Joshua and so I didn't tell him or the children.

It wasn't for another month that I stopped Stephen Jackson, the breast surgeon, in the corridor.

'I've found a lump in my breast,' I said. 'Would you mind having a look at it for me?'

'No problem, Abby. Don't worry, it's bound to be benign. I'll have finished my list by about two. Come up at about three? Give me time to write up my notes.'

I wasn't sure how I felt about taking off my clothes in front of a colleague who was also a friend, but I told myself not to be silly.

'My hands are a bit cold,' he said as he felt one breast and then the other. 'I'll just do a fine needle aspirate.'

I tried to gauge from his face whether he thought the lump was cancer or not.

'This may hurt a bit.'

He probed around with the needle to get a good sample.

'There,' he said. 'All done. I'll send this off to cytology. They'll look at it straight away.'

'What do you think, though?' I said.

He looked serious.

'I'm 50% sure it's not benign.'

I knew what he really meant.

'Look, Abby. The chances are that even if it is malignant it's still localised. The lump is quite small. You're lucky you found it.'

I rubbed the back of my hand across my eyes.

'If you call that lucky.'

'I'll ask the cytologist to phone me with the result. I'll be in touch. Try not to worry.'

As I got home that evening the phone was ringing.

'I've got your result. I'm sorry, Abby. It's not good news. It's definitely malignant. There's absolutely no doubt. I've got a theatre slot at St Margaret's next Monday.'

I tried to keep my voice even.

'I want that thing out of me. For two pins, I'd ask you to operate on the kitchen table tonight.'

'I'll see what I can do. Would you mind being operated on at the Chester Clinic? I'll need a chest X-ray and a full blood count beforehand.'

'Anywhere. Just get it out.'

He rang back an hour later to say that a theatre was available late the next afternoon, provided I got all the tests done in the morning.

I finally told Joshua. He held me tight, near to tears himself.

'You'll be OK, Abby, you'll see. Only the good die young.'

I attempted a smile.

'59 is hardly young.'

Next morning, I went into St Margaret's as usual. One of the junior pathologists had a report for me to check.

'I'll get the extra stains done, Dr Waterman, and bring them back tomorrow.'

I quite enjoyed saying 'You'll need to show them to one of the other consultants. I'm afraid I won't be here tomorrow. I'm going in to have my breast cancer removed this afternoon.'

I went to see the Head of Department and asked him to tell as few people as possible. I didn't want a stream of visitors with long faces coming in and commiserating with me.

The atmosphere in the Chester Clinic was friendly but brisk and efficient. The anaesthetist was another colleague.

'You'll be fine, Abby,' he said. 'Better than 70% five-year survival. By the millennium it'll be over 80%.'

If I'd been giving a lecture on breast cancer, of course I'd have said how good the survival was, but virtually everyone I'd met with breast cancer was dead. I was a pathologist so I only met patients with breast cancer in the post-mortem room. What your head knows is one thing, and what you feel in your heart is another. My heart said I would one of those who died.

I am not sure whether it's better or worse to be 'in the trade' when something like this happens. In some ways, it was much easier for me as a doctor, familiar with hospitals and medical jargon, but in many ways, it was more difficult. I was only too aware of everything that could go wrong, all the possible complications. Like most women I thought, 'Why me?' and 'I don't want to die'. I felt that, even more than other women, I had to put a brave face on things and 'be good'.

When I woke from my operation the surgeon was at my side.

'The drains can be removed in a couple of days, Abby. The lump came out with a good margin of normal tissue. I've sent the specimen over to pathology, but I'm sure we're well clear.'

When he left, the nurse came in and helped me to the bathroom.

'That's a nice tinkle,' she said. 'Well done.'

I looked out of the window as she settled me into bed.

'Snow's forecast,' she said.

Large flakes began to fall, and soon there was a thick layer of snow on the outside window sill.

Joshua came with some large hothouse grapes and a whodunit to read. I drifted off to sleep as soon as he left.

I was out of bed the next day, and after two more days the drains were taken out. My breast wasn't very sore though my armpit was stiff where the lymph glands had been removed.

By now there was thick snow covering the church opposite making it look like Christmas. It felt very cosy in my warm room.

'Better than working any day,' I thought, until I remembered my cancer.

There was a knock at the door.

'Come in,' I called.

A large woman bustled in, brandishing an envelope.

'I'm the breast clinic nurse,' she said. 'Your surgeon asked me to give you this. It's a copy of the pathology report.'

'Ductal carcinoma of the breast Grade 1. Well clear of the surgical margins. No evidence of malignancy in the 15 lymph nodes submitted.'

For the first time, I let myself go in front of someone.

'I'm so sorry. I've had to hold myself together for Joshua and the children but it's been so hard,' I sobbed.

She put her arms around me.

'There, there,' she said. 'You have a good cry. You've been a brave girl.'

It was lovely being mothered and lovely having such a positive report.

I went back to work as soon as the stitches were out. I was to have a six-week course of radiotherapy and I had my first tattoos – two tiny blue spots to enable the radiographers to position the X-ray beam exactly. One was in my left armpit, and the other in the middle of my breast bone at the same level.

The problem with being a doctor is that everyone expects you to know all about your treatment, but I didn't. My fields were routine pathology and research. I had little knowledge about treatment and I really appreciated having everything explained to me as if I was an ordinary person. Not patronising, just factual. I knew radiotherapy to my chest wouldn't make my hair fall out but I still worried how I would cope. I was prescribed Tamoxifen but it made me feel ill, so I had to stop taking it.

I tried not to stare at the other patients waiting for treatment and try to guess what kind of cancer they had. Was it I who made the diagnosis on their surgical biopsy?

I arranged to have my radiotherapy first thing in the morning so I could go up to the pathology department as usual. I found it difficult to deal with breast cancer specimens but for the best part of three weeks I managed to carry on with my routine work and lecture the medical students. Gradually I became more and more fatigued but I told myself it was silly. Surely radiotherapy to just one half of my chest shouldn't be affecting me, but it was getting worse. The Head of Department called me in.

'I know how you feel. Abby, about being stout-hearted and all that, but I think you should take a couple of months' sick leave. You look completely worn out. Come in when you feel like it to write up your research but I'll take you off the diagnostic rota. I promise you the department won't fall apart. We'll cope.'

I was a bit miffed at not being considered indispensable, but I was feeling sick and bone tired.

I was due to have a long weekend in Barcelona toward the end of my course of radiotherapy, and tried to persuade the oncologist to let me miss the last treatment.

'Look, Abby,' he said. 'Change your booking. I'd never forgive myself if something happens because I didn't insist that you had the full course.'

'OK. I'll be good,' I said.

I had coped with my breast cancer but I couldn't cope with the new professor. At first, he was very friendly and full of plans for my future in the department. Then he published a paper that conflicted with my own work, work that I'd shown him. I felt strongly that the work shouldn't stand as it was. I went to see him.

'I think I should write a letter to the journal saying that your test should be viewed with caution, but that your results are interesting and warrant funding for further research.'

He seemed to accept it, but soon he began to persecute me. I'd never liked doing post-mortems. It didn't help that being five foot nothing I had to stand on a special platform to reach the fixed post-mortem tables at St Margaret's.

'I don't know why you don't climb inside and just toss the organs out,' the jokey Professor of Forensic Pathology said.

The new professor said I would have to supervise autopsies every alternate week, instead of every six weeks as at present and spend less time supervising the junior pathologists which I enjoyed.

Even worse, he said that he would expect my research to wind down within two years. I was nearly 60, with only five years to go. He wouldn't budge, even when I told him that my grant from a cancer charity was about to be renewed. With only two years to go I wouldn't be able to start any major work or recruit new technicians. Those already working in my laboratory would feel threatened, and start looking for posts elsewhere.

I was desolate. I couldn't sleep and didn't want to eat. I fell into a deep depression and saw a psychiatrist at St Margaret's. He admitted me to the psychiatric ward at the Chester Clinic and kept me completely sedated for several days, only allowing me to wake for light meals and use the bathroom. When he allowed me to resurface, he put me on stronger antidepressants. It took six weeks before I felt I could face going home for a weekend. When Joshua took me shopping in Selfridges I panicked. I sat in a corner on the floor until I could move again and go back to the clinic. The psychotherapist advised me to take early retirement.

'I can't. My staff depend on me' I said. 'They have mortgages to pay and some need my help to finish their theses. I'd be letting them down.'

She put it bluntly.

'What would they do if you died?'

Finally, I accepted her advice and took early retirement on the grounds of ill health. I started a new chapter of my life – not working at a job but at a wide variety of art, music and literature studies. Joshua was still working but I went regularly to see Louise, our elder daughter who was working as an English language teacher in the north of Spain.

It was vanity, sheer vanity. I'd missed out on Doc Marten's when they were all the rage and when I saw the thick-soled boots in the ECCO shoe shop I couldn't resist them. I should have given them to Oxfam after I tripped hurrying to get to the Post Office before it closed. That time I only skinned the palms of my hands and tore a hole in my jeans. When I tripped crossing the road in San Sebastian, I broke my hip.

I was in Spain to look after Louise, who was expecting her second baby any day. When she had gone into premature labour three weeks earlier, the obstetrician gave her drugs to stop the contractions and sent her home. We were on our way to her obstetrician for a check-up, when I tripped crossing the road. I'd once again stubbed those extra thick soles and went flying, landing hard on my right side. When I got up, I couldn't put any weight on my right leg. It wasn't hurting so, leaning on Louise, I hopped to the far pavement and sat down on a bench in the sun.

I sent Louise off to her appointment, but decided to see if, after I'd rested a bit, I could stand on my right leg. The pain was excruciating and I cried out, collapsing back onto the bench. My hip had to be broken. Standing up had scrunched the broken ends together. I suspected the worst – that I had a fracture through bone weakened by secondary spread from the breast cancer I'd had 10 years before. If it had spread to my bones the outlook was grim.

When Louise got back, I was fighting hard not to cry, it hurt so much. Neither of us had a mobile phone, but a pizzeria nearby let Louise ring for an ambulance. It came quickly. The ambulance man started to help my very pregnant daughter up the steps until she explained it was her mother who needed the ambulance. Between them they got me into the ambulance.

The driver took us to the main hospital, the *Residencia*, with me crying out at every bump and apologising for making a fuss. He was most concerned about getting my form E111, which would cover my treatment in Spain. Without it, the driver said he wouldn't be paid. Louise promised him that she would go back to her flat and collect my form as soon as she could.

Casualty was crowded. I lay on the stretcher hardly able to breathe for the pain. Then it was my turn to have an X-ray and I was shunted into the examination room.

'It's a displaced fracture of the right neck of femur,' the casualty officer said, with hardly a trace of a Spanish accent. 'You'll need a full hip replacement. The *Residencia* is full with this flu' epidemic so I'll send you to *San Juan de Dios*. You'll be well looked after. And,' he added, 'there's nothing to suggest it's a pathological fracture through a secondary. I'm sorry I can't prescribe anything for the pain, just in case they decide to operate today.'

Louise asked where he learnt his English.

'I had a registrar post at St Margaret's.'

'It's a small world,' Louise said. 'My mum was a consultant there.'

'Is Stephen Jackson still at St Margaret's? He was my boss.'

I said he was a very good friend and the surgeon who'd dealt with my breast cancer.

'Small world,' he repeated.

San Juan de Dios was a small private hospital up on the hillside above San Sebastian. Because the *Residencia* couldn't take me, my treatment would be covered by the European Health scheme. I was put to bed in a small double room and soon visited by the surgeon. Louise translated his Spanish.

'I'll get your leg in traction and then I'll see when I can operate.

Tomorrow my list is full, but I can operate the day after. I'll write you up for some painkillers.'

The injection was bliss. I was now floating and almost pain-free. The nurses brought in a traction pulley and attached it to my leg so that the broken ends of my femur were no longer grating on each other.

'You go,' I said to Louise. 'Phone Dad and tell him I'm fine and not to worry and to bring some crutches. He'll want to book a flight.'

Joshua had broken his leg two years before and had it pinned. His crutches were still in the cupboard under the hall stairs.

I turned to the patient in the other bed, a little old lady who looked about a hundred. I had been learning Spanish for two years and could understand most of it, if people spoke slowly. She said she'd had her hip replaced for osteoarthritis and that it was done under an epidural anaesthetic.

I felt ill for weeks after I had a general anaesthetic to have my varicose veins operated on years before so, when the surgeon came back to confirm when I would have my operation, I asked if I could have an epidural.

'Of course,' he said.

He was a young-looking surgeon from Peru with prematurely white hair. Yes, he could speak some English but, if I didn't mind, he'd rather speak in Spanish.

One of the nurses spoke a little English. She'd been an *au pair* in Epsom years before. With goodwill on both sides and a lot of '*¿Cómo se dice en Español . . . ?*' I managed to get by. Some words like *una bacinilla* – a bedpan – just hadn't come up in my Spanish lessons, nor the fairly obvious *hacer pis*. When a nurse offered me a *calmante* I protested that I was calm, I really was, though the pain was bad. She explained that *una calmante* was a painkiller.

The nights were the worst. I'd been written up for 6 hourly injections of a painkiller but the pain was often unbearable long before the 6 hours were up. I had to stick it out. The nurses had no discretion to change the timing.

The day of my operation arrived but I didn't get my pre-med until early evening, because they'd had to send out for blood of my type. I remembered being wheeled out of my room and then no more until I heard hammering as my prosthesis was forced into place. I felt a slight pricking as clips were inserted to close the incision.

Joshua's flight to Spain was delayed six hours and Louise was worried that there had been an accident, but he was now with her. The surgeon didn't finish my operation until around 11pm but took the time to phone Louise and tell her that I was fine.

The next two days passed in a fog of pain, but then I was finally allowed to get out of bed and sit in an armchair. No more struggling to use a bedpan while lying down.

'Don't cross your legs,' the nurses said.

I don't think they got the joke when I said, 'But my mother said I should always keep my legs crossed.'

I started to walk first with a Zimmer frame and then with the crutches Joshua had brought from England. All the patients had visitors, lots of visitors. One had been a merchant seaman and prided himself on his English. I had to pretend I understood him, but his pronunciation was so awful, I only got one word in ten.

Joshua said he'd been told 'Heaven up; Hell down,' to help remember which foot to use first when going up and down stairs, after his broken femur was pinned. The Hell part certainly described what it was like going down. In Spanish, it was *'La mala, la buena,'* the bad, the good, that you said as you attempted stairs.

The Spanish visitors overflowed into the corridor and shouted *Brava* and *Una mujer fuerte y valiente* as I struggled up the stairs – quite easy – or down – horrid.

There was no nonsense about being woken at six in the morning as I would have been in an English hospital. Food seemed to arrive every couple of hours. It started with coffee and croissants at 8am, then mid-morning coffee and biscuits, a delicious three course lunch, a mid-afternoon snack, an equally delicious three course dinner and, of course, a snack before bedtime. The nurses worried that I didn't eat enough, but I couldn't eat all that food, delicious as it was, and I worried that I'd never be able to lose the weight I would put on.

A round little priest, a *cura*, who spoke no English, came to see me every day, nodding and smiling at the end of my bed saying: *'Bueno, bueno, bueno.'* Louise's partner, who'd hated his Jesuit school and the monks who taught him, was horrified, but I found the *cura's* visits comforting and I looked forward to them.

Then Louise went into labour and her bouncing four kilo son was born. Unfortunately, she had the baby in the *Residencia* in the middle of town and I was still up the hillside at *San Juan de Dios*. I asked the surgeon if I could go and see my grandson.

'No,' he said. 'It's not safe. Your wound is not yet healed.'

I used the oldest trick in the world and started to cry.

'Vale, vale. OK you can go but only for one hour,' he said writing out a pass for me.

The taxi took ages to come but finally I hobbled up to Louise's bed.

'He's so beautiful,' I said, in tears again. 'May I pick him up?'

When I was discharged back to Louise's flat I heard Samantha, my three-year-old grand-daughter telling a visitor:

'Grandma slipped on an apron and broke her hip.'

I was puzzled.

'Grandpa told her to pick her apron off the kitchen floor or someone would slip on it,' Louise explained. 'Now she's got into her head that that's how you broke your hip.'

I told my daughter how the nurses had praised my Spanish though it was still very elementary. Louise was by now fluent.

'Just shows,' Louise said. 'At the *Residencia* they complained that I'd lived in Spain all these years and still spoke with an English accent.'

When I got back to the UK I gave those bloody shoes to Oxfam as soon as my crutches would take me there.

I went to see Mr Alan Wells, an orthopaedic surgeon who checked me over said the operation was well done. For the first two years all was fine until I took up a trial offer at a nearby gym and was taken through some painful stretches. I started having pain in my hip that got worse and worse. I tried injections and physiotherapy but nothing helped.

I went back to Alan Wells. He arranged to have my hip x-rayed and then under general anaesthetic visualised the joint by injecting it with a dye opaque to x-rays. He still had no idea why I was having pain, so he ordered a bone scan. This would show whether the cause of pain was in my bones, particularly my spine.

On the request form under past medical history he had, of course, put *Lumpectomy for Breast Cancer 1990*.

A week later he phoned.

'Could you come and see me later today, Abby? I have your bone scan report.'

When I went in, he had a serious look on his normally jolly face.

'I'm sorry to tell you, Abby, but you have secondaries in your spine and they're the source of your pain. I think you'd better see an oncologist. I can recommend someone if you like.'

I didn't know what to say. Mine had been a small low-grade cancer with no evidence of spread to the lymph glands. The surgeon's resection edges were completely clear of the cancer and then I'd had a full course of radiotherapy. Follow-up mammograms and check-ups had never shown any evidence of recurrence. I'd had a bit of lower back pain ever since having the children, but this was only occasional and certainly I had no pain elsewhere.

He handed me a copy of the bone scan report:

'There are multiple hot spots in the spine. In view of the history these are cause for concern.' By hot spots was meant areas of increased take up of the dye and the site of some abnormality.

I walked out of the clinic stunned. How could I tell Joshua and the children? Spread of secondary cancer throughout my spine was a death sentence. I didn't allow myself to cry in the street as I walked home.

I knew the chairman of the cancer charity BACUP and decided to ring him when I got home. Of course, I knew that breast cancer can recur years later. When I was working on tumour markers, I had collected specimens of secondary deposits of breast cancer in the scalp and little finger from women who'd had their primary breast cancers removed up to twenty years before.

But I felt there was something wrong about the diagnosis. I'd carried out hundreds of autopsies on women dying of breast cancer during my three years at St Justin's and it just wasn't like the natural history of the breast cancers I'd seen. Perhaps if my hip had broken through a bone weakened by secondary cancer I'd have been more convinced.

351

I re-read the bone scan report.

'There are multiple hot spots in the spine. In view of the history these are cause for concern.'

Maybe the radiologist reporting on my bone scan was inexperienced or just stupid, but he should have written 'warrant further investigation' instead of 'are cause for concern'. He couldn't tell from the scans what those abnormal spots meant.

By the time I got home I was moderately optimistic, but the surgeon's words filled Josh with despair. I told him that I was unconvinced, but he thought I was trying to make the best of it.

I had an appointment with the oncologist two days later. We looked at my x-rays and scans together.

'Maybe I'm trying to kid myself,' I said, 'but it doesn't seem like the usual clinical picture of late cancer spread.'

He put his arm around my shoulders.

'I agree with you, Abby, but I think we have to consider the possibility. I'll write you up for an MRI scan.'

An appointment was available after the weekend, but then the hospital phoned to say there were problems with the scanner and they'd have to put me off for a week. Day by day my early optimism was vanishing. By now, I was convinced Alan Wells was right after all, that I really did have a spine full of cancer.

After the scan, the technician came out to tell me the scans were satisfactory and didn't need repeating. I looked at her face trying to see whether her serious expression meant the worst.

'Did you find anything abnormal?'

'Dr Waterman,' she said, 'you know I'm not allowed to answer clinical questions. The radiologists are here and they will see you soon.'

Joshua was at work and I was on my own, dreading the result. I was sure they would say that my cancer had spread to my bones.

A man and a woman doctor came out with outstretched hands and introduced themselves. To me they hardly looked old enough to be qualified doctors, let alone consultant radiologists.

'Come into the viewing room and we'll look at your scans together.'

I tried to interpret their smiles. Were they pitying smiles or just friendly? I feared the worst.

'Really enjoyed your pathology lectures at St Margaret's,' the male consultant said. 'Where are you working now?'

I didn't want to waste time on chit-chat. Did I have a spine full of cancer or not?

I said I'd been retired for 10 years and anticipated his next question.

'No, and I don't miss it. I'm doing lots of other things.'

The three of us sat down in front of the screens.

'First of all, Dr Waterman, there's absolutely nothing to suggest cancer deposits in your spine. We see a typical wear-and tear picture consistent with your age and there is evidence of osteoporosis. I've read your work on the demonstration of individual cancer cells in bone samples but there's no indication that you should have a bone marrow aspirate to check. '

I could have hugged them both.

'I suppose that's what I got from stomping around on two legs all these years. Perhaps if I'd gone on all fours . . .' I said.

Mr Wells reopened my hip joint but found only a bit of tightness in the hip capsule. Over the years, I tried physiotherapy, Pilates, massage, acupuncture, steroid injections. Nothing helped. The pain was variable but bearable. I have learned to live with it.

There was one good thing about having broken my hip and

having my walking limited by the pain, I was issued with a Blue Disabled badge and could park near the Further Education colleges and the Oxford Street shops.

Joshua had booked tickets for Clint Eastwood's *Gran Torino* and, as we were going by bus, we had to hurry. On Saturday evenings, the buses could be far apart.

As I started down the short flight of steps outside our block of flats, I tripped and fell hard onto my left ankle. I tried to get up but couldn't put weight on that foot. Joshua helped me up and said he would collect the crutches we still had. He was soon back and helped me through the lobby, down the next flight into the court-yard and up in the lift to our 9th floor flat.

My ankle was already swelling up. I hoped it was just a sprain and put an ice bag to cool in the freezer. I phoned Alan Wells, but he was away at a conference. I put the cold bag back on my ankle and decided to phone the Chester Clinic the next day to see if another surgeon was available.

Jonathan, another orthopaedic surgeon, was free at 10am next morning. We parked outside and Joshua went in to collect a wheelchair.

'I suspect you've done it again, Dr Waterman,' Jonathan said. 'Come back here when you've had your x-ray.'

'Fractured your left lateral malleolus,' he said, when I returned. He turned his computer screen to show me the image. 'I'll just get physiotherapy to fit you with an air boot.'

Two weeks later we went to see *Gran Torino*. Clint Eastwood plays a surly elderly widower who initially rejects all contact from his Asian neighbours, but finally sacrifices his life for them.

A good film but not worth breaking an ankle for.

CHAPTER 26

Further Education Classes

I enrolled for lots of classes, some at one Further Education college and some at another – painting, drawing, cooking, history of art, Spanish, creative writing, pottery, dressmaking, machine knitting, felt making – everything I hadn't had time for when I was working. It wasn't just that I hadn't had the time, I hadn't had the inclination. My mind was always so full of work. Even when I was at the theatre, I would find myself thinking about a difficult diagnosis or a hiccup in our research.

Now I enjoyed the freedom of doing things that weren't important, things that weren't a matter of life and death.

'It's wonderful,' I said to my art teacher. 'Nothing I do now is critical. If my drawing of the model looks like a human being, great. If not, at least I produced something. If my new cookery dish tastes good, or if I can't eat it and have to throw it out, if I manage to remember whether Rubens came first or Constable, it just doesn't matter. You can't imagine the relief and feeling of freedom. My life is no longer constantly punctuated by drama, by death, by irrevocable mistakes – where every word I put in a report is critical. It could be a matter of life or death if what I said in my report was misinterpreted by the surgeons and the wrong treatment given.

We bought a piano when our youngest, Jane, was five. The children all had piano lessons until they complained it was too boring. Both Simon and Bernard learned to play the acoustic guitar and all of us, Josh included, played the recorder. We sang and played nursery and folk songs and had a great time. When Louise learnt to play the clarinet and Jane the flute, I played duets and trios with them.

Once all four children left home to go to university, and I was working full time, we sold the piano. I didn't play again until I retired, using part of the £500 legacy from my Aunt Jenny to buy an electronic keyboard.

I applied to enrol in a piano class. I didn't realise I was meant to bring some music to my audition, so I had to sight-read my way through one of the piano tutor's pieces.

'A bit rusty, aren't you?' the tutor said rather disparagingly. 'I'll sign you up for Level Three.'

The fifteen of us played on electronic pianos, wearing headphones. We took them off to play in turn on the upright normal piano in the front of the class. Over the years I gradually progressed to a class in which we played on a grand piano.

I was going to play Bach's *Invention No 13* at the concert at the college the following month. I'd been practising the piece for weeks but, although I'd got the notes sorted, I wanted advice on the 'dynamics' – the crescendos and diminuendos. I felt I needed some private lessons as well as the classes, and arranged to have some with my college tutor.

It was my first private lesson with him. Mason Street is a short street. One side is lined by offices and warehouses and the other by the sprawling Sir James Morgan council estate. My piano teacher lived there, in Elizabeth House.

The pavement outside the estate was obstructed by building works, so I walked on the pavement on the opposite side, looking across for Elizabeth House. Just as I saw its name, I caught my foot in the gap between two broken paving stones and tripped. Putting out my left hand to save myself, I fell hard onto my left side and wrist.

The driver of a furniture lorry parked nearby came over to help me up.

'Nasty fall, love,' he said. 'About time the council did something about this pavement. No wonder you fell. I'd sue them if I was you.'

'A drop too much of the hard stuff,' I said, trying to sound non-chalant. My wrist was sore but not too bad really. Perhaps it was only a sprain.

I crossed to Elizabeth House and pressed 83, my tutor's button.

'Come up to the 3rd floor,' a muffled voice said.

I did, but flat 83 wasn't there. I got back into the lift and tried the 8th floor, but still no luck. I held my swollen, painful wrist cradled against me as I went back down to the ground floor. There was nothing to show which flats were on each floor.

I pressed the intercom button again. I'd misheard. His flat was on the 10th floor.

He tut-tutted over my swollen wrist and brought some ice cubes wrapped in a towel.

'I'm so sorry, Abby. I think we'd better cancel, don't you? It might be broken. You should go to Casualty.'

'I'm fine. It could be just a sprain. I can play with my right hand.'

We went through all the crescendos and diminuendos and, when he was finally satisfied, we played the *Invention* as a duet, with him playing the left-hand part and me playing the right.

'That's good, Abby. I like that. Hope it's only a sprain. Shall I call a taxi for you?'

'No, I'm fine. The car's parked just outside. It's an automatic so I'll be OK. I can drive with my right hand.'

I wasn't fine really. My wrist was now more swollen and it was agonising as I got into the car to drive home using only my right hand. The scary part was driving round Trafalgar Square and taking my hand off the wheel to reach across to indicate that I was turning into St James's Park.

When I got home I phoned an orthopaedic surgeon friend, Stephen Butterworth at the Chester Clinic.

'I'm operating in half an hour but I could see you later tonight,' he said. 'I'll be finished about ten or, if you think it can wait, I could see you first thing tomorrow.'

'Tomorrow's fine. I'm hoping I've just sprained it.'

Joshua said I ought to go to Casualty but I persuaded him I could wait until morning. I took a painkiller but it didn't help and I had a bad night. Whichever way I turned I seemed to be lying on my painful wrist. Around three I gave up, had a glass of milk and got out *Tales of the City*, but it was hard to concentrate. I watched the clock creep slowly round until it was time to get up. Joshua drove me to the clinic.

'I'm pretty sure you've broken it,' Stephen said. 'We'll just get an x-ray.'

I had chipped the corner of my ulna, the smaller bone in my forearm. It felt better as soon as I had a lightweight plaster cast fitted. It kept my broken bone supported and stopped the broken ends rubbing together.

When I got home, I emailed my piano teacher.

I'm afraid my wrist is broken. If you like we can play the Invention at the concert as a duet.

He emailed back:

OK. If you're sure.

Until Joshua bought a plastic sleeve that I could slip over my arm I had to have a stand-up wash – little more than a lick and a promise. That first shower was bliss, though dressing and undressing was a pain. I got frustrated at how many things need two hands, like pulling up my jeans and fastening my belt. Going to the loo was a struggle.

When the plaster came off after six weeks, I looked at my left wrist with dismay. There was an ugly bump where the bone had broken.

'You're lucky,' the physiotherapist, said. 'You should see how crooked some wrists end up. I'll just rub the dead skin off.'

I put my elbow on a towel with the hand straight up and she started to rub my forearm. Masses of grey skin flaked off.

'I know most hospital dust is composed of human skin flakes. No wonder, when you see the amount coming off my arm,' I said.

She laughed.

'That's nothing compared with how much skin I get off some men.'

I saw her weekly until I could move my wrist more or less normally. Now and again I felt a twinge when I picked up something heavy, but it was fine, even if it looked a bit odd.

I only missed my piano class that first week. After that I mainly listened to the others playing. Once, to loud applause from the others, I played the right-hand part of the Bach *Invention* while our tutor played the left.

Over the next couple of weeks, I began to feel it was a crazy idea playing at the concert. The thought hung over me like a black cloud. I sent another email.

I'm so sorry but I don't think I'm up to playing at the concert. Maybe next year?

I was sorry I'd broken my wrist, of course I was, but it was good to have a respectable excuse not to have to play in the concert. As a child, I'd never felt nervous playing the piano in public, but I had been dreading the concert. I knew I wasn't even as good as I'd been as a schoolgirl, and when I listened to recordings of Bach's *Inventions* I realised just how amateur I was – forgivable in a child but not in an adult.

I hadn't been able to think of a good enough excuse not to put my name down to play at the concert when all the others had agreed to play. A broken wrist trumped everything.

The next year I had no excuse to get out of the end of term concert. We joined with the other class at our same level and I was on to play fifth. I went to the loo before the concert started and nipped out again when the third person sat down to play. The young woman who played before me was very tall and I had to adjust the piano stool to my height before I sat down.

I announced my piece, Erik Satie's *Gymnopoedie No 1,* and said a little about Satie and his eccentricity. I've always found it difficult to memorise music and relied on my sight-reading, but this was one piece that I learned by heart without trying. I loved its mournful meandering melodies and I stopped being nervous once I started to play.

There was a wonderful moment of silence when I finished, then everyone started clapping.

Our tutor handed us our assessments at our next lesson.

'Beautiful performance. Very expressive. Congratulations.'

But I'd had enough of the auditions that were held at the end of every term to determine whether we would move up a level or stay in the same class, and the critical looks the audition tutor gave me. I arranged for private lessons with a handsome young tutor who is critical, but always encouraging and supportive.

Most of us in the art class were retired, but there were some younger people. A few weeks into the term, a new young man came to our life class. Tall, with bleached blond hair and green eyes fringed with long dark lashes, he was gorgeous. Instead of getting out an easel, he went over to chat with our tutor. Minutes later he vanished behind the screen and came back nude. Of course, I had seen lots of nude men, alive as well as dead – seen them, felt them, prodded them. But there was something very different about a beautiful young man posing naked.

The tutor fussed about, getting him in a crouching position on the rug, head pointing forward as if ready for a race.

'Right. Ten-minute sketch only. This is a tough position for Nick to hold'.

I washed over my sheet of paper with water and began to draw in brown ink on the wet paper with firm strokes.

As I looked at the blond shining hair now fallen over the young man's face, I saw him as a wolf, the curls of gold hair on his lower belly spreading over his body, forming a tawny pelt. His face became elongated and his ears pricked up, turning to catch the sound, his deep purple tongue hanging out of his mouth between sharp jagged teeth, tail swishing angrily, chest heaving as he panted, powerful and fierce.

The tutor released that pose and this time Nick lay on the couch resting on his elbow. I drew him in purple with washes of colour showing the angular curve of his hip, the muscles of his chest.

At the break Nick put on a dressing gown and wandered around looking at the drawings.

'I like that,' he said to me. 'Powerful but controlled.'

'Is that how you see yourself?' I asked.

'Perhaps,' he said.

'I'd like a portrait this time,' the tutor said.' You've got an hour'.

I changed to a soft pencil. My drawing was dark and brooding. Although it captured Nick's features, it portrayed an older more serious man. As he pushed back his hair with the heel of his hand, someone groaned. He smiled ruefully, said sorry, and pulled his hair back down over his forehead.

Our class always had lunch together in the college canteen. Nick went down with us and sat next to me. We laughed when we saw we had chosen the same mixture of salads, the same brown rolls sprinkled with sunflower seeds and a bottle of sparkling mineral water. We chatted about this and that, and got onto our childhoods. When I mentioned I'd been brought up in the East End of London, Nick said he was going to an exhibition at the Whitechapel Art Gallery, and would I like to come with him.

I took Nick to Blooms, the famous salt beef restaurant nearby. He was hungry again and wolfed down a salt beef sandwich thickly spread with mustard, reminding me of my vision of him in the art class.

After we went round the exhibition of new work by young artists, I wanted to look at the children's library from which I had borrowed six books every week.

It was horribly changed. Instead of thousands of books there were hundreds. The tall stacks that had stretched from floor to ceiling in the adult library were replaced by low bookshelves.

Dated 1892, the copper plaque at the foot of the stairs was as shiny as ever. It was dedicated to J Passmore Edwards Esquire, in recognition of his generosity in defraying the cost of the building. The little museum with its fierce stuffed animals, pottery and copper utensils had gone. The librarian said it had been dismantled twenty years before. I felt cheated of my memories.

We walked to Petticoat Lane. It too had changed. Once a virtually an all Jewish enclave, most of the Jews had moved out and the new immigrants, the Pakistanis and Bengalis, had moved in.

'If you're not doing anything tomorrow afternoon would you like to come to a chamber music concert at the Wigmore Hall?' Nick asked. 'A friend of mine is the second violin.'

A beautiful young man, he had that way of looking at me, listening to me as if I was really important to him. But I wasn't sure I wanted to spend the next day with him.

He bought the tickets and got vouchers for coffee in the interval. We were only just in time and had to inch our way into seats in the middle of a row.

The music was glorious, Haydn, Mozart and Bartok, the players tossing the melodies back and forth between them. My eyes were pricking, ready to overflow, at the beauty of the music.

Nick took me backstage to meet the musicians. I was surprised at just how young they were. I wondered if the pretty second violinist was Nick's girlfriend, but she was a distant cousin.

WOMAN in a WHITE COAT

Nick insisted on seeing me home and gave me a peck on each cheek as he left.

'I'll be in touch,' he said as he strode off, but he never appeared at our class again.

It was because Louise was teaching English as a foreign language in San Sebastian, in the north of Spain, that I decided to learn Spanish.

When I started my second year, our tutor asked if we would like to take the Part 1 of the Royal Society of Arts exam in Spanish. It would be good for the tutor and good for the college to have external exam successes. As I enjoyed the class very much, and liked the tutor, I agreed she could put my name down, even though I had a bad history with exams.

The Spanish oral examination seemed to go well. I always had plenty to say whatever the language. We talked about the open-air food markets you can find everywhere in Spain and about Louise. The main part of the exam consisted of an audio section, where we listened to a tape and then answered written questions. The tapes the tutor used in class were worn and scratchy. The one used in the exam was much clearer but, even though the examiner played it twice, I couldn't catch all of it. For the comprehension section, we had a piece about the nougat they manufacture in Gerona. A box of nougat was one of the presents I always bought for the class when I'd been on a visit to Louise. I felt quite pleased with myself when I handed in my exam papers.

I went for lunch in the canteen with the others. It was a big, big mistake. Max, the know-all in the class, went on and on about his answers and my spirits dropped by the minute.

'What did you think about the concert the young couple on the tape went to?'

I had clearly not understood everything the Spanish speakers had said. I thought they were middle aged and I realised I'd made some silly mistakes in the comprehension too.

I went home miserable and upset. How could I have been so stupid? I'd wanted to be nice to our tutor and say thank you to the college, and let myself in for highly predictable misery.

Joshua was less than sympathetic. He'd been through the same scenario over each of my exams. He was sure I hadn't failed and changed the subject whenever I got upset waiting for the results.

He didn't say 'I told you so' when I got 'A's in all three parts. Just a quick cuddle and 'Well done, goose.' I thought I'd sound spiteful if I crowed about the fact that Max had only got a B and two Cs.

I swore I'd never ever take another exam, not in Spanish and not in anything else.

The college organised a Spanish day on the last Saturday of term. Joshua came to pick me up lunch time so we could choose some new saucepans in Heal's cookshop.

Joshua was driving when I started to tell him about the *paella* someone had brought in. Suddenly I couldn't speak properly. My tongue felt thick and my words were slurred.

'I think we'd better go home, Josh,' I managed to get out. 'I'm not feeling good.'

He turned the car around and looked at me anxiously.

'What do you think it is? Something you ate for lunch? I always worry about everyone bringing in food from home. They might have kept it out of the fridge somewhere warm for hours.'

I shook my head. I was sure it wasn't the food. When we got home I lay down on the living room sofa.

'Had I better to get our GP to come round?' Josh asked.

'No. I'll just rest a bit.'

Next day, a Sunday, I had recovered completely and on Monday morning I phoned my friend, Phillip Thomson, at St Margaret's. He said he was free at 11.30.

When I thought about how lucky I was to be able to get expert medical advice so quickly, I told myself I'd earned it. I recalled how much scorn and sarcasm was directed at medical students by the registrars and consultants, how as housemen we were on 24/7 and about the long training to reach consultant status. The other consultants were my friends, specialists I worked with, whose cases I reported on. Of course, I would go to them if I was in trouble.

'Good to see you, Abby. How's retirement suiting you? Missing us?'

'Not at all. I'd hoped never to darken St Margaret's doorstep ever again but I had this weird attack on Saturday.'

He tested my central nervous system carefully, first each of my cranial nerves, checking my sight and hearing, my muscle movements and my reflexes, and he examined my eyes with an ophthalmoscope.

'There's no sign of raised intra-cranial pressure,' he said 'so it's not what you're thinking. I'm pretty certain you've haven't got something nasty growing in your head.'

I had been sure I had a brain tumour. It would have fitted my symptoms. When I thought about the differential diagnosis of any new aches and pains, cancer was always top of my list.

'Better have a Doppler scan of your carotid arteries in case you have a blockage and then I'll arrange an MRI of your brain. You've either had a transient ischaemic attack, or it could be a recurrence of the migraine you had as a child.'

'But it was nothing like my migraine attacks. It was mainly loss of speech.'

'All sorts of weird things can happen during a migraine attack. Some patients even have a temporary unilateral paralysis.'

'Thanks very much,' I said grimacing.

I had my Doppler scan next day and it was normal. Phillip was a bit reticent when I asked about my MRI.

'If you look at your left cortex, you can see that you appear to have lost an area about 3 centimetres in diameter, though when I examined you I found no neurological deficit. We're finding all sorts of anomalies with these scans in people who are symptom free.'

'I guess you'll have to wait for my post-mortem to find out what it means,' I said. 'Just think what I might have achieved if I'd had a whole brain. Might have got a Nobel Prize for starters. Do you think if I dressed up as the Scarecrow, the Wizard of Oz would help me get a whole brain?'

We had finally paid off our mortgage and decided to use the lump sum I was due when I retired to buy a holiday home in the sun. A friend visiting Nerja one Christmas brought back a brochure offering an inspection weekend. The agent met us in Gibraltar. He drove like mad along the motorway until it petered out beyond Malaga and then crawled bad-temperedly along the narrow coast road to Nerja. He showed us several thoroughly unpleasant flats with rusted railings and broken-down dusty furniture. He was barely sober when he arrived to take us out to dinner. The stove in the villa where he put us up had run out of paraffin. It was so cold we slept in all our clothes.

On Sunday, the day we were due to return home, he persuaded us to look at a two-bedroomed terraced house in a development, completed two years before. Because of the depressed state of the economy only three had sold. The house we chose was perfect for us. Only a few minutes from the sea, its roof terrace had views both over the market gardens of Nerja and of the mountains behind. A small delicatessen-cum-supermarket on the corner, a furniture shop and a hairdresser would supply us with everything we needed.

For ten years we went there Christmas, Easter and Summer – Joshua was still teaching at the dental hospital and had to take time off in August when the students had their summer holiday. Most holidays, one or other of our children joined us. The simple fish restaurant 100 yards away served the catch of the day with crisp delicious chips cooked in locally pressed olive oil. Several restaurants in the centre served excellent local food.

Until they widened the road to accommodate the tourist buses that besiege the Sunday market at Frigiliana, I spent much of the winding journey up from Nerja with my eyes closed. Joshua always did the driving in Spain and he seemed able to ignore the sheer drop at the side of the road. Over coffee and a toasted baguette at our favourite outdoor café, we looked down an almost vertical slope to the river far below. On the other side, there was a gentle hillside crowded with olive trees. In the distance, we could see the Mediterranean and coast of North Africa.

Frigiliana is one of the white-walled villages of the Alpujarras, that stretch of Andalucía south of the great Sierra Nevada mountains, whose peaks are covered in snow except in the very height of summer. It is a bye-law that all the houses must be painted white, so we were surprised one day to find a woman painting her house pale blue. She was using a roller tied to a very long stick while a rickety home-made ladder stood leaning idle at her side. By the time we'd walked through the village, peered through gated archways full of flowering plants and had lunch, the paint had dried to a brilliant white. I later learned that the white paint particles are suspended in a blue solvent that evaporates on drying. Though the streets of Frigiliana are narrow there were none of the splashes of colour from car grazes you see in towns like Arcos de la Frontera, where there is barely a hand's breadth between your car and the wall. Frigiliana residents must immediately rush out and paint over any offending paint marks that do occur.

The local Spanish pottery ware is fragile – unlike china, it doesn't bounce when you drop it – so we often needed to buy replacements in a new non-matching design from one of the many craft shops perched on the steep stairways up to the top of the town.

One Sunday the gate of the oil refinery at the end of the road stood open and the foreman showed us over the silent factory. We saw the huge round presses ready to crush the olives – leaves and all – and the enormous blackened rush mats for filtering the oil. We bought a small bottle from him but we preferred the extra virgin olive oil we got at the Cooperative in *Perriana*, further along the coast. This was a much larger more modern establishment and we'd stock up on one litre bottles for us, and five litre plastic containers for Louise to take back to San Sebastian at Christmas. We were always offered a taste before we bought – a crusty slice of bread to dip in the latest pressing.

Most of the ceramic plaques decorating the walls of Frigiliana were religious or purely decorative but there was one celebrating the fact that this was the site of the last battle between the Moors and the Christians. However, it was at Granada that Boabdil, Mohammed XII, finally surrendered in 1492. Legend has it that as

369

he looked back from above the city he was scolded by his mother who said:

'Why do you weep like a woman for what you could not defend like a man?'

The hillside from which he was said to have looked on Granada for the last time is known as *'El ultimo suspiro del Moro'* – 'The Moor's Last Sigh'.

However, my favourite plaque is one in Nerja which says *'En mil novecientos noventa y tres nunca ocurrió aquí'* – in 1993 nothing happened here!

When we bought *No 6 Los Huertos*, Nerja was a sleepy seaside village with cobbled streets, the occasional horse-drawn carriage and the classic white painted houses of the *Alpujarras*. Most of the voices you heard in the streets were Spanish, some were Scandinavian. Few were British.

Gradually the language changed, and we mainly heard loud British voices, voices complaining that though the treatment at the local hospital was fine, why couldn't the nurses and doctors speak English? And why can you never get a decent cup of tea here?

Burger bars appeared. Our favourite fish restaurant became a fish and chip shop with smaller portions, tea available as well as wine and tomato ketchup on the tables. We had only ever seen one beggar in Nerja – an old man who stood quietly outside the church on Sunday mornings. Now young people appeared with guitars, Mexican blankets and begging bowls. At night, there were drunks vomiting in the streets. They were almost always British.

At first, we were the only non-Spanish owners in our development and then several English families bought houses. Their teenage children kept everyone awake at night larking about in the pool and having noisy parties. One of the English owners got himself elected as President of the Residents' Committee and did nothing but grouse. Our long honeymoon was over.

To begin with, we missed our house in Nerja but now, with our four children scattered around the world, we can spend our holidays in more exotic places, contributing to mass tourism there instead.

CHAPTER 27

Recurrence

I was fed up with my hip pain. It not only limited how far I could walk before it got too painful, but where I could go. If there wasn't a nearby bus stop, or a disabled parking space, I couldn't go there. Travelling on the underground was a nightmare. It was a fair walk to the nearest underground station and too much walking and too many stairs once there. My destination station was rarely near enough to wherever I wanted to go.

All my contemporaries at St Margaret's had now retired, so I looked up hip surgeons on the web. The blurb about a hip surgeon at St Aidan's sounded convincing and I arranged to see him.

It is normal for us to have a small flat space filled with a little fluid forming a little pocket, a bursa, to help the muscles slide over the bony tuberosity at the top of our thighs. The surgeon thought that the cause of my pain might be an enlarged bursa over the top of my femur, the greater trochanter. I had an MRI scan and the radiologist said that my bursa was huge. I was advised to have it removed.

It was half past five and still dark as I struggled to free myself from the bedclothes. I had been tossing and turning all night worrying about my operation and I was still agitated. I swung my legs onto the floor and pulled on my silk kimono and the espadrilles I wore as slippers.

I went into the kitchen to get a drink of water and looked at the black cross on the calendar, Tuesday March 5th. The surgery was today. I wasn't allowed to eat anything but I didn't feel hungry.

The living room was softly lit by the LEDs on my computer and the four-gang adaptors scattered about the room. Trying to calm myself, I unlocked the glass door to our balcony. It slid back with a soft groan and I stepped out into a grey chilly morning. The rain had stopped but the floor tiles were still wet. I picked at the moss growing between them and pulled up the weeds that always came up again, however many times I tore them out.

The view from the ninth floor was stunning. It stretched from the London Eye in the East to the MI6 building in the West. In front of me was a cityscape of grey rooftops. Most of the buildings were still dark, but here and there a few lighted windows showed people already at work. The flags on the Houses of Parliament flapped in the breeze and the long sharp leaves on our dwarf palm tree rustled. At this time of day, the pods on the Eye were still empty. In the far distance, the warning lights on the cranes looked like constellations of red stars. A lone airplane roared overhead on its way to Heathrow Airport and there was already a steady hum of traffic along Horseferry Road. Big Ben's face was lit up. At six o'clock I heard it toll the hour.

There were no birds on the balcony, but in the past, we've had thrushes, blackbirds, finches, magpies and a peregrine falcon. Once there was a Mallard duck standing on the balcony wall. I told one of the porters about it.

'A pair nested on the roof opposite you three years ago,' he told me. 'We had to go up onto the roof and bring the ducklings down. We put them in the fountain but next day they were gone. No idea what happened to them.'

The smell of bacon and eggs coming from our neighbour next door was appetising, but I wasn't tempted. She came out holding her ancient Siamese cat.

'How's Sultan this morning?' I asked, just to be polite. She'd told me his kidneys were failing and I knew it was only a matter of time.

'Bit better today. He even had some breakfast,' she said as she went back inside.

I switched on my computer and looked at my emails. The usual stuff:

Dear Mum, Good luck for tomorrow. Arriving April 17th. OK if I bring a friend to stay? Love Simon

Yes

Dear Mum, If I send you the returns note, will you send the book back to Amazon for me? Love Bernard

Will do.

Dear Mum, I need to make a cake for Rebecca's birthday. Can you send me your fruit cake recipe? Love Louise

Herewith.

RECURRENCE

Dear Mum, OK for us to stay with you for a couple of days at the end of the month? Love Jane

Yes. OK.

There was just time for me to practice Tchaikovsky's *October* that I was going to play for my friends later in the month. It was getting late. I would have to hurry. I got out the case I'd packed the night before and put in my laptop. I checked on Joshua. His face was serene, relaxed. I didn't want to wake him so I left a note.

'Gone to St Aidan's. I'll text you with where I've parked the car.'

In the lift, I noticed that the numbers on the buttons were raised. In a more modern lift the numbers would also be in Braille. I thought about my blind friend in our Monday creative writing class. She uses a voice-activated computer that she calls *Mr Windows* and composes beautifully crafted pieces, full of remembered images from before she went blind. A college assistant reads out her pieces in class.

There was a strong smell of lemon as I got out of the lift. It was the floor cleaner that the porter uses to wash the hallway. He smiled as I passed.

'Bit chilly today,' I said.

'Much warmer in the Philippines where I come from,' he replied.

I changed lifts to go down to the car park. As I drove out I saw that the ornamental cherry trees on the pavement opposite were already covered in a haze of pink blossom. A lorry beeped as it suddenly backed out in front of me.

By the time I crossed Lambeth Bridge the clouds had blown away and the sun was sparkling on the Thames. A group of tourists waited at the bus stop for the Duck Tour that uses amphibian assault craft from the WW2 Normandy landing, the khaki now painted bright yellow. The tour goes around Westminster and into the Thames for a short distance. The driver will point to the carved stone lion heads on the south wall of the embankment.

'The water is dangerously high if it reaches the lions' mouths,' he says. *'If the lions drink, London sinks.'*

I drove on towards Waterloo Bridge and then up Kingsway listening to Beethoven's 5th Piano Concerto on *Classic FM*.

It was important to see everything, hear everything. It could be for the last time.

I knew the surgeon would read out the list of possible complications before asking me to sign the consent form for reopening my hip. I'd seen most of them in the post-mortem room – deep vein thrombosis leading to fatal lung embolism, broncho-pneumonia – especially in people of my age confined to bed – and wound infection. I was concerned about MRSA, though St Aidan's had one of the lowest rates in the country.

I asked to have my operation under an epidural anaesthetic, as I had for the original operation to replace my fractured hip. I was wheeled down to theatre. Being now 79, my spine had grown little excrescences – osteophytes – that blocked a clear passage to my spinal cord. After a few painful attempts, the anaesthetist gave up. She couldn't get the needle positioned and I had to have a full general anaesthetic instead.

I woke to find her at my bedside. She held up her mobile in front of me.

'What do you think?' she asked, showing me a photo of a large blood-covered oval object suspended from a pair of surgical forceps.

'It's the largest bursa we've ever seen,' she said. 'Here's hoping it was the cause of your hip pain. It's certainly big enough.'

When the surgeon came to see me, I asked him to give me the specimen when the pathologist had taken a sample for diagnosis. I would stand it next to the formalin-filled pot containing the head of femur fractured when I was in San Sebastian to look after Louise when she was having her second baby.

When my hip pain first occurred, back in 2002, I had taken out the specimen to have a good look and check if there were any of the tell-tale white areas of secondary cancer after all. Perhaps the Spanish surgeon had missed them but I couldn't see any and I couldn't face taking it to St Margaret's pathology department to examine it under the microscope.

The surgeon said I could go home the following day. Provided I was sensible, and kept the dressing over the wound site clean and dry, I could take gentle exercise.

It was lovely to be home in my own bed but I awoke at 2 am wet and sticky. I threw back the bedclothes to find a large blood stain soaking the dressing, the underlying sheet, our electric under-blanket and the mattress. I had been given some dressings to take home and Josh rewrapped my wound. I waited until 8am before phoning the surgeon.

'Don't worry,' he said. 'Come in when you're ready and the nurses will put a firm dressing on.'

The nurses fussed over me, bringing Josh and me tea and biscuits, before replacing the dressing.

I was already sick of staying at home, so next day we went to Tesco. I sat in front of the tills until Josh had collected up our shopping and then joined him to pay. As I took back my credit card, I felt something run down the outside of my leg. Soon there was a

WOMAN in a WHITE COAT

small pool of bloody fluid on the floor by my foot, and a wet patch on the side of my jeans. The man behind me looked at me with disgust. No doubt he thought I'd wet myself.

Josh helped me back to the car. Luckily, we had an old towel in the boot I could use to protect the car seat.

I phoned the surgeon again and he told me the nurses would put a firmer dressing on. All was well for two days and then I awoke to find the dressing soaked through again.

'Can I see the surgeon on call, this time?' I asked.

After a long wait, a young surgeon in training arrived in her outdoor clothes. Having taken off her coat, she was about to remove my dressing.

'Don't you think you should wash your hands first?' I asked.

She grunted, complied and redressed my leg.

This time the leakage stopped. The wound had closed but it was now hot and swollen. I had an appointment with the physiotherapist.

'I'm not treating you with your wound looking like that,' she said. 'It looks as if it could be infected. I'll phone the surgeon.'

'Can you come in tomorrow?' he asked. No apology for leaving me coming back and forth to St Aidan's for nearly a week. 'I'll need to re-open it under general. I'll drain the wound and plug it to stop it happening again. Don't eat or drink after midnight and come in first thing.'

I hated the idea of another general anaesthetic. I couldn't have an epidural injection and at my age a general anaesthetic is a potentially hazardous procedure.

Next morning, he came up to see me after I checked in.

'Couldn't you just put in a needle and drain the fluid?' I asked.

'No. It wouldn't work. I need to open it up and seal it properly.'

This time the incision healed without further trouble but the operation had done nothing to relieve my long-standing hip pain, and I was left with a permanent, though painless, swelling at the site.

I couldn't deal with the trauma of it all at the time. It took a year before I could bring myself to write to the surgeon and complain about the way I had been treated. His feeble excuses fell on deaf ears.

I learned to accept the limitations imposed by my hip pain – often I am hardly conscious of its presence. However, if I asked myself the question the physiotherapist always start with 'What is your pain like, on a scale of one to ten?' The answer is rarely 'Zero.'

Then the pain changed. It started to radiate down the outside of my leg and was unrelieved by a visit to the physiotherapist. The lower back pain I'd had on and off since having children got worse. My GP ordered an x-ray and the spectre of cancer recurrence reared its ugly head again.

> *'There is destruction of the L5 posterior vertebral body and endplate. Taken in conjunction with the patient's known breast malignancy, this raises the possibility of metastatic disease.'*

It was agony getting into bed, agony lying in bed and, after a few hours of interrupted sleep, agony struggling out of bed.

The spinal surgeon ordered an MRI and I had two anxious days waiting for the results. Had my cancer finally caught up with me? Was my spine full of secondary deposits?

This time it was all too credible. I tried to think whether I would agree to have chemotherapy. Could I cope with the nausea and having my hair fall out?

I knew the score. When I was working at St Olave's I'd carried out autopsies on hundreds of women who had died of breast cancer. I tried to keep from Joshua how likely it was that this time my cancer had recurred and spread to my spine. One morning he caught me in the kitchen crying. Near to tears himself, he tried to comfort me, to reassure me it would be OK, but I couldn't be comforted. A kiss and a hug wouldn't make it better.

It was the toughest two days I've ever spent.

Once again it wasn't cancer, but it wasn't all good news. My vertebral column had deteriorated further and a large spinal nerve was being compressed. The situation wasn't severe enough for surgery, but I could get pain relief by an injection of local anaesthetic and cortisone – a manoeuvre carried out in hospital under sedation. There was a slot available the following Monday. It was up to me. I said I'd think about it, but by Friday I was ready to have the injection.

Then I looked up the procedure on the web. To my horror, one of the possible, though rare, complications was paraplegia. I am a master of rare side effects. Colleagues who treated me were always sure I've been looking up the rare complications of my drugs, when I reported side effects they'd read about but never seen.

It was a no-brainer. I couldn't take the risk of waking up paralysed. I'd soldier on, take painkillers and accept the situation.

But I didn't have to. Gradually the pain eased. It was difficult taking the painkillers – they made me feel sick all day but at least I could get out of bed – and the nausea helped me lose weight.

Within four months I was practically back to where I had been before the pain changed. Most of the pain had been due to swelling around the nerve, compressing it further, and with time the swelling had gone down.

CHAPTER 28

Death Knocks at My Door

Death came knocking at my door in August, came right in, cold bony fingers at my throat and foul charnel-breath in my face. I had a major heart attack – blocked my coronary arteries and killed off areas of the left ventricle of my heart, the part that pumps freshly oxygenated blood around the body.

My heart attack was a searing pain in the centre of my chest radiating down my left arm. Was it bad? Not as bad as having three of my four children without analgesia, but after labour you get a lovely present. There are no rewards for having a coronary artery occlusion.

Was it expected? Yes and no. I had several 'risk factors'. I was old – nearly 85, had high blood pressure, albeit well controlled with medication, and high 'bad' cholesterol (LDL). Statins – cholesterol-lowering drugs – made me depressed, utterly miserable, so I couldn't take them.

On the plus side, my 'good' cholesterol (HDL) was high. I had never smoked more than four cigarettes a year and was just on the

381

right side of my BMI – Body Mass Index. I had even managed to lose the few extra pounds I felt I didn't need.

But I had been having occasional chest pains, was a bit breathless on exertion and was being investigated by my GP.

Not feeling well, I went to bed early. I had cooked dinner for Josh, my husband, Louise, my elder daughter, her husband, Mark, and their two teenage children, Samantha and Daniel, and washed up.

Louise and Mark live in the Basque Country in the North of Spain. Being teachers, they get school holidays so they and their children come to stay with us in our London flat at Christmas, Easter and August.

The pain struck at around 8.30pm. I stumbled into the living room and asked Joshua to ring 999. In what seemed only minutes, two very calm and competent paramedics were at the door. They carried out an ECG (electro-cardiogram) and confirmed that I had indeed had a major heart attack.

From then on, things are a bit vague. I remember the paramedics taking me down in a stretcher-chair to the courtyard from our 9th floor flat and lifting me into their waiting ambulance. They had Josh and Louise stand outside as they carried out some further manoeuvres. Fortunately, the August night was mild. I have a vague recollection of being wheeled into the hospital and then remember nothing more until I was thanking the cardiologist for saving my life. He had inserted stents – tiny perforated metal tubes – into two of my blocked coronary arteries. These are the arteries that supply oxygenated blood to the heart itself. My third coronary artery was beyond salvation.

Next day, in the Cardiac Care ward, it was apparent that my heart wasn't coping and the cardiologist decided to insert an intra-aortic pump – a tubular pump that is threaded into the aorta, the main artery that supplies the body with fresh blood. It is powered by a large external pump. I remember having my groin dry-shaved in preparation and apparently told Louise that having the pump inserted was uncomfortable. I have no memory of being asked for my consent, though I must have been asked, nor of telling my elder son, Simon, that the pump sounded like a washing machine. Later, in a period of delirium, I became convinced that the circular air vents in the ceiling were the portholes of washing machines.

I was then moved to the ICU (Intensive Care Unit) where I remember my bed being in the corner of the ward next to a window and seeing my two English grandchildren, Simon's two, standing at the end of my bed. Though Josh and my children visited me every day, sometimes twice a day, I have no memory of seeing any of the rest of them for the five days I was in ICU – five days lost to me. I only know of most things that happened while I was in Intensive Care from being told about it by one of my children.

It became clear that my heart couldn't cope with supplying enough blood to my lungs for me to breathe unaided. I was asked if I would agree to being put on a ventilator but said I'd prefer to wait another day before taking such a major step, to see if it was really necessary.

It was, and I was on a ventilator for the next three days. My only memory of that time was that at one stage I was wearing white linen mitts – fingerless mittens like 'scratch mitts' for babies. My son, Bernard, told me later that I apologised to the nurse looking after me for attacking her when she tried to stop me pulling out my various tubes. I thought she was trying to kill me – a delusion experienced by many critically ill patients.

There is a memory I'm glad I don't have. One day when Louise and Mark came to see me, I held out my hand to each of them and then waved them goodbye, as if I was about to die. It was too much for Mark and he burst into tears.

My younger daughter, Jane, had flown over from Switzerland, where she lives. After three days, an attempt was made to take me off the ventilator and, thinking that all was well, she booked a flight home for the next day as she had urgent commitments at the University. However, I became very confused and my heart couldn't cope, so I was re-intubated and kept heavily sedated.

It was my turn to knock back – for me to repeat the favour and knock at Death's Door. Although I was very close to dying, I never had any 'near-death' visions – no bright lights, no celestial voices. Perhaps you need to be deeply religious to have such experiences.

The nurses couldn't have treated me with more care and respect, so I didn't really need advocates to impress on the staff that I was not just a little old gaga lady, whose life had run its course and whose value was less than that of the 40-year old plumber in the next bed. However, during the time I was near to death, sedated and on a ventilator, my family felt they had to be sure everyone knew that I was worth saving. They told them about my achievements, such as they were; that I lead an active mental and physical life and hadn't lost my marbles; and that I wouldn't wish to give up but would want to survive. I love them for it.

Simon had been visiting daily and I tried to communicate with him while on the ventilator by writing, but I was too shaky and produced only a scribble when I tried to write 'Am I dying?' – something I'm told I asked many times. He finally wrote out the alphabet so I could communicate by pointing. The anaesthetist who came to remove the ventilator tube had a Scottish accent which I was lucid enough to recognise, so I proudly pointed to S-C-O-T. Fortunately, this time when the ventilator was removed, my heart picked up and I no longer needed it. Simon compares me to the Duracell Bunny in the TV commercial that showed how much longer their batteries last.

Once I was conscious, the Critical Care consultant came to ask me whether if I collapsed I would want to be resuscitated. I was surprised that he asked me. It was not until after I was discharged from hospital that I discovered that it was decided that having the ventilator replaced once was my last chance. A medical decision had been made. If I couldn't be extubated in a couple of days that would be that. I was only alive because the intra-aortic pump was keeping my blood circulating and a ventilator was breathing for me. Since my heart and lungs were being supported artificially and my body was shutting down, there would be no point trying heroic measures like open heart massage if the ventilator couldn't be successfully removed. I was labelled 'Do Not Resuscitate'. It's a frightening thought for me – even now.

I told the consultant that I had a good life, with four wonderful children. Of course, I would want to be resuscitated unless it was clear that I was brain-dead and would remain a vegetable.

I was then transferred to the High Dependency Unit (HDU – dependant on care not alcohol or drugs). There, I was conscious most of the time but, like up to 80% of critically ill patients, I experienced several episodes of delirium which seemed absolutely real to me. These are thought to be due to a derangement of the brain's neurotransmitters compounded by the drugs used for sedation. Whatever the ultimate cause, my days in HDU were punctuated by a series of delusions and hallucinations, mainly at night but sometimes during the day – though I had some periods of lucidity.

Louise had brought in some of my personal possessions including the soft tartan shawl she had given me for one of my birthdays, my mobile and some toiletries. It was comforting having some of my own things around me. During a period of lucidity, I took some selfies of me and my children and of the circular vents in the ceiling I had been so sure were the portholes of washing machines. I also snapped some pictures of Joshua dozing in the chair beside my bed. He was too worried about me to sleep properly at night, too anxious about what he might find when he next visited the hospital.

Not only did my delusions seem real to me but sometimes I convinced my family that they were real. Early on the day after I left the ICU, I phoned home and spoke to Louise. I told her she must get Josh to drive to the hospital and park around the back as I was to be discharged. Even though I was obviously deluded – it was only a day after I had been taken off the ventilator for the second time and couldn't yet walk unaided – I sounded so normal that to begin with she believed me. This is another memory I don't have. I have no idea why some of my delusions are still so clear and detailed to me, while others, like this call to Louise, have gone from my memory.

The only really distressing part of my stay in hospital was being incontinent of liquid faeces. I had a urinary catheter, so that was taken care of, but I can remember feeling absolutely awful as the smelly stuff oozed out of me. The nurses were kindness itself – assuring me that it was a natural function, that they were used to it and not to worry – but I was 'with it' enough to feel deeply ashamed. I well remember the first time I was able to control my bowels, use one of the disposable papier maché bedpans and pass a solid stool. It was one of the highlights of my stay in HDU.

Josh and I, and the rest of the family had been to see Jeff Koons' artefacts at Damien Hurst's gallery. During a period of delirium, I told Louise that I didn't like the look of the HDU ward. It was untidy and full of objects from Damien Hurst's collection and the clock was bent at a right angle like Salvador Dali's pocket watches in his 1931 painting *The Persistence of Memory*. I obviously thought either Jeff Koons or Damien Hurst had been ultra-generous to the hospital. The objects I thought I saw would have been worth millions.

My bed was moved around during the time I was in HDU and at one stage I was by the window with a splendid view of the river and the Houses of Parliament. I told Bernard that the hospital was about to be privatised because the view was so good. A room overlooking the river was worth a lot of money and I insisted that we were to be moved out of the ward that day.

On an occasion when I was about to have a blanket bath, I was convinced that I was going to be washed in an apparatus rather like an automatic car-wash, and that a notice with the prices was suspended above it. I asked Simon whether it wouldn't be too expensive. He assured me that I was in an NHS hospital and that everything was free.

I went back to visit HDU several weeks after being discharged. My mental image from my episodes of delirium was completely different from reality. For me, the end of the ward was curved to form an oval and there were floor-to-ceiling windows, through which I could see a panoply of stars in the night sky. In reality, all the walls are straight and none of them extended from the floor to the ceiling.

The beds could be screened off by dark blue concertina blinds. In one of my episodes of delirium at night, the nurses closed all the blinds and spent their time cleaning them top to bottom. In fact, they are never washed, just changed when necessary. The nurses were interrupted in their washing when one of them brought in fish and chips wrapped in cream-coloured paper. Towards dawn, I saw police bring in a wounded man, to what in my delirium was an all-female ward. In fact, although the nurses try to keep each bay of the ward for the same sex, the HDU is a mixed ward.

Another night, when all the other patients were asleep, I felt sticky all over. I told the male nurse in charge that I had been promised a shower at 2 am when a particular nurse came on duty. When she came in, she helped me out of bed and gave me a shower and shampoo and then dried my hair with a hair dryer. Is that memory real or another of my delusions?

Louise recounted that one day I was particularly agitated. I was having trouble sleeping and had been awake for 24 hours or more. I told her that I had muskets hidden under the bedclothes and that we had to go out and fight, though we had to have a rest first.

On another occasion, I was taking part in a 'Dirty Protest' by women – against what I have no idea. Draped in white sheets, we daubed our faces and clothes with paint and slept on open demountable structures rather like market stalls. Some of the women spoke in French and I felt certain we were in Paris.

One night, the ward had changed, with the beds scattered in a big open room. I could hear the rain beating on the windows and saw that the river outside had come up to the ward which was on the tenth floor. The other patients had left for 'the barracks' where they were employed making small rugs. I begged the nurse in charge to take me there before we all drowned. It was 3am but he phoned my son Simon and gave me his mobile to speak to him. Simon said he would go outside and see. Moments later he said it was OK, that it wasn't raining and that I could go back to bed. And I did.

One of the most frightening occurrences was visiting a village where adults and children were all involved in paedophilia. They also made a kind of liqueur which they gave to the children as well as selling it. The adults wore thin black plywood costumes that were shaped like double-bass cases. They made a sinister clattering sound, as they moved and chanted in a language I didn't recognise.

On my last day in HDU, I saw a woman drop dead on a sailing boat in the river outside the window. The other passenger was a famous painter, who was also the wounded man of my previous delusion. He was sitting up in the bed next to mine and the nurses said that the woman who died was his wife, though I knew she was his mistress. The nurses told me I needed to have intra-nasal oxygen but I refused. I thought it was just to persuade me to agree with the official version and save the painter from scandal.

I experienced one last attack of delirium as I was being transferred from HDU to a geriatric ward and lucidity. My bed was pushed through the main hospital and I became confused. My sons were with me and I kept asking them which television channel I was on and who were the director and producer as they weren't any good.

I had no further attacks of delirium in the four days I spent learning to walk and recovering the manual dexterity I had lost while unconscious. For some reason, even though he visited me every day and sometimes twice a day, I never told Josh about my delusions while I was having them. I confided only in my children and the nurses.

Some of my episodes of delirium occurred during the day when one of the children was present, so I can be sure these were delusions, not dreams. Those that occurred at night could have been dreams, but I seemed to be awake. Only on the night that I thought the river had risen up to the tenth floor did I involve Simon, so I know I was delirious on that occasion and not dreaming. It would be difficult now to contact any of the nurses who were on night duty at that time, but the memories are powerful and very clear. I was told I had several periods of delirium during the night so I doubt that those I have related above were dreams. But what is the difference between dreams and delusions, except that I was awake while being deluded?

While in some of my attacks of delirium the delusions were related to real events, in others I can find no such link. Was it a news item that was responsible, a recent novel I had read or an older memory? And why do I recall some things that happened in the ICU and not others? Those that I remember are crystal clear. Does it mean that a part of my brain died? Certainly, by the time I was lucid in the HDU I knew I had lost some manual dexterity and remember Simon congratulating me on being able to eat peas with a fork. A physiotherapist gave me some tube stoppers to practice screwing them into each other to get my fingers working again.

I also had difficulty remembering exact words or expressions. I know it's a common experience – feeling that a word is on the tip of your tongue – but it was not a frequent experience for me before my heart attack. Now it was, though in the succeeding few weeks both my dexterity and command of language more or less returned to normal.

Having a heart attack wasn't as terrible an experience as it might have been. As a doctor who had worked in that hospital as a consultant pathologist, I felt at home, in familiar surroundings. Everyone was very kind and though some of my hallucinations were frightening in themselves, overall my feelings about them are that they were exciting and probably a good basis for short stories or a mystery novel. Perhaps my memory loss was a protective mechanism, saving me from memories of the worst times.

So, what now? Well, I am well aware that it may happen again, that I might not be so lucky next time and that I must live the time I have left to the full. I can't help getting frustrated when getting out of the bath makes me breathless, so that I have to wait to catch my breath before I can dry myself. But I try to make myself remember how near to death I was and how fortunate I am to have had such brilliant care that I am still in the land of the living.

I had to cancel my further education classes last term but now I have enrolled for Art History and Photoshop as well as finding a splendid young piano teacher. With Josh, I have been to most of the art exhibitions presently on in London and have seen the latest movies.

It's all a bit of an effort for me but I am determined to make every day count and hope that there will be plenty of them.

Now that I am so much nearer to 100 than to one, I look back and see that there is much to be said for the peaceful life of an octogenarian couple who have been together in a loving relationship for over 60 years. The rough edges have been worn away and we have so many shared memories and experiences.

I was born and grew up in London's impoverished East End and fought disappointment, prejudice and sexism to succeed in a male orientated society. I have been in turn a Harley Street dentist, a toy shop owner and member of the Design Centre Committee, a consultant pathologist running a cancer research laboratory as well as a wife and mother of four children. I have gained great satisfaction and fulfilment in all of these.

Since retiring. I have been to classes in painting, drawing, print making, literature, creative and non-fiction writing, pottery, cookery, art history, philosophy, dressmaking and machine knitting, and I have learned to speak passable Spanish.

I can now make my own clothes, design my own cards and

knock up a more or less gourmet three-course meal for my family without too much angst. I managed to survive head lice, scarlet fever, thyrotoxicosis, breast cancer, depression and fractures of my hip, wrist and ankle.

The flap of our letter box rattles. The post has arrived and with it the latest prospectus for Adult Education. I will definitely take Art History and Literature. Perhaps I will enrol for Classical Greek as well, and read the classics in the original.

I already have a small Greek vocabulary from when I was a dental student at St Margaret's. I learned to say *kallimera* (good morning) and *anoíxte to stóma sas* (open your mouth) to patients from the local Greek Cypriot community. I have a larger Greek vocabulary derived from the many medical terms we had to learn. Maybe learning Greek will exercise my mind and grow some new brain cells to replace those I've lost over the years.